CULTURE IN AN AGE OF MONEY

CULTURE IN AN AGE OF MONEY

The Legacy of the 1980s in America

Edited with an Introduction by
NICOLAUS MILLS

 Chicago Ivan R. Dee 1990

Most of the contents of this book appeared in slightly different form in *Dissent* magazine, copyright © 1989, 1990 by the Foundation for the Study of Independent Social Ideas. Grateful acknowledgement is made to the following for permission to reprint other previously published materials:

Esquire, for "The Short Happy Life of the American Yuppie" by Hendrik Hertzberg, copyright © 1988 by *Esquire*.

The *New Republic*, for excerpts from "God and Man at Lynchburg" by Sean Wilentz, copyright © 1988 by the *New Republic*; for "Presidency by Ralph Lauren" by Alessandra Stanley, copyright © 1988 by the *New Republic*; and for "The Treason of the Critics" by Irving Howe, copyright © 1989 by the *New Republic*.

Pantheon Books, a division of Random House, for excerpts from *Selling Culture* by Debora Silverman, copyright © 1986 by Debora Silverman.

Library of Congress Cataloging-in-Publication Data:
Culture in an age of money : the legacy of the 1980s in America / edited with an
    introduction by Nicolaus Mills.
        p.   cm.
    ISBN 0-929587-35-9
    1. United States—Civilization—1970–   2. Arts, American. 3. Arts, Modern—20th
Century—United States. I. Mills, Nicolaus.
E169.12.C78   1990
973.927—dc20   90-37347

For Barb Pequet and Si Kahn,
and in memory of Arthur Wohl

CONTENTS

CULTURE IN AN AGE OF MONEY

Nicolaus Mills

THE CULTURE OF TRIUMPH AND THE SPIRIT OF THE TIMES

In early 1981, as the Reagan administration was getting under way, its first cultural controversy began. Nancy Reagan wanted new china for the White House. The cost of the china was the problem. The Lenox pattern with a raised gold presidential seal in the center that the president's wife chose came to $209,508 for 220 place settings. At a time when her husband was talking about cutting welfare eligibility and the misery index (inflation plus unemployment) was over 20 percent, Nancy Reagan's desire for new china seemed like an idea borrowed from Marie Antoinette.

Nicolaus Mills is Professor of American Studies at Sarah Lawrence College and a co-editor of *Dissent*. His books include *The New Journalism*, *Busing USA*, and *The Crowd in American Literature*.

Democrats rubbed their hands in glee. What they failed to understand was that a new era was starting. American culture in the 1980s would be a culture based on triumph—on the admiration of power and status—and nothing would be more important to that culture than its symbols. Especially at the start, they were what allowed the president to insist, "We have every right to dream heroic dreams."

The America that the Reagan administration inherited was an America still in shock from a decade of humiliation. The country had lost the longest war in its history. A president had resigned in disgrace. The economy was in shambles. Only a quarter of the voting-age population felt the government could be trusted to do what was right most of the time. New White House china would not erase these past humiliations, but like the president's pledge "to make America proud again," new china would be a start in the right direction.

During his final year in office, Jimmy Carter had talked about the country's "malaise." But for the Reagans, triumph would be the watchword. "The cynics were wrong. America never was a sick society," Ronald Reagan declared. In the 1980s his America would not look or act like a weakling nation. The president and his guests would eat off china that proclaimed, "The era of self-doubt is over." The demeaning humility of a Jimmy Carter, who allowed Iran to hold Americans hostage for 444 days and insisted he liked peanut butter sandwiches, was past.

Two decades earlier, John Kennedy made social commitment seem glamorous, and what followed was a counterculture in which civil rights, the antiwar movement, and Woodstock all had their place. Ronald Reagan's version of Camelot was Disneyland, and what followed was a culture in which the "magic of the marketplace" replaced the Magic Kingdom. "The marketplace will take care of children," Reagan's Federal Communications Commissioner Mark Fowler announced shortly after taking office. His remarks were intended for critics of children's television, but what lay behind them was a much deeper faith in the way things worked.

Money words—yuppie, upscale, privatization, takeover—became the key language of the 1980s, and they signaled a culture with an insatiable need to proclaim its triumphs. Even more important, especially after the Nixon-Ford-Carter years, they signaled a culture that was coherent in its promise. In the culture of triumph, the past was modern because it held the key to the future. Image was crucial because we needed to see ourselves afresh. Getting rich was justified because it left the nation better off. Cutting aid to the poor was humane because welfare hurt initiative.

A century earlier, government helped pave the way for the Gilded Age by ending both the inheritance tax and the income tax. In the 1980s the Reagan administration moved in a similar direction, cutting personal taxes and establishing Justice Department guidelines that all but ended antitrust activity. Businesses and individuals were given the green light to create the kind of America Ronald Reagan had in mind when he declared, "What I want to see above all is that this remains a country where someone can always get rich." It did not take long for the green light to be noticed. "Conspicuous consumption," Gilded Age critic Thorstein Veblen's phrase for the ostentation of the leisure class, became in the 1980s "flaunting it." For a figure like real estate mogul Donald Trump, it was not enough to be seen in all the right places. It was essential to brand the world one occupied: to live in Trump Tower, to fly Trump Shuttle, to sail on the Trump Princess.

In *Liar's Poker*, an account of his days on Wall Street in the 1980s, Michael Lewis described his work at Salomon Brothers as occurring in the center of a modern gold rush. "Never have so many unskilled twenty-four-year-olds made so much money in so little time as we did in this decade," Lewis wrote. He was not indulging in hyperbole, not in a decade in which Drexel Burnham Lambert executive Michael Milken made $550 million in one year. On Wall Street the culture of triumph was king, and the key to it was the creation of a paper economy in which the buying and selling of companies was more profitable than running them.

For the "hot" brokerage firms, ethics became irrelevant. Shortly before filing for bankruptcy in 1990, Drexel Burnham Lambert paid its executives $350 million in bonuses—almost as much as it owed its creditors. And even among conservative brokerage houses, new rules and a new psychology reigned.

The 1980s became the decade in which the hostile takeover was made possible by the leveraged buyout and the junk bond, when greenmail was paid to avoid a takeover, when companies were attacked by raiders and saved by white knights, when fired executives floated into retirement on golden parachutes. Only a cynic or the special interests (labor unions, the civil rights movement) would oppose such a culture. As Secretary of Education William Bennett bragged to the Heritage Foundation in a 1986 address, "American conservatism now sets the terms of our debate. It does so because, without in the least abandoning its principles, it has succeeded in identifying itself with the quintessential American appetite for new challenges and new opportunities."

In foreign policy the most dramatic indication of the new culture of triumph was reflected in the revival of an imperial America committed to showing its power. Between 1980 and 1987 the military budget more than doubled, climbing to $282 billion annually. But the real change was in the country's inner psychology, its abandonment of what Ronald Reagan called our "Vietnam syndrome." The Grenada invasion of 1983 showed how serious the president was when he insisted Vietnam "was, in truth, a noble cause." The invasion came less than seventy-two hours after Lebanese terrorists killed 241 Marines in their Beirut barracks, and it refocused attention on a part of the world that had been an American sore spot since the Nicaraguan revolution of 1979.

The fighting itself was over in days. The casualties were light: nineteen killed, 115 wounded. The army, nonetheless, gave out 8,612 medals, and for the country there was an enormous release of tension. We were no longer a helpless giant. It was now clear what the president meant when during the 1980 campaign he declared, "There is a lesson for us all in Vietnam . . . let us tell those who fought that war that we will never again ask young men to fight and possibly die in a war that our government is afraid to let them win."

The philosophical groundwork for such interventionism had been laid in 1979 by Jeane Kirkpatrick, later Reagan's United Nations ambasssador, in an article entitled, "Dictatorships and Double Standards." Now such thinking had a base in reality. After Grenada it became easier to reimagine Vietnam as a war that America could have won. No longer did the Vietnam vet have to be a 1970s figure like the sensitive, crippled hero John Voight played in *Coming Home*. The vet of the 1980s could be Sylvester Stallone's John Rambo, whose rage and muscularity argue that we did not lose Vietnam on the battle-field, and who, on going back to rescue his POW buddies, asks the perfect Reagan question, "This time do we get to win?"

The domestic equivalent of Rambo was the Wall Street buccaneer, the takeover artist that financier Asher Edelman sought to cultivate in his Columbia Business School course "Corporate Raiding—The Art of War," when he offered a $100,000 bounty to any student who found a company he could acquire. The real economic hero of the culture of triumph was, however, the dream consumer, the yuppie. It was the yuppie lifestyle that the Reagan administration had in mind when it adopted the logic of the Laffer curve, which said that if tax rates, especially at the upper level, were lowered, the rich would try to get even richer and in so doing improve the economy and government revenues.

There were, of course, jokes about the materialism of yuppies and their passion for brand names. But the yuppie was someone the 1980s culture quickly learned to love. As the popular television sitcom *Family Ties* showed, the yuppie was the button-down kid who knew the path to the good life. His 1960s baby-boom parents might not understand his ambitions, but they

could not help being impressed (particularly when he was as
likable as Michael J. Fox's Alex Keaton) with how good he was at
looking out for number one.

For Ronald Reagan the roots of an America in which patriotism and prosperity reigned supreme lay in the Revolution. There
we had established our independence. There, as he told the
nation in a July 4th radio address, we "began with a tax revolt."
The key was to go back to the future. "Our new beginning is a
continuation of that beginning created two centuries ago," the
president declared in his second inaugural. He did not, however,
rely on rhetoric or legislation alone to define the "Second
American Revolution" he was after. As he knew from his
Hollywood days, the essence of modern America was image.

For Reagan and the culture of triumph, the extravaganza thus
became the crucial public event of the 1980s. Nothing else so
clearly dramatized what both were about or showed what the
president meant when he said, "When I spoke about a new
beginning, I was talking about much more than budget cuts and
incentives for savings and investment. I was talking about a
fundamental change . . . that honors the legacy of the Founding
Fathers."

The first inauguration with its $8 million price tag for four days
of celebration set the tone for the extravaganzas that followed. It
began with an $800,000 fireworks display at the Lincoln Memori-
al, followed by two nights of show-business performances presided over by the Reagans, and finally, on the fourth day, nine
inaugural balls which conjured up the image of an American
Versailles. From Almaden Vineyards came 14,400 bottles of
champagne. From the Society of American Florists $13,000
worth of roses. From Ridgewell's caterers 400,000 hors d'oeuvres.
"When you've got to pay $2,000 for a limousine for four days, $7
to park, and $2.50 to check your coat at a time when most people
in the country can't hack it, that's ostentation," Senator Barry
Goldwater groused. Goldwater had missed the point. The extravaganzas of the 1980s, like the culture of triumph, were not

concerned with the work ethic of small-town America. They were advertisements for America the Grand, and their aesthetic, as Reagan-era historian Sidney Blumenthal shrewdly observed, was one in which the beautiful was the expensive, the good was the costly.

The inaugural aesthetic was repeated at the 1984 Olympics in Los Angeles. The president did not attend the games, instead contenting himself with urging the American team to "Do it for the Gipper." But in every other respect he was the dominant Olympic figure. His "new patriotism" was reflected in the crowds chanting "USA, USA" every time an American athlete competed. Most of all, the "resurgence of national pride" that the president wanted the country to feel was captured in the $6 million opening and closing ceremonies directed by Hollywood producer David Wolper. "The tone of the opening ceremony is going to be majesty," Wolper promised, and what followed were the most political Olympics since 1936. Wolper's plan to have an eagle take off from the west rim of the Coliseum and soar down onto the field during the playing of the national anthem was canceled at the last minute. But everything else went like clockwork. Church bells rang throughout the city. A plane wrote "WELCOME" across the sky, and a cast of nine thousand—including 125 trumpeters, three hundred placard bearers, and eighty-four pianists playing "Rhapsody in Blue"—performed on cue.

The peak in extravaganzas came two years later, on July 4, 1986, with the hundredth anniversary of the Statue of Liberty. It was the perfect Reagan moment, an occasion to match the politics of restoration with the restoration of a national monument. On opening night, as the faces of the president and his wife were superimposed on the image of the relit statue, he took the tribute in stride, as if such a blending of iconography were only natural. Later he spoke of his tax bill putting a smile on Liberty, but here, as at his inaugural, the president knew that the best way to be effective was to play a role. The spectacle of Liberty Weekend, like that of the Olympics, was left to David Wolper to orchestrate. With a $30 million budget and no athletes to worry about, Wolper had few constraints. Television rights for the weekend went to ABC for $10 million. Millions more came from sponsors paying to use the statue in their advertising. Like the candy makers who carved a fourteen-foot chocolate replica of Liberty or the caterer who molded her likeness out of sixty pounds of chopped liver, Wolper was free to let scale dictate choice.

On Thursday a 1.4 million-watt series of laser beams shot across New York harbor to illuminate the relit statue for the first time. On Friday, following the largest assembly of ships since the end of World War II, the evening concluded with the largest fireworks display in U.S. history (twenty tons of materials, forty thousand projectiles) computer coordinated to music played aboard the carrier *John F. Kennedy* by the Marine Corps band), and on Sunday the greatest spectacle of all at Meadowlands Stadium in New Jersey: a cast of twelve thousand, including two hundred Elvis Presley impersonators, three hundred Jazzercise dancers, and an eight-hundred-voice chorus, performing on a twenty-tier stage with five waterfalls. The extravaganza's message was again unmistakable. To be American was to be powerful, and to be powerful was to be rich.

What about the homeless, whom Los Angeles police swept off the streets during the Olympics? Or the poor, whom the Statue of Liberty welcomed but who were not welcome at Liberty Weekend? "The social safety net for the elderly, the needy, the disabled, and the unemployed will be left intact," the president promised. But the crucial point was that such a safety net, like the safety net for the circus aerialist, was to be kept out of sight. The problem with our concern for the poor, both the Reagan administration and the culture of triumph held, was that in the past it had crippled them. In his influential 1984 book, *Losing Ground*, conservative Charles Murray of the Manhattan Institute described how, as a result of relaxed welfare standards and liberal court rulings, the 1960s had made it easier for the poor to get along without jobs and get away with crimes. For Ronald Reagan, the Murray view of poverty offered the perfect reason to cut back on aiding the poor. "Federal welfare programs have created a massive social problem," he insisted. "Government created a poverty trap that wreaks havoc on the very support system the poor most need to lift themselves out of poverty—the family."

"Reagan made the denial of compassion respectable," New York governor Mario Cuomo complained. "He justified it by saying not only that the government wasted money, but also that poor people were somehow better off without government help in the first place." The country was, however, in no mood to listen to Cuomo or bother with figures showing that in the 1980s the living standard of the bottom fifth of the country dropped by 8 percent while that of the top fifth rose by 16 percent. Indeed, the kind of denial Reagan and Charles Murray had made respectable with regard to the poor was part of a much larger pattern of denial that was inseparable from the culture of triumph.

Irangate, the stock market crash of 1987, the scandals at the Environmental Protection Agency, the influence-peddling trials of White House aides Michael Deaver and Lyn Nofziger might easily have changed the country politically. But the culture of triumph made dwelling on such negatives a repudiation of what was best in America. We had gotten ourselves into trouble during the 1970s by imagining we were weak when we were not. There was no point in going through that again. In the president's words, "We've stopped looking at our warts and rediscovered how much there is to love in this blessed land."

A powerful counterculture might have challenged such a selective approach to events, but even at its best the counterculture of the 1980s found itself checked by the culture of triumph. The precedent set in 1980, when the mourning for John Lennon's Christmas-season assassination was quickly overshadowed by the first Reagan inaugural, continued throughout the decade. Two years after its installation, Maya Lin's elegiac, black granite Vietnam Memorial was sharing space in Constitution Gardens with Frederick Hart's bronze statues of three battle-weary infantrymen. In even less time, Bruce Springsteen's *Born in the USA* album, with its haunting portrait of a young vet trying to eke out a living in a declining industrial town, became the musical inspiration for Chrysler automobile's upbeat "Made in the USA" commercial.

Most important, the liberal tradition that might have provided the counterculture of the 1980s with a political base collapsed. When accused of being a liberal during the 1988 presidential debates, Michael Dukakis complained about being labeled, before declaring weeks later that he was a liberal in the tradition of Franklin Roosevelt and John Kennedy. But the damage was done. By the end of the second presidential debate, the liberalism of Dukakis and the Democrats lay exposed as a narrow proceduralism—"scolding," Congressman Barney Frank called it—that made upholding the law the remedy for everything from crime in the street to Irangate.

In the end the 1980s offered no antidote for the cult of success which the culture of triumph made the centerpiece of the decade. When the public extravaganzas of the Reagan administration ended, the private extravaganzas of the superrich replaced them. The excesses of the Bradley Martins' famous party of 1897, in which the Waldorf ballroom was done over to resemble Versailles at the cost of $400,000, were given new life. In the summer of 1989, Wall Street financier Saul Steinberg's $1 million fiftieth birthday party was not even the event of the season. That honor went to publisher Malcolm Forbes for a $2 million seventieth birthday party in Morocco. There he and eight hundred guests, flown from the United States on three jet airplanes, were entertained by six hundred acrobats, jugglers, and belly dancers, had an honor guard of three hundred Berber horsemen, and consumed 216 magnums of champagne in toasts.

"How do you defend it? I don't try to defend it," Forbes said of his party. A few years earlier, shortly before his conviction for insider trading, Wall Street arbitrager Ivan Boesky put the same sentiments in even blunter language. "Greed is all right, by the way," he declared in his 1986 commencement speech at the

University of California Business School in Berkeley. "Greed is healthy."

In Oliver Stone's film *Wall Street*, Boesky's words were echoed by Michael Douglas playing Gordon Gekko, a ruthless corporate raider who relies on insider information to make his deals. "Greed, for lack of a better word, is good. Greed is right. Greed works," Gekko, sounding for all the world like a revivalist preacher, tells a group of worried stockholders.

In all the arts, however, not just film, a Boesky-like obsession with money set the tone for the 1980s. "Plutography," Tom Wolfe's neologism for the "graphic depiction of the acts of the rich," became the decade's guiding aesthetic. Plutography defined novels like Wolfe's own best-seller, *The Bonfire of the Vanities*, with its portrait of Sherman McCoy, a Wall Street broker who lives in a world where at forty either you are making a million a year or you're an incompetent. In an even more obvious way, plutography defined television's hit series. *Dynasty* and *Dallas* made family money wars the heart of weekly programming and paved the way for Robin Leach's *Lifestyles of the Rich and Famous*, which took viewers on shopping trips along Rodeo Drive and into the homes of the wealthy before ending with Leach's trademark sign-off, "May you have caviar wishes and champagne dreams."

Even the fine arts were not immune to the 1980s cult of success. The new art hero was not the starving painter living in a Greenwich village walkup. The new art hero was the promoter who knew how to make art pay. In New York's SoHo, once a sweatshop and warehouse district, gallery-owner Mary Boone got as much attention as the artists in her stable, among them David Salle and Julian Schnabel, for her ability to sell their work to the right collectors (those with museum connections), then promote it so that its secondary-market value (resale) skyrocketed. Uptown a similar phenomenon was going on at normally staid Sotheby's, which from 1979 to 1989 did more than $10 billion in business. Even for people who never went to museums, Sotheby's prices were news, and before the decade was up, its chief auctioneer,

John Marion, acquired the celebrity of a television game-show host for his suave handling of sales which brought in $53.4 million for Van Gogh's *Irises* and $20.7 million (a record for a living artist) for Willem de Kooning's *Interchange*.

The ultimate link between consumerism and high art was however, the Bloomingdale's–Metropolitan Museum alliance. In 1980 both turned their attention to aristocratic China and to what the Bloomingdale's ads called "forty years of opulence." But the link did not end here. As art historian Debora Silverman pointed out, what Bloomingdale's was packaging as fashion, the Met was packaging as art. Robes from the Met's "Costume of China" exhibit were first shown to the public at Bloomingdale's along with the reproductions for sale in the store. Then, on being returned to the Met, the robes were displayed on mannequins dressed by Met curator and former *Harper's Bazaar* fashion editor Diana Vreeland. The problem, as critics were quick to point out, was that the Met mannequins were not dressed according to Chinese custom. Their clothes should have shown their bearers' places in the caste system and in the hierarchy of man and nature. Instead what dictated their layered look in the museum was what had dictated their look at Bloomingdale's: the illusion of fashionable luxury they could be made to convey.

In the eyes of Diana Vreeland and the Met's Costume Institute, the China show was, nonetheless, a stunning success, and for the rest of the 1980s it set the tone for the Met's alliance with the fashion world. Two years later the Met mounted a costume exhibit on aristocratic womanhood, "La Belle Epoque," which was closely followed by what Bloomingdale's called a "dazzling salute" to the products and style of France, "Fete de France." In 1983 came a Met exhibition "Twenty-Five Years of Yves Saint Laurent," and one year later "Man and the Horse, presented by Polo/Ralph Lauren." By the end of the decade, the museum–department store alliance which the Met's Costume Institute made a norm had spread to other cities as well. In 1987 Boston's Institute of Contemporary Art and Filene's joined forces to sponsor Richard Avedon's photography exhibit, "In the American

West." Avedon's Western portraits were used not only to promote a "Wild Cactus Ball" at Filene's but on Filene's ads in the *Boston Globe* and on the inside cover of its spring catalog.

The Metropolitan Museum of Art's belief that in the 1980s high culture and consumerism could be combined was no mistake. As the decade's personal fashion showed, nothing was so sexy as the look of money. While the Met's Chinese costume exhibit was going on, the *New York Times Magazine* carried an article by Francesca Stanfill, "Living Well Is the Best Revenge," heralding the arrival of an era in which the successful "have no fear of ostentation, nor are they inhibited by the presence of discretion that often characterizes those with old fortunes." The article was about Oscar and Françoise de la Renta, but it was no less applicable to the Reagans. The president in his jodhpurs and Nancy Reagan in her $25,000 worth of inaugural gowns (later, $46,000 for the second inaugural) were once again paving the way for the culture of triumph. As novelist and style critic Alison Lurie observed, "The rich need to look secure now, and to look secure you need to look rich." Before the decade was up, even the stores selling the new elegance figured out ways to flaunt it. To make its flagship store in New York fit its clothes image, Ralph Lauren's gutted the inside of the 1898 Rhinelander mansion, changing it to look like a cross between an English country house and a gentleman's club.

Nor did the changes stop here. The 1980s were not only the decade of the power lunch and the power tie, but the power physique. A decade earlier the middle class had jogged its way to health. In the 1980s it powered its way to health with the Nautilus machine, and when that didn't work, there was always liposuction. As the Calvin Klein Obsession for Men cologne ads—with their muscular male and female nude models—showed, the point of the new elegance was to make it clear that what lay below all the surface luxury was raw power.

Even romance was unable to resist the success ethic of the culture of triumph. The essence of romance in the 1980s became the successful marriage. (By 1989 even *Playboy* founder Hugh Hefner had remarried.) In the age of AIDS, such a change made sexual sense, but nothing fueled the change so much as money and the vision of a home in which husband and wife were proven wage-earners. As Mike Nichols's 1988 film *Working Girl* showed, even office romance was now different. The Staten Island–born secretary of *Working Girl* proves herself lovable not by being helpless but by being a financial wiz. When her Wellesley-educated boss gets hurt in a skiing accident, she substitutes for her and pulls off a takeover that wins the heart of her future husband, a Wall Street broker. What dazzles him is that she is better in business than he. He can marry her with the assurance that rather than taking a financial risk he is forming a partnership that will leave him better off. At the end of the film, there is no romantic talk about babies or housework. As music floods the soundtrack, we see the former secretary, now with an office and secretary of her own, starting her work day confident that she has at last arrived where she wants to be.

"They called it the Reagan Revolution, and I'll accept that, but for me it always seemed like the Great Rediscovery: a rediscovery of our values and our common sense," Ronald Reagan declared in his farewell address. The sentiments were vintage Reagan. In his 1986 State of the Union address, he had even used a line from the hit film *Back to the Future* to illustrate his belief that our pre-1960s past was the key to our future. As the decade progressed, far less gifted politicians than the president learned from his example that if the past could be appropriated, it was a powerful weapon for discrediting anyone who opposed the culture of triumph and the traditions it stood for.

Attorney General Edwin Meese justified his attacks on the Warren Court by charging that the Court had violated the "original intention" of the Constitution. Secretary of Education William Bennett opposed the liberalization of college curriculums on the grounds that it disregarded "the American common culture." Even the media found that they could gain new legitimacy by wrapping themselves in the past. Trying to regain readers it had lost to the feminist movement of the 1960s and 1970s, *Good Housekeeping* magazine appealed to a woman it called the "New Traditionalist." "She's a contemporary woman," the *Good Housekeeping* ads declared, "who has made a new commitment to the traditional values that some people thought were old-fashioned."

The *Good Housekeeping* ads could be written off as self-promotion. But the nostalgia of the president and men like Meese and Bennett was another story. It was rooted in the kind of historical absolutism that prompted the president's favorite televangelist, Jerry Falwell, to call America "back to biblical morality, back to sensibility, and back to patriotism." What lay behind such calls to action was the belief that the foundations of contemporary precedent were shaky. They could be challenged wherever they conflicted with the country's authentic past. There was no need for the modern conservative to adopt traditional conservative restraint.

The legal consequences of such thinking were immediately apparent in the willingness of the Reagan appointees to the Supreme Court to overturn precedents established a decade earlier in affirmative action and abortion rights. But the most dramatic indication of what the historical absolutism of the culture of triumph meant for the 1980s came with the Bush administration's response to a Supreme Court decision it did not expect: the 1989 ruling upholding flag burning as symbolic speech protected by the First Amendment.

"The flag represents and reflects the fabric of our nation—our dreams, our destiny, our very fiber as a people," the new president declared angrily as he called for a constitutional amendment to make flag desecration illegal. His language, his insistence that the fabric of the flag and the fabric of the country were the same, was pure Reaganism, as was the backdrop, the Iwo Jima Memorial, he chose for his speech. But the moment was also one that summed up how much the culture of triumph, with its symbolism and claims on the past, had come to dominate

American life in the 1980s. Even the low-cal Reaganism of George Bush could not escape its hold. In the final year of the decade, it was no longer hubris to think that what the Founding Fathers really meant by the First Amendment needed to be spelled out with another amendment.

Nor was it hubris to think that the climactic international event of the decade—the dismantling of the Berlin Wall—could be commodified. Within three weeks of East Germany's November 1989 opening of the Wall, a Missouri-based gift company was selling "authentic cuts" from the wall in stores across the United States. By year's end 750,000 cuts—neatly boxed and costing up to $14.95—had been sold. The cuts were, their ads declared, "a proud tribute to freedom," but within the context of the 1980s, they were more than that. They were mirrors of a culture rooted in the belief that possession is the key to authenticity.

Who in 1980 could have imagined such an irony: chips from the most hated communist symbol of the Cold War on sale in American department stores for the price of a paperweight? In the final year of the decade, it was, however, an essay by Francis Fukuyama, "The End of History?" published in the conservative quarterly the *National Interest*, that provided the culture of triumph with its ultimate compliment. Hailed from the start by such leading conservative intellectuals as Allan Bloom, Gertrude Himmelfarb, and Irving Kristol, before the year was up "The End of History?" had achieved the notoriety that forty years earlier George Kennan, writing as Mr. X, had won for his famous article "The Sources of Soviet Conduct" in *Foreign Affairs*.

Fukuyama, like Kennan in 1947 a member of the State Department planning staff, based his article on Hegel's theories about the relationship between consciousness and history. But what brought "The End of History?" immediate attention was not Fukuyama's reworking of Hegelian theory. It was his bold assertion that "something very fundamental has happened in world history"—the universalization of Western liberal democracy and the free-market economy supporting it. By that Fukuyama did not mean that historical conflict was over or that all governments had actually become Westernized. His point was rather that the last systemic rival to Western liberalism, Marxism-Leninism, was dead as a mobilizing ideology. The "triumph of the West" was complete.

"The End of History?" was the perfect coda to the 1980s for the culture of triumph and its supporters. Their ideal America had always been America the Grand. Now Fukuyama was saying that the values of America the Grand dominated the world. "The End of History?" not only held that America's ideological battle with communism—in Reagan myth, the Evil Empire—had been won. It also held that on the domestic front America could justifiably abandon any concern with systemic change. Poverty in America, Fukuyama went on to conclude, did not stem from underlying legal and social structures but from the cultural and social character of the poor and the premodern legacy of racism and slavery.

The authors of the fifteen essays that make up *Culture in an Age of Money* take a very different view of the last ten years. If anything emerges from the essays collected here, it is a sense that, while the victories of the culture of triumph have been frequent, they have been largely hollow. Wall Street's takeover psychology may have left brokers rich, but it has spawned an unproductive paper economy. Glitz architecture may have changed our cities, but it has given us a series of overdone, flashy buildings. Television news may have gotten better at predicting elections, but it has depoliticized political campaigning.

What follows here is not, however, a running debate over Francis Fukuyama's endism or the culture of triumph. The essays that make up *Culture in an Age of Money* are, above all else, a practical attempt to explain why the new conservative culture of the 1980s was so dominant and what we can learn from the opposition to it, whether it came from antiwar Vietnam films or a "New Black Aesthetic." The essays in this collection are thus not—to use Todd Gitlin's phrase—built upon zeitgeist mongering.

They concentrate instead on specific trends and cultural types: on yuppies, pluggies, televangelists, the end of the common reader, the rise of a new success novel.

After a decade in which the political party that promoted and identified itself with the culture of triumph swept every presidential election, such a focus is more crucial than ever. Those who gave Ronald Reagan and George Bush their overwhelming victories were not voting out of simple self-interest, especially in a year like 1984 when they were 54 percent of blue-collar workers, 59 percent of white-collar workers, and 57 percent of those with incomes between $12,500 and $24,999. They were voting for a culture they saw as hopeful and with which they identified, even when it failed to benefit them directly. As we enter the 1990s, it is essential to understand that culture and how it overshadowed its opposition. Nothing less will do if the 1990s are to be different from the 1980s, if our post–Cold War budgets are to yield a peace dividend.

Todd Gitlin

BLIPS, BITES AND SAVVY TALK

In the pilot film for the 1987 television series *Max Headroom*, an investigative reporter discovers that an advertiser is compressing television commercials into almost instantaneous "blipverts," units so high-powered they can cause some viewers to explode. American television has long been compressing politics into chunks, ten-second "bites," and images that freeze into icons as they repeat across millions of screens and newspapers. The 1980s were saturated with these memorialized mo-

Todd Gitlin is Professor of Sociology at the University of California, Berkeley. His five books include *The Whole World Is Watching, Inside Prime Time*, and *The Sixties: Years of Hope, Days of Rage*. His articles appear regularly in *Dissent, The Nation*, the *New York Times*, and the *Los Angeles Times*.

ments. Think of Ronald Reagan at the Korean DMZ, wearing a flak jacket, field glasses, keeping an eye on the North Korean Communists; or in the bunker at Omaha Beach, simulating the wartime performance he had spared himself during the actual World War II. Think of the American medical student kissing American soil after the troops had evacuated him from Grenada. Think of Star Wars animation and Oliver North saluting. The sense of history as a collage reaches some sort of twilight of the idols when we think of the 1988 election. There it is hard to think of anything *but* blips and bites: the Pledge of Allegiance; George Bush touring the garbage of Boston Harbor (leaving aside that some of the spot was shot elsewhere); the face of Willie Horton; the mismatch of tank and Michael Dukakis. The question I want to raise is whether chunk news has caused democratic politics to explode.

Although I pose the question in an extreme form, it is hardly alien to 1988's endless campaign journalism. Indeed, the journalists were obsessed with the question of whether media images had become the campaign, and if so, whose fault that was. That obsession is itself worth scrutiny. But consider first the coverage itself. According to the most relentless of studies as well as the evidence of the senses, the main mode of campaign journalism is the horse-race story. Here is that preoccupation—indeed, enchantment—with means characteristic of a society that is competitive, bureaucratic, professional, and technological all at once. The big questions of the campaign, in poll and story, are *Who's ahead? Who's falling behind? Who's gaining?*

This is an observation only a fool would deny. I recall a conversation I had with a network correspondent in 1980. I criticized the horse-race coverage of the primaries. "I know," he said. "We've been trying to figure out what we can do differently. We haven't been able to figure it out." To a great though not universal extent, the media still haven't. They can't. The popularity of unexamined military and sports metaphors like "campaign" and "race" shows how deep the addiction runs. This is a success culture bedazzled by sports statistics and empty of criteria other than numbers to answer the question, "How am I doing?" Journalists compete, news organizations compete—the channeled aggression of the race is what makes their blood run. In the absence of a vital polis, they take polls.

By 1988 the obsession had reached new heights, or depths: one night, ABC News devoted fourteen minutes, almost two-thirds of the news section of the newscast, to a poll—a bigger bloc by far than was given to any issue. In a perverse way, the journalists' fancy for polls is a stratagem directed toward mastery. Here at least is something they know how to do, something they can be good at without defying their starting premise, which is, after all, deference. Their stance is an insouciant subservience. They have imposed upon themselves a code they call objectivity but that is more properly understood as a mixture of obsequiousness and fatalism—it is not "their business" in general to affront the authorities, not "their place" to declare who is lying and who is right. Starting from the premise that they haven't the right to raise issues the candidates don't raise or explore records the candidates don't explore, they can at least ask a question they feel entitled to answer: "Who's ahead?" How can racing addicts be chased away from the track?

By 1988 the fact that the horse race had become the principal "story" was itself "old news." Many in the news media had finally figured out one thing they could do differently. They could take the audience backstage, behind the horse race, into the paddocks, the stables, the clubhouse, and the bookie joints. But this time horse-race coverage was joined by handicapping coverage—stories about campaign tactics, what the handlers were up to, how the reporters felt about being handled: in short, *How are the candidates trying to do it to us, and how are they doing at it?* Anxiety lay behind this new style—anxiety that Reagan really had pulled the Teflon over their eyes, that they had been suckered by the smoothly whirring machinery of his stagecraft. So handicapping coverage was a defensive maneuver, and a self-flattering one: the media could in this way show that they were immune from the ministrations of campaign professionals.

The result is what many people call a postmodern move, in two senses: enchantment with the means toward the means and ingratiation via a pass at deconstruction. There is a lot of this in American culture nowadays: the postmodern high culture of the 1960s (paintings calling attention to their paintedness, novels exposing their novelistic machinery) has swept into popular culture. An aspirin commercial dizzyingly toys with itself ("I'm not a doctor, though I play one on TV," says a soap opera actor); an Isuzu commercial bids for trust by using subtitles to expose the lies of the overenthusiastic pitchman; actors face the audience and speak "out of character" in *Moonlighting*. Campaign coverage in 1988 reveled in this mode. Viewers were invited to be cognoscenti of their own bamboozlement.

This was the campaign that made "sound bite," "spin control," "spin doctor," and "handler" into household phrases. Dukakis handlers even made a commercial about Bush handlers wringing their hands about how to handle Dan Quayle, a commercial that went over far better with hip connoisseurs than with the unhip rest of the audience who had trouble tracing the commercial to Dukakis. This campaign metacoverage, coverage of the coverage, partakes of the postmodern fascination with surfaces and the machinery that cranks them out, a fascination indistinguishable from surrender—as if once we understand that all images are concocted we have attained the only satisfaction the heart and mind are capable of. (This is the famous Brechtian "alienation effect" but with a difference: Brecht thought that actors, by standing outside and "presenting" their characters, could lay bare social relations and show that life could be changed; paradoxically, campaign metacoverage, by laying bare the campaign's tactics and inside doings, demonstrates only that the campaign is a juggernaut that cannot be diverted.) Thus, voiceovers explained knowingly that the candidate was going to a flag factory or driving a tank in order to score public relations points. Here, for example, is ABC's Brit Hume narrating the appearance of George Bush at a flag factory on September 20, 1988: "Bush aides deny he came here to wrap himself in the flag, but if that wasn't the point of this visit, what was it?"

In the same vein was the new postdebate ritual: the networks featuring campaign spin doctors, on camera, telling reporters why their respective candidates had done just fine, while the network correspondents affected an arch superiority and print reporters insisted that the spin doctors couldn't spin *them*. Meanwhile, the presumably unspinnable pundits rattled on about how the candidates performed, whether they had given good sound bite— issuing reviews, in other words, along with behind-the-scenes assessments of the handlers' skill in setting expectations for the performance, so that, for example, if Dan Quayle succeeded in speaking whole sentences he was to be decreed a success in "doing what he set out to do."

These rituals exhibited the insouciant side of insouciant subservience—reporters dancing attendance at the campaign ball while insisting that they were actually following their own beat. Evaluating the candidates' claims and records was considered highbrow and boring—and potentially worse. For to probe too much or too far into issues, to show too much initiative in stating the public problems, would be seen by the news business as hubris, a violation of their unwritten agreement to let the candidates set the public agenda. Curiously, the morning shows, despite their razzmatazz, may have dwelt on issues more than the nightly news—largely because the morning interviewers were not so dependent on Washington insiders, not so tightly bound to the source-cultivating and glad-handing that guide reportage inside the Beltway. It was a morning show that discovered that the Bush and Dukakis campaigns had hired the same Hollywood lighting professionals to illuminate their rallies. (Possibly the Dukakis handlers had learned from Mondale's blunder in turning a 1984 debate lighting decision over to Reagan's more skilled poeple, leaving Mondale showing rings under his eyes—so Michael Deaver told Mark Hertsgaard, as reported in Hertsgaard's *On Bended Knee*.)

As befit the new and sometimes dizzying self-consciousness,

reporters sometimes displayed, even in public, a certain awareness that they were players in a game not of their own scripting; that they could be had, and were actively being had, by savvy handlers; and that they were tired of being had. The problem first acquired media currency with a tale told by Hedrick Smith, in his 1988 book *The Power Game*, about a 1984 campaign piece by Leslie Stahl. Here is Stahl's own version of the story as she told it the night after the election on ABC's *Viewpoint:*

> This was a five-minute piece on the evening news . . . at the end of President Reagan's '84 campaign, and the point of the piece was to really criticize him for—I didn't use this language in the piece—but the point was, he was trying to create amnesia over the budget cuts. For instance . . . I showed him at the Handicapped Olympics, and I said, you wouldn't know by these pictures that this man tried to cut the budget for the handicapped. And the piece went on and on like that. It was very tough, and I was very nervous about going back to the White House the next day, Sam [she is talking to fellow panelist Sam Donaldson], because I thought they'd never return my phone calls and they'd keep returning yours. [This is Exhibit B on factors inhibiting press criticism: the competition of the pack, which can produce protracted press honeymoons and pile-ons.—T.G.] But my phone rang, and it was a White House official [Richard Darman, according to a reliable source], and he said, "Great piece, Leslie." And I said, "Come on, that was a tough—what do you mean, 'great piece'?" And he said, "We loved it, we loved it, we loved it. Thank you very much. It was a five-minute commercial, you know, unpaid commercial for our campaign." I said, "Didn't you hear what I said? I was tough." "Nobody heard what you said. They just saw the five minutes of beautiful pictures of Ronald Reagan. They saw the balloons, they saw the flags, they saw the red, white and blue. Haven't you people figured out yet that the picture always overrides what you say?"

The 1988 answer was, apparently not. For the networks and

the candidates (successful candidates, anyway) share an interest in what they consider "great pictures," that is, images that evoke myths. Curiously, the famous cynicism of journalists does not keep them from being gullible. Indeed, in this setting, cynicism and gullibility are two sides of the same con. The handlers count on the gullible side when they gamble that cameras, to paraphrase the ex-president's masterful slip on the subject of facts, are stupid things. That is why the Reagan staffers were proud of their public relations triumphs; their business was to produce what one of them called "our little playlets"—far-flung photo opportunities with real-life backdrops. Print reporters, meanwhile, were unable or unwilling to proceed differently. Although the pressure for "great pictures" doesn't apply, at least in the establishment press, the print people are unwilling to cede the "playlets" to television; they compete on television's terms, leaving the handlers free to set their agendas for them.

What is not altogether clear, of course, is whether the Reagan staffers were right to be proud of their public relations triumphs. We don't know, in fact, that "the picture always overrides what you say." Possibly that is true for some audiences, at some times, in some places, and not for others. What is clear, though, is that when the picture is stark enough, or the bite bites hard enough, journalists, especially on television, are unwilling to forgo the drama. To be boring is the cardinal sin. Embarrassed by their role as relay stations for orchestrated blips and bites, even amply rewarded journalists purport to resent the way Reagan's staff made megaphones of them; at the least they have become acutely self-conscious about their manipulability. The White House and the television-led press have been scrambling for relative advantage since the Kennedy administration; metacoverage was the press's attempt to recoup some losses.

Too Hip for Words
But to make sense of metacoverage I want to look at

the dominant form of political consciousness in a formally open but fundamentally depoliticized society, which is savviness.

Already in 1950, David Riesman in *The Lonely Crowd* described what he called the inside dopester—a consumer of politics who

> may be one who has concluded (with good reason) that since he can do nothing to change politics, he can only understand it. Or he may see all political issues in terms of being able to get some insider on the telephone. [In any case] he is politically cosmopolitan. . . . He will go to great lengths to keep from looking and feeling like the uninformed outsider.

The goal is "never to be taken in by any person, cause, or event."

Over the past forty years, Riesman's inside dopester has evolved into another type: a harsher, more brittle and cynical type still more knowledgeable in the ways in which things really work, still more purposefully disengaged, still more knowledgeable in a managerial way, allergic to political commitments. The premium attitude is a sort of knowing appraisal. Speaking up is less important—certainly less fun—than sizing up. Politics, real politics, is for "players"—fascinating term, for it implies that everyone else is a spectator. To be "interested in politics" is to know how to rate the players: Do they have good hands? How do they do in the clutch? How are they positioning themselves for the next day?

Savviness flatters spectators that they really do understand, that people like them are in charge, that even if they live outside the Beltway, they remain sovereign. Keeping up with the maneuvers of Washington insiders, defining the issues as they define them, savviness appeals to a spirit both managerial and voyeuristic. It transmutes the desire to participate into spectacle. One is already participating, in effect, by watching. "I like to watch" is *the* premium attitude. If you have a scorecard, you can tell the players. The ultimate inside dopesters are the political journalists.

Today, both advertising and political coverage flourish on, and suffer from, what Mark Crispin Miller has called "the hipness unto death." Miller argues that television advertising has learned to profess its power by apparently mocking it, standing aside from vulgar claims, assuring the viewer that all of us knowing types are too smart to be taken in by advertising, or gaucherie or passion of any kind. In the same way, the postmodern savviness of political coverage—whether in the glib version of a Bruce Morton or the more sedate version of MacNeil/Lehrer—binds its audience closer to an eerie politics of half-truth, deceit, and evasion in which ignorant symbols clash by night. If the players evade an issue, the savvy spectator knows enough to lose interest in it as well.

Coverage of the horse race and metacoverage of the handicappers both suit the discourse of savviness. They invite and cultivate an inside dopester's attitude toward politics—vicarious fascination coupled with knowing indifference.

It might well be, then, that Leslie Stahl's 1984 piece, like many others, was really three pieces. A critical audience got her point—Reagan was a hypocrite. An image-minded audience got the White House's point—Reagan personified national will and caring, even as the nice-guy martyr to wise-ass Eastern commentators. And inside dopesters got still another point—Reagan, master performer, was impervious to quarrelsome voiceovers.

Perhaps, too, there was a fourth piece—the backstage drama in which the White House made a point of showing Leslie Stahl her place. This must be humiliating for any reporter so old-fashioned as to want to take the measure of images against realities. Stahl's story reveals that the only alternative to complicity would be the damn-it-all spirit of an outsider indifferent to whether the handlers will favor her with scoop-worthy tidbits of information the next time. While telling Stahl that she's been had, the White House knows that, given her understanding of her job, she's going to be coming back for more stories; Deaver, the public relations man, knows that the surest way to make a reporter complicit is to treat her as an insider. As long as the agenda is set by the White House, or the campaign, the watchdog is defanged.

An Audience for the Spectacle

More must be said about what I just called the image-minded audience. For 1988 was not only the year of metacoverage; it was the year of the negative commercial, the bite, the clip, the image-blip. In theory, these chunks are television's distinct forte: the emotion-laden image in which an entire narrative is instantly present—Willie Horton, the flag, Bush with his granddaughter. The image is what rivets; the image is what is remembered. Research done by Ronald Lembo in the sociology department at Berkeley shows that some television viewers are inclined to follow narrative while others, disproportionately the young, pay more attention to distinct, out-of-context images.

What professional handlers and television journalists alike do is find images that condense their "little playlets," images that satisfy both lovers of story and lovers of image. Then blip-centered television floods the audience with images that compress and evoke an entire narrative. The 1980s began with one of these: the blindfolded American featured on the long-running melodrama called "America Held Hostage," sixty-three weeks of it during 1979–81, running on ABC at 11:30 five nights a week, propounding an image of America as a "pitiful helpless giant" (in Richard Nixon's phrase). Those were the months when Walter Cronkite signed off at CBS night after night by ticking off "the umpty-umpth day of captivity for the American hostages in Iran." In this ceremony of innocence violated, the moment arose to efface the national brooding over Vietnam. Now it could be seen that the Vietnam trauma had eclipsed the larger truth: it was the anti-Americans who were ugly. In the 1980s the American was the paleface captive of redskins. It was the the anti-American blindfold that disfigured him. The image cried out for a man to ride out of the sagebrush on a white horse into the White House.

The script for the Teheran playlet was not written by the Reagan handlers (although it is possible that they promised weapons to Iran's Revolutionary Guards in exchange for their keeping the hostages until election day), but they certainly knew how it would end.

We know how adept Reagan was at performing his playlets—he'd been doing them all his life. For eight years we heard endlessly, from reporters rushing about with spray cans of Teflon, about the mysterious personal qualities of the Great Communicator-in-Chief. But the mighty Wurlitzer of the media was primed for a figure who knew how to play upon it. The adaptability of the apparatus is exhibited by the media success of even so maladroit a figure as George Bush during the 1988 election. Having declared that Bush's central problem was to lick the wimp image, the media allowed him to impress them that once he started talking tough he turned out "stronger than expected." In their own fashion, Bush and his handlers—some of them fresh from Reagan's team—followed. Their masterwork was a Bush commercial that opens with a still photo on the White House lawn: Reagan to the right, at the side of the frame; Gorbachev at the center, shaking hands with the stern-faced Bush. The camera moves in on the vice president and Gorbachev; Reagan is left behind—having presided, he yields gracefully to his successor, the new man of the hour. As the camera moves closer, the stern face and the handshake take over, while the voiceover speaks the incantation: "strong . . . continue the arms control process . . . a president ready to go to work on day one." The entire saga is present in a single image: Bush the heir, the reliable, the man of strength who is also savvy enough to deal.

An American Tradition

How new is the reduction of political discourse to the horse race, the handicapping, the tailoring of campaigns to the concoction of imagery? What is particular to television? How good were the good old days?

Tempting as it is to assume that television has corrupted a previously virginal politics, the beginning of wisdom is history. As the campaigns invite us to read their blips, alarm is amply justified—but not because American politics has fallen from a pastoral of lucid debate and hushed, enlightened discourse to a hellish era of mudslinging and degraded sloganeering. Television did not invent the superficiality, triviality, and treachery of American politics. American politics has been raucous, deceptive, giddy, shallow, sloganeering, and demagogic for most of its history. "Infotainment" is in the American grain. So is reduction and spectacle—and high-minded revulsion against both.

Is negative campaigning new? In 1828, supporters of Andrew Jackson charged that John Quincy Adams had slept with his wife before marrying her, and that, while minister to Russia, he had supplied the Czar with a young American mistress. In turn, pro-Adams newspapers accused Jackson of adultery, gambling, cockfighting, bigamy, slave-trading, drunkenness, theft, lying, and murder. Jackson was said to be the offspring of a prostitute's marriage to a mulatto. Papers accused Jackson's previously divorced wife of having moved in with him while still married to her first husband. Not that all mud sticks. Some mud makes the slinger slip. In 1884 a Protestant minister called the Democrats the party of "Rum, Romanism, and Rebellion" as the Republican James G. Blaine stood by without demurral—which may well have cost Blaine the election.

Is the preference for personality over issues new? Once elected president, Andrew Jackson set to wiping out Indian tribes—but this was not an issue in the campaign that elected him, any more than the New Deal was an issue in the campaign that elected Franklin Roosevelt in 1932. (Roosevelt campaigned for a balanced budget.)

Are the blip and the bite new? "Tippecanoe and Tyler Too," the leading slogan of 1840, does not exactly constitute a Lincoln-Douglas debate. That year, according to Kathleen Hall Jamieson's *Packaging the Presidency*, followers of William Henry "Tippecanoe" Harrison carried log cabins in parades, circulated log cabin bandanas and banners, gave away log cabin pins, and sang log cabin songs, all meant to evoke the humble origins of their candidate—although Harrison had been born to prosperity and had lived only briefly in a log cabin. A half-century later, in 1896, Mark Hanna, McKinley's chief handler, was the first campaign manager to be celebrated in his own right. Hanna acquired the reputation of a "phrasemaker" for giving the world such bites as "The Advance Agent of Prosperity," "Full Dinner Pail," and "Poverty or Prosperity," which were circulated on posters, cartoons, and envelope stickers, the mass media of the time. Hanna "has advertised McKinley as if he were a patent medicine!" marveled that earnest student of modern techniques, Theodore Roosevelt. In that watershed year, professional management made its appearance, and both candidates threw themselves into a whirl of public activity.

I draw the information about Hanna from an important book by Michael E. McGerr, *The Decline of Popular Politics: The American North, 1865–1928*. McGerr presents considerable evidence that from 1840 (the "Tippecanoe" campaign) through 1896, vast numbers of people participated in the pageantry of presidential campaigns. Average turnout from 1824 to 1836 was 48 percent of eligible voters; but from 1876 to 1900, it was 77 percent. During the three decades after the Civil War, mass rallies commonly lasted for many hours; there were torchlight parades; there were campaign clubs and marching groups. "More than one-fifth of Northern voters probably played an active part in the campaign organizations of each presidential contest during the '70s and '80s" McGerr writes. And with popular mobilization came high voter turnout—up to 84 percent of the eligible (all male) electorate in 1896 and 1900 before it slid to 75 percent during the years 1900–16 and 58 percent in 1920–24. (It rose again in the 1930s, with the Great Depression and the New Deal, and then started sliding again.) Arguably the mass mobilization and hoopla turned out the vote; voting was the consolidation of a communal ritual, not an isolated act by which the isolated citizen expressed piety.

In the age of professionalization, reformers recoiled. What

developed in the 1870s and 1880s, with a push from so-called "educated men," was a didactic politics, what McGerr calls an "elitist" politics. The high-minded reformers insisted on a secret ballot; they approved of social science; they wanted enlightened leaders to guide the unwashed. Under their leadership, they worked toward a new-style campaign: a campaign of education. Independent journalism helped—newspapers no longer under party management. Alongside the waning partisan press, two new kinds of newspapers emerged: the high-minded independent paper with its educated tone, cultivating political discernment; and the low-minded sensational paper with its lurid tone, cultivating antipolitical passion. The way is already open to our contemporary bifurcation: the *New York Times* and the *New York Post;* Arthur Sulzberger and Rupert Murdoch; MacNeil/Lehrer and Geraldo Rivera. This split corresponds to the highbrow/lowbrow cultural split that developed around the same time, as traced by Lawrence W. Levine in his recent book of that title.

The sharply bifurcated media help divide the public: to oversimplify, a progressive middle class takes politics seriously while a diverted working class is for the most part (except for the Great Depression) disaffected. Although it took decades for this process to develop, and there were exceptional periods of working-class mobilization along the way, the lineaments of the modern campaign were already in place at the turn of the century: emphasis on the personality of the candidate, not the party; emphasis on the national campaign, not community events; a campaign of packaging, posed pictures, and slogans. Politics as a discretionary, episodic, defensive activity for the majority alongside moral politics for the few. In short, the politics of the consumer society.

The radio hookups of the 1920s made the campaigns still more national, made it possible for candidates and presidents to reach over the heads of the party apparatus directly to the electorate. The parties became gradually more redundant. Some of this was welcomed by reformers, and properly so: gradually, candidates found it harder to whisper to white Southern voters what they were afraid to proclaim out loud in the North. Above all else, though, the powers of the new media made it necessary for candidates and parties to manage them. Professionally concocted newsreels played a part in the defeat of Upton Sinclair's 1934 "End Poverty in California" gubernatorial campaign. A documentary newsreel spliced together at the last minute to counter a Dewey effort probably helped Truman squeak through in 1948.

But only with television and the proliferation of primaries did media management become central and routine to political campaigns. In 1952, Eisenhower, whose campaign was the first to buy television spots, was reluctant to advertise. After 1960, when Kennedy beat a sweating, five-o'clock-shadowed Nixon among those who watched the debate while losing among those who heard it on the radio, the handwriting was on the screen. The time of the professional media consultant had arrived. When his hour came round again in 1968, the new Nixon had learned to use—and submit to—the professional image managers. Nixon, the first president from southern California, moved advertising and public relations people into his high command. And not just for the campaign. The president in office could use the same skills. Haldeman and Ehrlichman, with their enemies lists and provocateur tactics, were the founding fathers of what Sidney Blumenthal later called "the permanent campaign"—a combination of polling, image-making, and popularity-building strategy that Reagan developed to the highest of low arts.

The pattern seems set for the 1980s: metacoverage for the cognoscenti, spurious pageantry for the majority. *The McLaughlin Group* for the know-it-all; Morton Downey, Jr., for the know-nothing. As the spectacle becomes more scripted and routine—the nominating conventions are the obvious example—more of the audience turns off. The spectacular version of politics that television delivers inspires political withdrawal along with pseudo-sophistication. As the pundits and correspondents pontificate in their savvy way, they take part in a circular conversation —while an attuned audience, wishing to be taken behind the scenes, is invited to inspect the strategies of the insiders, whether via the chilly cynicism of a Bruce Morton or the college-try bravado of a Sam Donaldson. Savviness is the tribute a spectacular culture pays to the pleasures of democracy. Middle-class outsiders want to be in the know, while the poor withdraw further and don't even vote. Politics, by these lights, remains a business for insiders and professionals. While the political class jockeys, the rest of us become voyeurs of our political fate—or *enragés*. Can it be simple coincidence that as voting and newspaper reading plummeted in the 1980s, Morton Downey, Jr. arrived with his electronic barroom brawl, and talk radio shows proved able to mobilize the indignant against congressional salary raises? Probably not. The vacuum of public discourse is filled on the cheap. Passions are disconnected from parties, moral panics disconnected from radical or even liberal politics. The talk show hosts did not mobilize against a tax "reform" that lined the pockets of the corporate rich.

Can This Generation Be Saved?

And the future? As the artist Folon says, "I work at forgetting I'm a pessimist." Ronald Lembo's research suggests that younger viewers are more likely, when they watch television, to pay attention to disconnected images; to switch channels, "watching" more than one program at once; and to spin off into fantasies about images. Of all age groups, the young are also the least likely to read newspapers and to vote. Do we detect a chain of causation? Does a fascination with speed, quick cuts, ten-second bites, one-second "scenes," and out-of-context images suggest less tolerance for the rigors of serious argument and the tedium of modern political life? Has the attention span been shrinking; and if so, is television the cause; and what would this prophesy for our politics? Is there, in a word, an MTV generation? Future apparatchiks of the media-politics nexus are assuming it: the politicians, the Deavers, the publishers of *USA Today* and its legion of imitators. David Shaw of the *Los Angeles Times* writes (March 15, 1989):

In 1967, according to the National Opinion Research Center at the University of Chicago, 73% of the people polled said they read a newspaper every day; by last year, the number of everyday readers had fallen by almost one-third, to 50.6%. During that same period, in the 18 to 29 age group, the number of "everyday readers" dropped by more than half, from 60% to 29%.

While 26.6 percent of *Los Angeles Times* readers are aged 18 to 29, 36.2 percent of *USA Today* readers are that age. And whereas young people used to acquire the habit of newspaper reading as they aged, this is apparently no longer happening. To recoup their losses, newspapers are trying to woo the young with celebrity profiles, fitness features, household tips.

In 1988, the Department of Education published a report—a summary of research hither and yon—on television's influence on cognitive development. The widespread publicity placed the emphasis on television's harmlessness. The Associated Press story that ran in the *New York Times* was headlined: "Yes, You Too Can Get A's While Watching 'Family Ties.' " But the report itself, by Daniel R. Anderson and Patricia A. Collins of the Department of Psychology at the University of Massachusetts, is inconclusive on the question of whether television watching affects the capacity to pay attention. "The possibility that rapid pacing may produce effects over longer exposure has not been examined," reads one typical hedge. "There does . . . appear to be some effect of TV on attention, yet the importance, generality, and nature of the effect is unknown": that is the summary sentence. Someday the grants may flow for the research obligatorily called for. But pending research, one still feels entitled to the pessimism that one must then work to forget. Television may not have eroded all possibilities for democratic political life, but it has certainly not thrown open the doors to broad-based enlightenment.

I have tried to show that there is precedent for a shriveled politics of slogans, deceit, and pageantry. But precedent is nothing to be complacent about when ignorance is the product. And the problem, ultimately, is not simply that Americans are ignorant. On this score, the statistics are bad enough. According to a 1979 poll, only 30 percent of Americans responding could identify the two countries involved in the SALT II talks then going on; in 1982, only 30 percent knew that Ronald Reagan opposed the nuclear freeze; in 1985, 36 percent thought that either China, India, or Monaco was part of the Soviet Union. But ignorance is sometimes a defense against powerlessness. Why bother knowing if there's nothing you know how to do about what you know? Why get worked up? What is most disturbing is not ignorance in its own right but, rather, the coupling of ignorance and power. When the nation-state has the power to reach out and blow up cities on the other side of the world, the spirit of diversion seems, to say the least, inadequate. Neither know-it-alls nor know-nothings are likely to rise to the occasion.

Ross Miller

PUTTING ON THE GLITZ: ARCHITECTURE AFTER POSTMODERNISM

Manhattan was first glitzed in late 1979 when developer Harry Helmsley and architects Emery Roth & Sons began making over a block-long property on Madison Avenue between 50th and 51st Streets. Under their direction, a mansion designed by McKim, Mead and White (1882) after the Palazzo della Cancelleria in Rome, was reborn as a luxury hotel. Helmsley

Ross Miller is Professor of English and Comparative Literature at the University of Connecticut. He is author of *American Apocalypse: The Great Fire and the Myth of Chicago*. His articles have appeared in *Interview, Progressive Architecture*, and *Architectural Digest*. He is at work on a study of the American skyscraper.

persuaded the city that simple preservation of this historic building was unprofitable. His plan took the existing structure, restored its lavish interior, and converted it to an elaborate lobby and pass-through for a sleek bronzed-glass and anodized aluminum tower that housed the guts of a new hotel. Only the color related the old building to the new. Helmsley was a pioneer.

At a time when austere functional glass office buildings defined serious East Coast cities, glitz with its brash concern for effect was thought acceptable only for the provinces: Las Vegas, Miami Beach, and Houston. The Helmsleys brought it to the heart of the city. The ripple effect has been widespread in art circles, high and low. The work of America's most prolific designers in the 1980s—Helmut Jahn, William Pedersen, John Portman, Philip Johnson, and John Burgee—reveals how glitz has gone upscale, transformed from a developer's strategy into a serious urban architecture. This transition has occurred at a time when architects have achieved celebrity status, finding themselves on the covers of *Time* and *Newsweek*. In the way that personality displaces ideas as a subject for the media, architecture's current love of glitz has made a difficult profession more accessible to the public, transforming the artistic process, not just the product, into a commodity to be bought, sold, and traded. New York's Max Protetch Gallery does a brisk business in contemporary architectural drawings, often of projects that will never be built. Prices are graded on the relative fame of the architect, not on the inherent quality of the work.

The loaves and fishes act of multiplying the value of a one-of-a-kind object was perfected by Andy Warhol. Posthumously awarded a retrospective at the Museum of Modern Art, Warhol's work holds no mystery. The mind-numbing reiteration of images from Brillo and Campbell's Soup to Marilyn and Mao is treated with no change of affect. In all instances, the artist refuses to get involved. He chooses instead to separate the aura from the soul and we are left with labels, masks, and trademarks. Warhol celebrates surface. To him the world is a flea market. A collector

Andy Warhol, Campbell's Soup
Can with Can Opener (1962).
Windsor, Inc. Collection.

of things, he despiritualizes reality. When he portrays serious subjects, like nuclear war, capital punishment, or the carnage of automobile crashes, he cannot go deep. He skims.

Architecture's adoption of surface over depth—elevation over section—in the 1980s is part of a large social trend, celebrating a society afraid of engagement. From videos to fast food the pace is manic and the style ironic. Like an alchemist changing dross to gold, Andy Warhol reprocessed kitsch, the horribly awful and grandiose, into art. He *knew* what he was doing. The ironic stance is inseparable from the work. His implied narrative is: "Sure this is junk and I know it. But isn't it fun? Aren't we all having a good time being in the know together?" Warhol's art initiates the viewer into a shared attitude that is marketed to look exclusive, like the Hard Rock Café, but admits everyone. The initiation into these experiences does not demand hard-won knowledge, only a willingness to be momentarily stimulated, then pass on. Between soup and war, all experiences are leveled. Warhol's success was not lost on the architectural profession.

Glitz is the developer's friend. Anyone can understand its meaning, its brash assertion of wealth. Harry Macklowe, who describes himself as an "architectural designer," built Metropolitan Tower (completed in 1985) on a sensitive site neighboring Carnegie Hall, whose own air rights are now being "utilized." In the spirit of the Helmsleys, a dark glass structure with a knife edge to the street, Metropolitan Tower violates, along with Edward Larrabee Barnes's IBM Building, the historic right-angled New York City grid. A building with such an aggressive profile in the city on one of New York's primary commercial streets does not engage the reciprocal relationship between public and private but glorifies ownership. Mr. Macklowe's words:

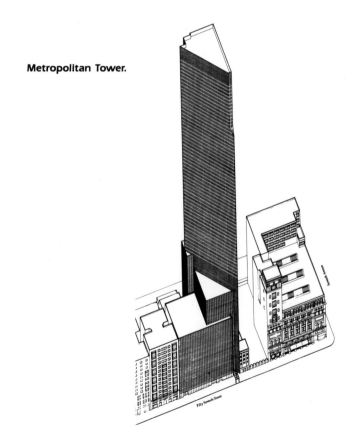

Metropolitan Tower.

I am Metropolitan Tower. The tallest. The most beautiful. Soaring proudly from the heart of New York, I gaze with pleasure upon the bustling rivers, graceful bridges, glittering avenues. Central Park is my garden. The sky and clouds reflect upon my face. And no matter in which direction I look, my city offers itself to me, an endless visual feast.

Born in Miami Beach

Architectural glitz of the 1980s has its roots in the postwar development of Miami Beach. Like a false diamond, this architectural ice developed out of the collaboration of a pragmatic architect, Morris Lapidus, and the new Florida hotel money. This, of course, was the old glitz, the sort of thing "Saturday Night Live" comedians and strict modernist architects still ridicule. Lapidus's Fontainebleau, Americana, and Eden Roc hotels are hybrids, employing the language of modern architecture with a Yiddish accent.

Miami Beach provided an upscale, unthreatening way to attract down south a new generation of prosperous Americans. The immigrant parents were lured to Art Deco Miami, their children to Miami Beach. Glitzy Las Vegas serves a similar function for vacationing Midwesterners. Both resorts sanction ostentation, for the architecture seems to license uninhibited display.

Miami's folklore of the glitzy fifties and early sixties included little about the native population, which was more or less invisible, seen only in service roles. In its prime the place inspired tales about the biggest sandwiches, pools, and showgirls. Contained as it was within an untainted white shell, Lapidus's glitz made the conspicuous consumption by a Depression generation, trained to accept austerity, appear to be a higher ethic. It was almost a duty to have fun in such a place. On a sandy strip that displaced the decaying city across the water, arrivistes had an architecture of their own. Morris Lapidus discovered a formula that combined his wonder as a young boy from Russia at seeing Coney Island in 1903 with the upscale cultural values he learned at school. The result, in his own words, was a "potpourri of anything I could put my hands on."

Miami's variety of the modern is not built to instruct. It carries none of its original associations with workers' housing and European utopian planning. But Lapidus was serious and did not patronize his clients; unlike later work, his architecture was not ironic. In his way, he transformed immigrant kitsch from a random collection of sentimental objects to a higher art version that assimilated into the larger culture. On a decidedly grander scale, he created a classy New World cultural context for what the migratory New Yorkers and New Jerseyites already knew and liked. Not surprisingly, Liberace was a favorite lounge act. Lapidus explains:

> You see, I try to understand people; my whole architecture is based on people. Who are they? What's their background, their training? They're going to come to Miami. They've heard that on the former Firestone Estate the fabulous Fontainebleau

Fontainebleau Hotel.

is going to be built. To begin with it had to be *fabulous*. It had to live up to this dream picture, the dream drawn by the advertising people. Where do these people get their culture? I finally came to the conclusion that most of them get their culture not from school, not from their travels, but from the movies, the cinema. If that's so, what was I to do?

Morris Lapidus was a sophisticated, classically trained architect, and his stylistic permissiveness can be misleading. His architecture was in fact responsive to his client, his audience, and booming postwar Miami. Lapidus disdained the condescending use of the knowing attitude, a main weapon in the generational conflict between American-born ethnics and their immigrant relatives. He created a vernacularized modernism to satisfy both fathers and sons, and in doing so succeeded in being contemporary while excluding the lingering protestant austerity of the International Style. Ridding architecture of its high-culture severity, he saved the modern skin and created a new core by filling the interior with colorful distractions. Glitz, as Lapidus originally conceived it, was populist, anti-elitist, and playful.

Fast to learn the lessons of Miami, John Portman elaborated on the Lapidus formula. When it came time for him to build on a large scale, he did not modestly sequester the glitter behind a modernist façade but saturated the entire building in it. Portman first gained wide attention with work for the Hyatt Corporation (1967) in his hometown of Atlanta, then quickly expanded a local practice into a national and then international phenomenon. His architecture is marketed and franchised. Easily replicated, like Warhol's multiples, Portman's work has the appeal of the familiar. A Hyatt in Chicago offers essentially the same experience as one in San Francisco. Because it creates its own context, integral to itself with little or no formal connection to the local streets, visitors to the city can avoid having to confront the world outside their hotel. Portman's hyperkinetic plans provide a sense of excitement in measured doses as the glimmering details offer the reassurance of the known. One is not confronted by the austere culture of high modernism. A Portman lobby is a celebration of kitsch not for its ironic effect as Bette Midler might play it, but for its sentimental and grandiose associations, like the costume jewelry in grandma's nightstand.

Portman's first hotel in Atlanta is composed around a giant square space, 120 feet to a side. Framing the square are twenty-two floors of "balcony-corridors" drawn as belts around the individual rooms. The plan turns everything inside out. Streets in this fake town are safely locked behind glass. Large planters hold greenery that drapes itself over the sides. On the ground are kiosks and other diversions that keep the lobby space filled with activity. The main attraction is an elevator tower with bronzed glass cars, lit like monster Christmas ornaments, running up and down an outside track.

By making the hotel complex the anchor for urban development planned and executed by the private sector, Portman was able to convince local governments to support a radical reorganization of neglected inner-city areas. In the late seventies he added the Bonaventure Hotel (Los Angeles) and Renaissance Center (Detroit) to the earlier Peachtree Center (Atlanta). To his credit, Portman, who began as a real estate developer, had the sense and energy to lead people back to the cities at a time when New York and other urban centers were in or near bankruptcy. Portman's strategy was simple enough. Take a hotel and dress it up: make it a magnet to attract people back to town. The Hyatt formula he settled on is now widely used in all its variations. He led the charge on the new Times Square with the Marriott Marquis, a fifty-story bunker fitted with its own shimmering atrium and revolving restaurant safely barricaded away from the city.

Out-of-towners particularly enjoy these spaces. The freedom to walk "outside" on a tenth floor balcony relieves both the claustrophobia of most large urban hotels and the anxiety of having to leave. Through the use of mirrors, lights, and shiny metallic surfaces, Portman partially creates the sensation of a real outside. A purely backlot affair, his streets are free of the perceived

Renaissance Center,
Detroit Plaza Hotel.
The Portman
Companies. Photo:
Alexandre Georges.

and real dangers of their inner-city locations. At Detroit's Renaissance Center and Los Angeles's Bonaventure Hotel, glitz is
used on the sleek façades to advertise a demilitarized zone within
the formerly dangerous and largely abandoned Central Business
District. A stiff flag on the moon, Portman's bright surfaces turn
away from the historical city. Modernism promoted transparency;
these glass boxes are opaque—one-way mirrors, framing beautiful views but allowing no way in.

A pioneer back to a territory thought lost, Portman proved the
inner city a good investment and helped define an architectural
language agreeable to the market conditions of the 1980s, where
everything seemed to be on sale. His architecture exploits a rich
provincial look. By importing the kind of planning and design
learned in developing the suburbs, Portman's architecture treats
the city as a colonial conquest. The existing city is shut out,
replaced by a fantasy urbanism in a climate-controlled and
secure mall. Like the English Club in prerevolutionary India or
the American corporate settlements in the Middle East, the

architecture of the 1980s is set off from existing buildings with little regard for context. It is an architecture for a new American generation born and raised in the suburbs. Suburbanized malls and atriums minimize the shock of living in the city within close proximity to different cultures and classes. For men and women fixated on the making of money, there is little interest in hassling the natural disorder of the street. The architecture eases the transition from work in a high-rise glass tower to play and consumption in a glassed-in mall. Order and control is the message as the city is exploited for its picturesque local color.

An outsider to architecture's primary axis—the Northeast, Chicago, California—Portman bridged the suburbs and the cities. Had not elements of his work been adopted by establishment designers whose work appears regularly in the prestigious European, Asian, and American architectural journals, Portman's work would have remained a provincial anomaly. But Establishment architecture's unexpected embrace of glitz made it the lingua franca of the 1980s, easing the formerly strained relationship between client and architect. The relationship between the two that had existed in the modern period was now reversed. No longer did the architect resist the developer or corporate client in order to educate him. Rather, he became his willing instrument.

Symbiosis with Corporate America

Philip Johnson was the first of the Ivy League establishment designers to understand how glitz could be used by "serious" architects to exhibit their good faith to clients uneasy with high art. He convinced developers and corporations that they could do business with him. He foreshadowed his plans, over a decade ago, in a lecture delivered at Columbia University. There he argued:

The day of ideology is thankfully over. Let us celebrate the death of the *idée fixe*. There are no rules, only facts. There is no order, only preference. There are no imperatives, only choice; or, to use a nineteenth-century word, "taste"; or a modern word, "take." . . . I am of the opinion we have no faiths. I have none. "Free at last," I say to myself.

Johnson's accomplishment was to void modern architecture of all political associations born in the days of utopian Weimar. Projects in Dallas, Houston, Minneapolis, and St. Louis completed in the late seventies reflect his cunning, as if he were doing the out-of-town tryouts of a show before it opened on Broadway. In this way, Johnson perfected a style that merged a glittering exterior and interior with a high-tech frame. Along with the last remnant of its kitschy innocence, Johnson purged glitz of its suburban provincial qualities before he transported it to the major cities.

In Johnson's work in the 1980s, the emphasis is on a building's surface and profile rather than the space it creates. A sense of the inappropriateness and infantilized nature of his skin-deep manipulations can be seen in Chicago at the heart of the city's financial district. There Johnson/Burgee in 1983, on a site diagonally across from Daniel Burnham and John Root's Rookery Building (1885–86), built a bloated version (forty stories to the original's twenty) of that historic firm's Masonic Temple. Once an associate architect with Mies van der Rohe on the Seagram Building, Johnson turned his back on the same modern architecture he and Henry-Russell Hitchcock zealously championed in 1932 in *The International Style: Architecture Since 1922*. This conversion was symbolically completed when Johnson and John Burgee relocated their firm from the Seagram Building, where it had been located since the building opened in 1958, to one designed by them on Third Avenue and 53rd Street.

The "Lipstick" Building is an oval structure on a typical New York right-angled lot. A thirty-four-story tower of glass and Swedish Imperial granite banding between floors, it is designed to stand out, to create its own context. Architectural historian Spiro Kostof calls this present state of urbanism the "one-of-each syndrome" and compares it to the turn-of-the-century battle of

53rd at Third, the "Lipstick" Building. John Burgee Architects with Philip Johnson. Photo: Gregory Murphey.

the skyscrapers, when press barons like the owners of the *New York Times*, *Tribune*, and *Sun* competed only "for the sake of prestige and image." The Lipstick Building revives that robber-baronial spirit. The nickname, "lipstick," has stuck because it somehow helps, through renaming in a vernacular way, to humble an object that appears so haughty and divorced from its environment that even *Vogue* describes it as "shine without luster."

But it would take a new generation of architects to bring glitz to its peak in the 1980s. Kohn Pedersen Fox (KPF) has exploited the developer's appetite for glitter and chrome by providing it with an endless variety of containers. A Manhattan-based firm, KPF specializes in a slick urbanism that can be read from a distance. It has brought postmodernism's mirror, its appetite for imitating past styles, closer to the present. In addition to overscaled Palladian detailing and other stale tricks of historicism, the firm has stimulated a new interest in Art Deco, setbacks, and other formerly distinguished urban strategies from the Golden Age of the New York skyscraper. An insatiable consumer, KPF's architecture recycles urban imagery of the distant and recent past, laundering it clean. KPF, along with a venerable Chicago firm, Perkins & Will, completed 900 North Michigan Avenue. There they provided the prime tenant, Bloomingdale's, with a cavernous atrium space, ornamented on the main floor with thin copies of metallic details from the New York store.

A fascination with shimmer and shine drives KPF to mistake reflection for what Montgomery Schuyler, the nineteenth-century American architecture critic, called the "thing itself." KPF built its critically acclaimed 333 Wacker Drive in 1983. Designed for a constricted site at an elbow of the Chicago River, the building appears inventive in form and unusually sensitive to its difficult site. But this Narcissus in the city, busy with its reflection in the river and its symbiotic mirroring of surrounding buildings, is in truth a clever copy in profile of an earlier building by Harrison and Abramovitz on the Connecticut River in Hartford. The

333 Wacker Drive. Kohn/Pedersen/Fox. Photo: Barbara Karant.

Phoenix Mutual Life Insurance Building (1960–64) is 333 Wacker Drive twenty years later. Mastery here is not concerned with authenticity but with proliferation. Even at its best, the essence of KPF architecture is not to be embarrassed by such transpositions but to embrace them. Glitz, in its perfected form, reflects and shines but has no memory.

The most gifted designer in the establishment axis is Helmut Jahn, who like Philip Johnson has roots in high modern architecture. After emigrating from Germany, Jahn was educated at Mies's old school, the Illinois Institute of Technology. Later, he apprenticed at C. F. Murphy (now Murphy/Jahn), a firm that, along with the Chicago office of Skidmore, Owings and Merrill, solidified Chicago's reputation as postwar America's premier architectural city. Murphy's principal designers after the war, Jacques Brownson and Gene Summers, established aestheticized Miesian principles. Structure was used as a prominent design element, exemplified by McCormick Place, on which Helmut Jahn worked when he first joined the firm. Working closely with Gene Summers, Jahn explored the ornamental properties of structure. Like New York's George Washington Bridge, McCormick Place revealed to Helmut Jahn the potential of an extroverted architecture that made visible its delight in pure display.

Jahn builds with uncommon freedom. At the beginning of the decade, he was asked to design a speculative office building in Chicago on the corner of Monroe and Dearborn. Now the Xerox Centre, it fuses high technology, a slick, enamelled aluminum-and-glass skin over a reinforced concrete structure, and a Euro-American image. The building's curved entrance evokes an unornamented version of Louis Sullivan's Carson Pirie Scott Department Store while its massing suggests Mies's "Designs for a glass skyscraper" (1921) and Erich Mendelsohn's Schocken Stores (1928). Jahn's mimesis is sophisticated, never literal. It often involves displacement of type and context, as in this case where an anonymous office commission symbiotically recalls two celebrated commercial projects. The mirroring of forms here is not dependent on literal quoting, as with most postmodernism.

Rather, Jahn codes into his work references to architecture history that are subtle and easily missed, as is the case with his highly publicized State of Illinois Building (1985), which plays with the classical orders to achieve a self-conscious civic effect.

The result is that Helmut Jahn's work in the 1980s has defined the boundary between glitz and genuine innovation. In his United Airlines Terminal (1987) at Chicago's O'Hare Airport, Jahn ably transformed the well-worked vernacular style of the railroad shed and exhibition hall into a finely integrated polychromatic mix of lights and color. The United Airlines terminal is an example of Jahn's best work in the 1980s. Less successful are forays into glitz that mark Chicago's North Western Terminal Project (1983), New York's 750 Lexington Avenue (1989), and Los Angeles's Wilshire-Westwood (1988). In each case, the architect was asked too quickly to arrive at a scheme. The one-of-a-kind syndrome leads away from analysis into pure display. Historical references in oddly divergent materials overshadow pure architectonic concerns. A Sullivanesque semicircular entrance attempts to break the oppressive impression of steel and glass at the North Western Terminal. But this small gesture to scale is overwhelmed by the inevitable anthropomorphic reading the building encourages. It is not the only one of Helmut Jahn's buildings that has the look of a broad-shouldered robot hulking above the street.

Jahn's recent work has included an unbuilt project for the world's tallest building for Donald Trump's grandiose Television City on Manhattan's Upper West Side and elaborate schemes throughout the world. His One Liberty Place now dominates Philadelphia's skyline, where a special high-rise zoning district was created to allow his sixty-one-story tower to be built. In the past, Philadelphia limited building height to a symbolic 491 feet, which was reserved for founder William Penn's statue on top of City Hall. Even Howe and Lescaze's Philadelphia Saving Fund Society tower (1932), the city's finest modern building, respected this traditional limit. But insensitivity to local tradition is part of glitz's international appeal. Particularity of place is not thought important as long as visitors find themselves safely in the eternal

**One Liberty Place.
Murphy/Jahn Architects.**

land of RICH. The lobby at One Liberty Place, with its marble walls, hanging American flag, baby grand, and palm tree, is a money vault, tucked away from the dwarfed older city outside. Helmut Jahn's work has none of the frantic insecurity of Trump Tower's six-story rose-colored atrium. However, with all its sophistication and energy the building can also be viewed as challenging the city. A famous building has been imported from another place and skinned for its image. One Liberty Place is a contemporary version of New York's Chrysler Building, a prime case of architecture that knowingly implies nothing in this time is unique or authentic.

Where Will Glitz Go?

How then should the decade be judged? In a recent interview, Helmut Jahn provided some insight. "The zeitgeist of Mies' time was technology; the zeitgeist for our time is marketing," he declared. "Mies believed that through technology and modern architecture you could make life better in society and in the city. Today we believe that through marketing and consuming we can make life better." Jahn's remarks explain how a fascination with surface and image led architecture into a decade-long romance with glitz. What for Morris Lapidus was a way to attract a paying audience to modern architecture became in the 1980s an expedient to satisfy a client without having to educate him to all the complex problems of urban architecture, particularly those that concern reviving the life of the street.

Glitz was a marketing scheme that got out of control. Meant to provide a commercially acceptable way to build in the city, with its own extraordinary momentum, it became an end in itself. It dominated the architecture of the 1980s just as the glorification of prosperity, exclusivity, and security dominated public discourse.

Ronald Reagan came into office "talking tough" about opposing the Evil Empire and glorified himself as Commander in Chief in Grenada, not Moscow. The stance was all important and the context rarely questioned, as Reagan took on personas from the Gipper to liberator at Normandy. Even when he got it wrong at Bitburg, be recovered instantly. He was incapable of embarrassment.

Dominated by large corporate firms, American architecture has manifested this same kind of smugness. Nonetheless there are some signs of change. Community opposition has forced developer Mortimer Zuckerman to scale down a gargantuan skyscraper project for Columbus Circle on Manhattan's West Side. Now in its third version and second architect, the building is still far from receiving approval. Architectural criticism has also forced alterations of plans at both the Guggenheim and Whitney Museums and scrapped proposals to build some large midblock towers

**Trump Tower Atrium.
Der Scutt, Design
Architect. Photo:
Norman McGrath.**

in Manhattan. To date, the most radical success has been the farcical dismantling of the top of the seventy-two-story Cityspire, on Seventh Avenue between 55th and 56th Streets, because the developer claimed eleven more feet than the city permitted.

There are other hopeful signs. Frank Gehry, 1989 recipient of the Pritzker Prize (architecture's version of the Nobel), has revived memories of a smaller-scale style of practice in America that produced Frank Lloyd Wright and Louis Kahn, who also worked in the shadow of great corporate firms but created the conditions for an opposition architecture. Following Gehry's example, a series of younger architects—George Ranalli, Steven Holl, Tod Williams, and Billie Tsien in New York, Ron Krueck in Chicago, Frank Israel and Morphosis in Los Angeles—has moved away from glitz. In their work and interest in teaching they are trying to take architecture out of the boardroom.

The result is that a greater awareness and interest in architecture has begun to develop nationwide. There is even a new architectural hero in the comics, Mr. X. A master architect responsible for "Radiant City," X became so revolted by his work that he went underground. Resurfacing recently, he vows to "undo the damage he believes he had done... even if it kills him." Never sleeping, pale, ghost-like, he haunts the city trying to reverse the process he helped initiate. Nice to think so.

Hendrik Hertzberg

THE SHORT HAPPY LIFE OF THE AMERICAN YUPPIE

It is gray dawn when they come for the last Yuppie. He is in an emergency detention center for cultural offenders, a loft building in lower Manhattan that has been converted many times. Built as a prison in the mid-nineteenth century, it has been, successively, a warehouse, a sweatshop, an artist's studio, and a luxury loft condominium; now it has come full circle. The Yuppie's cell is roomy but very dark, so dark the pressed-tin ceiling and exposed brick walls cannot be seen. His last meal—a simple poached salmon, an arugula and endive salad, a white

Hendrik Hertzberg is the editor of the *New Republic*. From 1979 to 1981 he was chief speech writer for President Jimmy Carter. He was earlier a correspondent for *Newsweek* and staff writer for the *New Yorker*.

chocolate mousse, a California Chardonnay, Saratoga water, decaf espresso—remains almost untouched on one end of the Alvar Aalto table. He has sat all night at the other end, writing final letters—to his wife, his mother, his broker—in the little pool of light given off by the Conran's lamp he was allowed to bring in with him. He looks tired, the skin of his youthful face drawn under the tan. His Perry Ellis shirt and his Giorgio Armani trousers are a little wrinkled but clean. He has lived well. He plans to die the same way. When the guards come, he rises and greets them with grave dignity, then walks between them to the elevator and out into the central courtyard. As he stands blindfolded against the wall, the pitiless sentence of the Zeitgeist Tribunal is read aloud. The Commissioner of Revolutionary Public Safety offers him a final cigarette.

"Certainly not," the last Yuppie says in a firm, even voice. "And as long as I am here, thank you for not smoking."

The Commissioner steps back. The members of the firing squad raise their rifles. "Ready . . . aim . . ."

Well, one can dream, no? But even if the revolution is not at hand, even if, on the contrary, the flow of Cajun restaurants, bijou grocery stores, futon dealerships, and vertical racket clubs is at this moment reaching a flood tide of unprecedented frenzy, there are ample signs that "the yuppie phenomenon" is doomed— that it is, as Nicholas von Hoffman said of Richard Nixon a few months before his fall, the dead mouse on America's kitchen floor, and the only question is when someone will pick it up by the tail and deposit it in the trash.

To all appearances, yuppiedom seems to be still thriving. But the yuptowns of our coastal cities, where one is seldom more than a few blocks from a designer ice-cream outlet or a branch of Banana Republic, have been overbuilt by speculators gripped by the delusion that trend lines never change direction. The gleaming, empty towers of yuppiedom betoken not prosperity but imminent collapse. The intimations—political, demographic, cultural, economic, journalistic, and culinary—are everywhere that yuppiedom is (to use a popular yuppie phrase, possibly connected with the well-known yuppie preference for grilled fish and crunchy vegetables) dead meat.

Intimations of Mortality

Political intimations: yuppiedom is essentially a phenomenon of the Ronald Reagan era, inextricably tied to the values, follies, and peculiar conditions thereof. The word *yuppie* shot from obscurity to ubiquity during the 1984 presidential campaign and became associated with the two politicians who squeezed Walter Mondale's head like the tongs in an Excedrin commercial, Gary Hart and Reagan himself. In 1987 Hart toppled off his perch like a coal-mine canary. As for Reagan, whose upscale economic policies, *The Wall Street Journal* once opined, "entitle him to inscription as the most aged Yuppie" —well, as of Inauguration Day 1989 at the latest, he's history.

Demographic intimations: Reagan notwithstanding, a yuppie is by definition young. Or at least youngish. And today's youngster is tomorrow's geezer. It would be cruel to dwell on what it is like to spend hours in the library squinting at the *Statistical Abstract of the United States*, but the bottom line (another yup favorite) is that a huge yuppie-age bulge, the famous baby boom, is moving through the population like a puppy through a python. The older members of this bulge have reached an age at which youth is something one feels nostalgic for. Just as crime dropped during the early 1980s when the younger baby boomers finally made it out of their teens, so yuppieness will fade when the older ones start moving to Florida. The Age of Aquarius ended when "aging hippie" became a routine sneer. We will soon begin hearing about "aging yuppies."

Cultural intimations: (1) for the 1989 fall season, ABC introduced a program called (and, irritatingly, spelled) *thirtysomething*, which treats the banal dilemmas of everyday yuppie life with *Masterpiece Theatre*–like reverence. (2) Your mother wears running shoes. (3) The *Readers' Guide to Periodical Literature*, which indexes magazines, had no items under "Yuppies" for the years 1900 to 1983 inclusive. For 1984 it had nineteen. For 1985 it had twenty-six. For 1986 it had fourteen. For the first three quarters of 1987 it had twelve. Now the bottom has dropped out. In the most recent monthly update of the *Readers' Guide*, the entry reads as follows, in its entirety:

Yuppies—*See also* Dinks

Economic intimations: Until the great Stock Market Crash of October 19, 1987, it had never occurred to yuppiedom that there might ever again be such a thing as a downturn in the business cycle. The crash wiped the condescending smile off many a smooth yuppie mug. The jokes began to circulate within hours of the Dow's 508-point tumble. (What's the difference between a pigeon and a yuppie stockbroker? A pigeon can still make a deposit on a new Mercedes.) But even before Black Monday, it was becoming clear that throughout the whole of the period of what was officially described as prosperity, the foundations of the economy were being systematically undermined by wild borrowing, excessive consumption, decreased savings, lunatic speculation, and unbridled corporate cannibalism—the full range of yuppieish follies that go by the name of Reaganomics. All this guarantees that the next recession will be extremely nasty. When it really takes hold, yuppiedom will be swept away, taking all the sushi-to-go outlets and chichi local business magazines with it.

Journalistic intimations: DROP SEEN AS BLOW TO YUPPIES—*New York Times* headline, after the crash. WILL THE YUPPIES RISE AGAIN? —same paper, two weeks after that. SUNSET FOR YUPPIES—*USA Today's* answer, two days after *that*.

The yuppie obits came in so thick and fast that in far-off England the editor of *The Daily Telegraph* sent a memo to his staff ordering a "complete ban" on the very word.

Culinary intimations: Burger King serves croissants.

The end, plainly, is near. It is time to quit wringing our hands and start pulling our chins. It is time to put the yuppie experience in—yes—perspective.

That Dirty Y-word

What we are dealing with here is something that began as a demographic category with cultural overtones and ended up as a moral category. *Yuppie* is now understood almost universally as a term of abuse. If you doubt this, try turning to the person next to you in exercise class and saying cheerily, *"You're* a yuppie. What's it like?"

At best, you'll get a slightly edgy, "I'm not a yuppie—I hate sun-dried tomatoes" or some such; at worst, the person may physically recoil. (You won't get punched, though; yuppies don't hit one another.) Why is everybody so defensive? The reason, of course, is that "you're a yuppie" is taken to mean not "you're a young urban professional" but rather "you have lousy values."

To understand how this came to be, it may help to draw back a bit and consider the history of the rise and picaresque adventures of the word and its many meanings.

The y-word itself seems to have been coined during the late 1970s, but hardly anybody used it until 1983. Bob Greene is generally credited with being the first to use it in print, in a syndicated *Chicago Tribune* column in March 1983. *Yuppie* became a national buzz word during the 1984 presidential campaign. It rose in lockstep with the political fortunes of Senator Gary Hart, but it did not fall with them. The media fad for yuppiedom continued to build, climaxing with a cover story, "The Year of the Yuppie," in the December 31, 1984, issue of *Newsweek*. The cover illustration, by Garry Trudeau, showed Mike Doonesbury, in business suit and backpack and, mounted on a ten-speed bike, crossing a bridge in a city park with a briefcase-carrying Joanie Caucus in skirt, blazer, pearls, Walkman, and New Balance running shoes.

Everybody agreed from the start that a yuppie had to be a baby boomer, one of the seventy million Americans born between 1946 and 1964. Beyond that, the category was, and is, played like an accordion. If yuppies are people who make $40,000 or more, live in cities, and work in professional or managerial jobs (the high end of *Newsweek's* several definitions), then there are only about a million and a half of them. If they are just baby boomers who went to college, live in metropolitan areas, and work in offices (the low end), there are more than twenty million.

Everybody also agreed from the start that yuppiedom was at least as much a matter of "life-style" as of statistics. Yuppies were defined more by what they consumed than what they produced. What they produced (as lawyers, brokers, bankers, accountants, consultants, executives) was intangible. What they consumed was quite tangible, a lot of it was imported, and a lot of it cried out to be made fun of. Right from the start, any random list of yuppie consumables—raspberry vinegar, Akitas, chèvre, Beamers (BMWs)—was good for a laugh, especially from yuppies themselves.

But along with the good-natured jokes, the moral demolition of this new category began almost at once. When Gary Hart started winning primaries in 1984, the press and the political community flailed about for an explanation. The forces of Walter Mondale were ready to provide one. "Mondale's aides cannily strove to diminish Hart's appeal by restating it as one of class," William A. Henry III wrote in his fine history of the campaign, *Vision of America,* "and helped persuade the press to adopt a shorthand term for a previously unrecognized group, the Yuppies."

Yuppie promptly went into a moral free fall that continued long after Reagan was reelected. In a Roper Poll taken in 1985, which found that 60 percent of adult Americans knew roughly what yuppies were (an impressive total, considering, for example, that only 34 percent know who is Secretary of State), six times as many people thought yuppies were "overly concerned with themselves" as thought they were "involved in working for the betterment of poor people." When a half-dozen young go-go Wall Street investment bankers—prototypical yuppie heroes—were indicted for insider trading in the wake of the Ivan Boesky scandal, yuppiedom's descent into moral squalor was complete in all eyes but its own. That was accomplished by the crash, which brought yuppies face to face with something worse (in their eyes) than dishonor: failure.

The word, once relatively neutral, is now in routine use as a weapon of contemptuous dismissal. Examples can be found in every day's newspaper. Here is one from the fresh copy of *The New York Times* on my desk. Frank Rich is reviewing a new play. It is, he writes, "a cuter, softened *Streetcar Named Desire* for the yuppie 1980s, down to its Windham Hill–style jazz-fusion score and its upbeat ending." Yuppie equals silly. Yuppie equals superficial. Yuppie equals mindlessly bland.

Because the moral opprobrium attached to yuppiedom is so severe, the yuppie is always someone else. Consider the Harvard Business School, which the rest of the world regards as the holy of holies of yuppiedom—the secular monastery where the orthodoxy of money and success will be cherished, the sacred texts *(In Search of Excellence,* et cetera) preserved, long after the dark ages return. Here we find a Cross pen in every inside pocket, an HP 12C calculator in every Gucci briefcase, a Hermès scarf around every throat. Here we find a studied disdain for the unsuccessful: "The guy's a complete loser" is the most feared putdown. Here "V.C." means venture capital, not Viet Cong. Yet even here, among the only group of people in the world consisting entirely of future Harvard M.B.A.'s, the reluctance to be tagged with the y-word is palpable. To normal B-School students, yuppies are the ones who want to become investment bankers. To the future "eye-bankers," yuppies are the ones who will settle for nothing short of a job with one of the "bulge bracket" firms, such as Salomon, Morgan Guaranty, or First Boston. And in the eyes of the aspirants to employment with these firms, yuppies are the ones who will under no circumstances consider a job in the Public Finance or Sales and Training departments, insisting on Corporate Finance or Mergers and Acquisitions. As a check, I arranged to have one of these exotic creatures pointed out to me. I approached him—he was a windswept-looking young man in a V-neck sweater and wide-wale corduroys—and asked him politely if he was a yuppie. "No, not really," he said. "I mean, hey, I drive an American car."

Our Yippie Forefathers

Yuppie, of course, is a play on words—many words. In the first instance, it is a play on *yippie*, the name adopted by Jerry Rubin and Abbie Hoffman for the "Youth International Party" they founded in 1968. The yippies were young, but they were neither international nor a party. They were a little band of anarcho-nihilist, media-manipulating politicos, who specialized in reducing solemn left-wing meetings to shambles with shouted demands for the abolition of pay toilets and who, gathering in Chicago's Grant Park during the 1968 Democratic National Convention, "nominated" Pigasus the Pig for President amid the fumes of tear gas and the thwack of police truncheons on long-haired heads. The connection between yippie and yuppie is direct. By 1983 Rubin, having dropped radicalism, was urging his former colleagues to join the "business community" and was promoting "networking" parties for young Wall Street types. It was one of those parties that was Bob Greene's hook for his column "Yippie vs. Yuppie," the one that introduced the new word to the general public.

Yippie, in turn, was a play on *hippie*, and here again the sinister, protean figure of Rubin makes an appearance. At the beginning of 1966, a year and a half before the "Summer of Love," hippies were still an embryonic phenomenon confined mostly to the Haight-Ashbury district of San Francisco. Apolitical and dreamy, the hippies had little contact with the radicals of Berkeley across the Bay. To bring the two communities of rebels, political and cultural, together, Rubin and others organized something called The Gathering of the Tribes for a Human Be-In, a rock-concert-cum-rally where some ten thousand people smoked pot, dropped acid, and listened to Allen Ginsberg chant *"Ommm,"* the Grateful Dead and Quicksilver Messenger Service play hypnotic electric music, and people like Jerry Rubin denounce the

Vietnam War and the established order. This event (which I attended, as it happened, a week before I went on active duty in the Navy) is as good a marker as any for the arrival of the counterculture as a mass movement. "Be-In" was itself a clever bit of wordplay (especially with "Human" in front of it), combining the political sit-in and teach-in with the psychedelic-mystical be-here-now to symbolize the marriage of the strains that produced the distinctive mass youth culture of the baby boomers, and eventually—so sinuously and unpredictably does the dialectic work its mysterious will—yuppies.

Hippies thought property was theft; yuppies think it's an investment. Hippies were interested in karma; yuppies prefer cars. Hippies liked mantras; yuppies like manna. Still, yuppiedom carried over from hippiedom an appreciation for things deemed "natural," an emphasis on personal freedom, and the self-absorption of that part of the counterculture known as the human-potential movement.

The etymological connection between yuppie and hippie is a reminder that the special power and poignancy of the yuppie idea cannot be understood without reference to that earlier time. And the 1960s get it coming and going. Among those members of the baby boom old enough to have experienced the '60s firsthand, yuppiedom is an expression of disillusionment (sometimes masking nostalgia). Among those too young for such direct experience, it is an expression of oedipal revolt (sometimes masking envy).

The Status Quotients

The cleavage is sharp between the two kinds of yuppies, older and younger. And the older ones—those aged about thirty-two and above—are much, much more defensive.

The other ancestor of *yuppie* is, of course, *preppy*. *The Yuppie Handbook*, by Marissa Piesman and Marilee Hartley, was a clever, best-selling knock-off of the even more popular *Official Preppy Handbook*, edited by Lisa Birnbach and published in 1980; the connection was strong enough that the authors of the former felt obliged to title their opening chapter "Beyond the Preppie." We thus arrive at the pseudo-social-science (to be redundant) formula—y = h + p—a handy way of summarizing the most important streams that fed the yuppie flood. Yuppies partook of the preppies' interest in law, banking, racket sports, and expensive clothes as badges of status. But yuppiedom, like hippiedom, is a democratic realm. Anyone can be a yuppie, just as anyone could be a hippie, while preppydom is, or pretends to be, an aristocracy of birth, a bastion of hereditary privilege. Ethnic minorities stand outside the charmed circle. Jews, for example, can go to prep school, and they have even been admitted to the most exalted eating clubs at Princeton, the most exclusive secret societies at Yale, the snootiest final clubs at Harvard; but even if they are named Guggenheim or Lehman, their preppyness is always provisional. No one named "Lisa Birnbach" can ever be a preppy in the fullest sense. What *The Official Preppy Handbook* did was enable Lisa Birnbach to become a yuppie. If one of yuppiedom's least attractive consequences was to make money the measure of all things, one of its not very numerous redeeming features was to reduce somewhat the prestige of inherited wealth.

In the preppy variant of snobbery, material objects—the clothes, the cars—were implicitly viewed as the outward signs of an innate superiority. In the yuppie dispensation, status was conferred by the objects themselves. One no longer had to be part of a class to acquire artifacts of that class. This was a logical result of the commercialization of bohemia and the reduction of "good taste" to a series of tidy, standardized formulas pioneered by *New York* magazine and eagerly picked up by the whole of the upscale press. Status became a commodity; sensibility became something that could be ordered out of a catalog. In the final nightmare, the Beatles "Revolution" was sold to be used as a jingle in an athletic shoe advertisement, and the Byrds' version of Pete Seeger's "Turn, Turn, Turn," was auctioned off for similar humiliation at the hands of a newsmagazine.

Part of the pathos of yuppiedom is that the products yuppies so assiduously consume are more upwardly mobile than the people who consume them. The nickel Popsicle went public and became the two-dollar Dove Bar. The workman's dungarees split two-for-one and became the fifty-dollar pair of Guess jeans. The neighborhood joint serving dollar burgers and working-class American beer (Budweiser) got its M.B.A. and became O. Henry's Drinking Establishment, serving $6.95 potato skins and working-class Mexican beer (Corona). The YMCA issued junk bonds and became a Nautilus health club. The repositioning of humble items of food and clothing as pricey, status-drenched luxuries is the signal triumph of yuppie marketing.

In Boston, where I've lived for the past couple of years, the restaurant of the moment is the Blue Diner. It is a "real" diner, built in 1947. The new people cleaned out the grease and spiffed up the old woodwork, but they serve "real" diner food: meat loaf, macaroni and cheese, American chop suey. But because this is a yuppie diner, the dishes are perfectly cooked and made with good, fresh ingredients. It costs three times as much as a "real" diner; on the other hand, the food is better—not three times better, but better. Such restaurants are yuppie culture at its best. The food's fine, but the customers' real appetites are social, not physical.

The Lie at the End of the Tunnel

The question remains: Why is everybody so mad at yuppies, including people who by any reasonable definition are yuppies themselves? "What, after all, is so terrible about quiche?" Michael Kinsley asks in a typically contrary 1984 essay entitled "Arise, Ye Yuppies!" Kinsley is comparing the 1980s to that previous era of self-satisfied consumption, the 1950s. "Are jogging and spinach salad really more decadent than golf and sirloin?" he asks. "Is the journey from an obsession with the perfect martini to an obsession with California Chardonnay really another stage in the decline and fall of American civilization?" Martinis have made a comeback, but the basic point remains valid. Many aspects of yuppie culture are clearly superior to what they replaced: small, efficient cars against gas-guzzling behemoths; neighborhoods of restored brownstones against suburban subdivisions; Woody Allen movies against Doris Day movies; gay friends against "homosexual panic"; the woman in the Liz Claiborne skirt against the man in the gray-flannel suit.

The fact is that, for the most part, today's yuppies have better taste than yesterday's well-off young adult Americans, are less ostentatious in their display of wealth, are far more apt to choose natural ingredients and fabrics over the chemical kind, set a far better example of healthful living, and are more tolerant. The source of the anger against them is not to be found in their own obnoxiousness or selfishness or hypocrisy, none of which is particularly striking. The source of the anger against them is to be found in the falseness of what they have been made to represent.

The premise of most of what has been said, written, filmed, and broadcast about yuppies goes like this: The Yuppie is emblematic of his time and generation. He is a synecdoche—the part that stands for the whole. In a time of prosperity, boundless opportunity, soaring hope, et cetera, he is the vanguard, the leading edge. He is like everybody else, only more so. We're all doing well; he's just doing a little bit better. He is simply a sharper, more dramatic instance of a trend that is general throughout the society. Therefore he is a fitting symbol of his age.

Implicit in the premise is a promise: that we all can be, will be, yuppies. Both premise and promise are false. The anger at the Yuppie is really anger at a lie.

Consider a few facts, dry but damning. They come from a just-published monograph called *Dollars and Dreams: The Changing American Income Distribution*, published by the Russell Sage Foundation and written by the respected economist Frank Levy.

During the decade between 1973 and 1984—the decade that ended by spitting out the word *yuppie*—the median American family saw its income *drop* from $28,200 to $26,433 (measured in 1984 dollars, as are all these examples). At the same time, the proportion of Americans classified as poor grew by nearly a third.

But who cares? The poor and the average are species yuppies scorn. What about our heroes? Well, the very rich got very much richer, but even people in yuppie income brackets had their problems. In 1973, families in what economists call the highest "quintile"—that is, the top fifth—were earning a mean average income of $68,278. In 1984 they were making less—$66,607, to be exact. That's nothing to hold a telethon over, of course, especially when the income of the poorest quintile was dropping at the same time from $9,136 to $7,297. But it's not the bonanza suggested by all the fuss about yuppies, either. It's stagnation.

The baby-boom generation was brought up in the 1950s and 1960s to assume that the little lines on the economic charts would keep going up and up forever. It hasn't worked out that way. Despite all the blather about "going for it" and "morning in America," despite all the gourmet mustard and CD players, reality has fallen sadly short of expectations.

Consider: In 1973, men who worked full time had a median income of $26,000. If things had continued to go the way they did when the yuppies were kiddies, this would have hit $31,000 in 1984. In fact, men who worked full time in 1984 had a median income of $23,218.

Consider: In the 1950s and 1960s, a man of twenty-five could expect that his real income would increase some 110 percent by the time he was thirty-five. But a twenty-five-year-old in 1973 saw his income over the next ten years increase by only 16 percent.

Consider: The proportion of young married couples whose income exceeded $35,000 (again, in constant 1984 dollars) was exactly the same in in 1984 as in 1973—and in 1973 many more of them were doing it on one paycheck.

Consider: In the 1950s, a typical thirty-year-old man needed 14 percent of his before-tax earnings to make the mortgage payments on a typical house. By 1973 this had risen to 21 percent, still not that bad. But by 1984, writes Levy emphatically, "a thirty-year-old man—now a member of the baby boom cohorts—would have had to spend *44 percent* of his gross earnings to carry a median-priced home."

One thing that did go up during the preyuppie decade was consumer spending per capita, which rose by 15 percent. But that was not because everybody cut their hair and went into investment banking. It was because more women were working and because of a greater willingness to go into debt.

Levy again:

"The other thing that kept going up was anxiety, reflected in the mounting emphasis young people put on making money. For twenty years the American Council on Education has been polling college freshmen about their values, including the importance to them of 'being very well off financially.' Before 1972 this was rated as 'essential' or 'very important,' the two highest possible ratings, by about half the freshmen polled. In 1973 it jumped to 63 percent, and now it's comfortably into the 70s."

One side of the yuppie myth tells college kids that a BMW, a condo, and a summer place in the Hamptons is the just and expectable reward for a bit of hard work and cleverness. What they actually see around them tells them nothing of the kind. The other side of the yuppie myth tells them that if they're worried about money it's because they're selfish little creeps who want to pig out on sushi. In reality, they're worried because there's plenty to worry about.

Connoisseurs of linguistic trivia will recall that for a brief time, *yuppie* had competition from *yumpie*. (HERE COME THE YUPPIES! —headline in *Time*, January 9, 1984. HERE COME THE YUMPIES! —ditto, March 26, 1984.) Lumpy, frumpy *yumpie* lost out because it had a discouragingly unglamorous sound, because it lacked yuppie's rich associational resonances, and because the "um" in it stood for "upwardly mobile," as against yuppie's more cautious "urban." If you define being upwardly mobile as having more status than your old man, then yes, those designated as yuppies are also yumpies. According to the Mayer Mobility Measure, a new social-science scam expressly created for this article (I won't go into the details, but the MMM entails impressive piles of computer printouts, the product of crunching University of Chicago numbers on a Harvard computer), fully 75 percent of yuppies work at more prestigious jobs than their fathers did, compared with just 48 percent of nonyuppie adults. But if upwardly mobile means you live better than your parents did and you're sure your children in turn will live better than you—the American Dream is another name for this—then no. The vast majority of those tagged yuppies by the media have been heading down, down, down for more than a decade, and the worst is yet to come. The very word *yuppie* is a taunt, a lie, a fraud: insult added to injury.

The Rise of the New Collar Class

One person who understood almost from the beginning that there was something wrong with the yuppie paradigm was Ralph Whitehead, a professor at the University of Massachusetts and a Democratic party guerrilla demographer whom Senator John Kerry once described as a cross between David Riesman and David Letterman. Since 1985, in articles and speeches, Whitehead has been arguing that the baby-boom generation is far too variegated and interesting to be stuffed into a single rubric. To take account of that variety, Whitehead came up with some alternative bumper-sticker categories of his own.

He pointed out that there are as many as twenty-five million baby boomers struggling along on family incomes between $20,000 and $40,000, a postindustrial working class whose members do the kinds of jobs that fall somewhere between physical labor and middle-management pencil pushing. They listen to rock 'n' roll and they know what marijuana smells like, but they have kids to support. They are trying in their own ways to fuse traditional values such as family and community with newer imperatives such as self-expression and individuality. Their idea of a good guy is Captain Furillo of *Hill Street Blues*, the tough cop who's not afraid to cry. These people are not yuppies. They are the sons and daughters of the old blue-collar class. With intentional rhyming resonance, Whitehead calls them the New Collars.

As for the new class of knowledge workers, Whitehead calls them, in another bit of postindustrial rhyming slang, the Bright Collars. Because the Bright Collars have some yuppie markings, they are sometimes victims of mistaken identity. There are nineteen million of them. They are knowledge workers—middle managers, social workers, teachers, bureaucrats, most lawyers, software engineers—products of the economic and technological transformation that has affected the age scale from the bottom up. ("As for yuppies," Whitehead says, "I haven't made up my mind yet if there's a thin, snotty stratum of them across the top of the Bright Collars or if *yuppie* is just the latest term for the top 3 percent of the American upper class. Or both.")

Unlike yuppies, neither New Collars nor Bright Collars are defined by consumption. They are defined by their place in a postindustrial society and economy that places a premium on differentiation and rejects the social principles of uniformity and patriarchy that have governed most of this century.

"If there's one thing that has come through in all the interviews and focus groups I've done with baby boomers, it's that these people have big egos but weak identities," Whitehead told me. "The big egos come from Dr. Spock, from the loosening of all kinds of moorings, from the sheer *size* of the baby-boom generation, which has gotten them used to being the center of attention throughout their lives. They really want to be somebody, but their culture and life experience no longer offer them the kind of off-the-rack identities that were available to their parents: 'Mom,' 'Dad,' 'homemaker,' 'soldier,' 'man,' 'woman,' 'American'—the big-ticket identities of the 1940s and '50s. American culture was an assembly line. A handful of identities rolled out of the factory and you fit yourself to one. If you weren't black or gay or an artist or an uppity woman, it was a pretty good system.

"But now the typical baby boomer is like a balloon stretched very tight. The air is the big ego and the thin, tightly stretched rubber is the identity. One pinprick and you're gone. Having to go elbow deep into the raw materials of American culture and fashion your own identity is tough. That's why a ready-made identity—especially if it has a nice sheen, like yuppie—was so attractive."

Whether or not one accepts Whitehead's terms, he is surely right that the drama of a generation trying to understand itself requires new ways of talking. A new social order requires a new language to describe it. The yuppie idea is one early attempt. But the first tremors of a new zeitgeist can already be felt, and when Wall Street laid its big egg the rumble came too loud to ignore. The eruption ought to be interesting. The shape of the postyuppie world cannot be predicted. What can be predicted is that it will be as different from what went before as the 1930s were from the 1920s or the 1960s from the 1950s. And it can be predicted that sometime around the year 2018, people will begin to wonder if the world is due for another decade of upheaval—like the one back in the 1990s.

In the new, second edition of *The Random House Dictionary of the English Language*, *yuppie* takes its place alongside *flapper* and *zouave*, just another word among 315,000 others. Entombed in the fine print, it will have a kind of existence—just as the carved letters on a tombstone have a kind of existence.

Shout out: Who killed the Yuppie? The answer is, It was you and I. We turned him into an effigy, and then we hanged him. He became the collective projection of a moral anxiety. We loaded onto him everything we hated about the times we had been living through—everything we hated about what we suspected we ourselves might have become. We made the Yuppie the effigy of selfishness and self-absorption, of the breakdown of social solidarity, of rampant careerism and obsessive ambition, of the unwholesome love of money, of the delusion that social problems have individual solutions, of callousness and contempt toward "losers," of the empty ideology of winnerism and the uncritical worship of "success." Then we strung the little bastard up.

Laura Bergheim

PLUGGIES

More insidiously than any other decade in our history, the 1980s have delivered unto us (and into our homes) the promises of past futurists: sit back, relax, and let your fingers do the walking across the universe of simulated experience. Quietly, almost magically, the middle-class home sweet home has been transformed into an environment that now doubles as office, schoolhouse, shopping mall, health club, printshop, restaurant, even electronic bordello. Television has been born again through television preachers, teachers, endless cable channels, and do-it-yourself satellite dishes. The lowly telephone has been redefined

Laura Bergheim writes frequently on popular culture and sociopolitical issues. Her most recent book is *Weird, Wonderful America*.

as the conduit for dial-a-porn, Domino's Pizza, call-waiting, and conference calls. Fax machines, PCs, VCRs, and CD players cast their spells on the most reluctant of technological inductees, while a mushrooming smorgasbord of byte-sized information sources continues to satisfy the appetites of hardened computer buffs.

Yuppies, once the most outwardly mobile of the upper middle class, have traded in their dancing shoes and one-night stands for sheepskin slippers and safe sex. Slides and swingsets stand empty as couches crowd with kids playing high-resolution video games. The great, electronic indoors beckons all but a stalwart few into the home technology whirlwind.

User-friendly technologies have given everyone the keystroke to the computer kingdom. When showrooms and catalogs for The Sharper Image and other elite-tech boutiques began appearing nationwide, larger and more mainstream retailers, including Radio Shack and Sears, jumped on the bandwagon. As the taste for high-tech toys trickled down to the masses, manufacturers began producing lower-priced, simplified versions of the top-of-the-line items. Entire computer systems now can be purchased for less than the cost of a single component ten years ago.

Pluggies—those who are plugged in but tuned out—are fast developing as the heirs to the yuppie. This new asocial animal is a creature of comfort and convenience, overstimulated by artificial intelligence and instant gratification, but underexposed to genuine experience and the virtues of patience. Although the Pluggie character is still fermenting, the modus operandi for a society of selectively self-sufficient shut-ins is already in place. Activities that once demanded human contact, involvement, and interaction now can be performed by a dazzling array of consumer technologies. Letters can be delivered by fax in seconds with nary a growling dog in the foyer. More information can be downloaded in an hour by computer modem than a librarian could dig up in a month. Banking now can be done via computer in most major cities, as can shopping, bill paying, travel planning, and other minor errands. People can even engage in civic activism without leaving home: citizens in Santa Monica can link their computers to city hall, electronically communicating questions and opinions on matters that once would have required a trip downtown.

Even when Pluggies interact meaningfully with those on the outside, it's often through a technological middleman: lonely Pluggies meet, make love, even marry each other via video dating, phone chat lines, and computer message boards—all without facing the pressures of unrealistic expectations or the threat of AIDS. The worst they can catch is a computer virus.

But why should they shun such natural human contact? The sociopolitical landscape of the 1980s holds a few clues. Early in the decade, the Reagan White House managed to erect a glittering, if shallow, façade of materialism and economic prosperity that helped camouflage the nation's unaddressed social problems. But by the mid-1980s the Hollywood-in-Washington scene began slowly to dissolve, fading out and then refocusing to reveal the scourges of crack addiction, AIDS, and homelessness. America, still primed to "stay the course" with Reagan, responded by backing away in horror from its modern-day plagues, embracing a full-scale siege mentality of ethnic and economic elitism. "NIMBY" ("Not In My Back Yard") became the battle cry of neighborhoods and communities fiercely opposed to the local placement of proposed substance-abuse clinics and homeless shelters. Indeed, pressure from NIMBYs led Nancy "Just Say No" Reagan to withdraw her support at the last minute from the Nancy Reagan Drug Rehabilitation Center, which had been slated to open in California. Mrs. Reagan's sudden reversal caused many of the center's wealthy supporters to demand that their donations be returned. With such carefully tended home fires blazing away, even baby boomers are looking back to the future, settling down to remake the domestic ideal in their own image.

The greatest indicator of the new closet culture is the rapid change in the role of white-collar workers and their workplace environment. The aggravations of commuting to and from work, combined with the growing number of two-career couples now starting families, have helped make the home-based office a popular alternative to the nine-to-five rat race. According to the Bureau of Labor Statistics, in 1985 some eighteen million Americans worked at home, either full-time or as a supplement to their day jobs. But by 1988, according to the National Work-At-Home Survey conducted by New York's LINK Resources, the number of home workers had jumped to about twenty-five million Americans, a 40 percent increase in only three years. The LINK survey also queried participants on their reasons for working at home: Of those who were self-employed, the largest group (24 percent) said they had set up their offices at home to start their own businesses, while nearly half of those who chose to work at home for other companies said they had done so because the home was a more productive environment.

Until Pluggies began setting up shop, the home office was seen as either the book-lined den where one paid the bills and hid out from kids and cohorts, or the lair of writers and artists in need of solitude. All that changed with the 1980s lionization of entrepreneurial stars like Steve Jobs, whose Apple Computers started a wave of high-tech equipment that was so user-friendly it jeopardized the role of the family dog. Suddenly, working at home became glamorous. New breeds of furniture and machinery began appearing in spare bedrooms and alcoves. The battered typewriter and cubby-holed desk were replaced by Scandinavian curvilinear computer stations outfitted with the latest in mini-computers, laser printers, and fax machines. Cushy old polyester deskchairs were traded in for state-of-the-art ergonomic seats and knee chairs designed (no doubt on computers) to reduce back strain during those long hours at the terminal.

This new work environment not only exudes high-tech, if spartan, good looks; it also functions tightly and efficiently. The once-necessary work of accountants and bookkeepers, researchers, secretaries, typesetters, telex operators, mailroom managers, and other support staff is now handled by myriad software programs, databases, desktop publishing systems, modems, and fax machines. Although such a set-up might have cost upward of $20,000 in the early 1980s, much of the basic hardware—a PC clone with a hard disk, monitor, and modem—now can be bought for under $1,000. Functional (if not top-notch) printers and fax machines can be had for under $1,000.

Database systems like DIALOG and CompuServe provide a central point of access to hundreds of information sources around the country. A writer working on a story about pig farming in Indonesia can log on and quickly search for related magazine and newspaper articles, doctoral dissertations, statistical abstracts, State Department reports, agricultural studies, soil maps, and practically any other resource material known. Once the information has been located, the writer can pick and choose what's appropriate, download it through the modem, and store it on disk or print it out—all within the time it might take to drive to a library with far fewer research materials.

Research isn't the only job that has been tamed by technology. Most time-consuming facets of paperwork have been all but eliminated. Fax technology has quickly replaced the overnight letter and telex as hard-copy communication. Contracts now can be read and revised, plans approved, and itineraries established within minutes rather than days. Likewise, desktop publishing has also revolutionized the way people communicate—slick publications and advertisements can be designed and reproduced using a home computer rather than paying and waiting for typesetting and paste-up.

Thanks to modern technology, the home office has come into its own during the past decade. Unfortunately, for all the benefits of efficient home employment, the very nature of the beast isolates people from their coworkers and colleagues. The level of contact with others becomes a matter of choice. Some home-based workers meet for lunch every day, just to get out of the house; but those more addicted to the insular society of the closet culture may never meet their clients or employers face to face. Although most people who work at home are either self-employed or on the staff of small firms, large organizations are now poised to start allowing employees to work at home. IBM is experimenting with flexible schedules for some workers (especially new mothers), allowing them to split their work time between home and office.

Over time, the home office can be expected to chip away at the established hierarchies and cycles of workplace structures and ethics. Where the office was once a place of social as well as work-related interaction, it may soon become merely the electronic switchyard and archival repository for home workers. With coworkers communicating by fax or modem instead of at the coffee machine or in the conference room, the spirits of teamwork or head-to-head competition that many workplaces promote may soon be a thing of the past. If home work catches on in big business, conglomerates and large corporations, already compartmentalized by virtue of their size and scope, will be further split up by their increasing number of off-site workers. Specific projects will be contracted out more frequently to independent specialists, leaving full-time employees (both in and out of the office) with the more amorphous, and perhaps less fulfilling, tasks of management and development.

Since the once-sacred concepts of company loyalty and personal commitment undoubtedly will be weakened by the lack of direct contact with the employer and coworkers, home workers simply may soak up all they need to know about a business and then quit to start one of their own. Thus, competition for clients and customers will heat up considerably amidst this breeding ground for small companies, many of which may not survive the battle.

Such faltering companies could then become buy-out fodder for the very same conglomerates the workers left behind in the first place. Such business recycling will have an intriguing impact on the way an employee moves up the corporate ladder, not to mention the ways in which product patents are enforced and corporate secrets protected.

Unions, primarily white-collar ones, will undergo a dramatic change as at-home employment increases. Unions have long fought against the concept of piecework—that is, paying employees by the piece (for instance, a nickel per shirt-sleeve sewn) rather than by the hour. But with no in-office time clock to punch or manager watching, at-home workers with untrusting bosses will undoubtedly be forced into the position of accepting just such productivity pay. Unless employers institute a universal honor system, there will be invasive, home-based monitoring systems that will justifiably raise the ire of Pluggies and will provide fodder for unions well into the next century. Another issue will be benefits or reimbursements related to the use of home equipment for office use. Once workers move back home such issues as work environment quality, child care, and commuting benefits will recede in importance.

Just as workers will be telecommuting to their offices, so will they be telecommuting to union meetings. The social aspect of local chapter gatherings will fade as national and international organizations stage meetings on screen. In the end, specializations will take the place of locals as the common denominator that unites and forms smaller groups. And the unions themselves, lacking the hands-clasped camaraderie engendered by the friendship of coworkers and local meetings, will evolve into watered-down professional societies with massive data bases and electronic bulletin boards. When the group workplace is thus broken up into self-contained, single-unit Pluggiedoms, the unions representing those workers will be forced to address the cries of a thousand separate complaints. With no central focus, unions will seek ways to universalize their negotiation and labor protection efforts by developing self-help computer programs to diagnose and resolve virtually any difficulty, possibly through direct negotiation with the computers of the employer. Soon, if history does indeed repeat itself, there will be management programs developed to do nothing but "bust" union programs.

The at-home office is an established fact of life for many workers, but a new twist is swiftly being added. High-tech tools now can follow their owners to the bedroom or to the BMW:

laptop computers, portable fax machines, and mobile phones (the granddaddy of tech totes) are turning the home office into a movable feast of labor. Although on the surface this may sound as though it defeats the stay-at-home purpose of the closet culture, mobile technology actually promises to change the concept of home as society has defined it.

"For millions, and particularly for the 'people of the future,' home is where you find it," wrote sociologist Alvin Toffler in his 1970 bestseller *Future Shock*. Toffler, noting the growing transiency inherent in modern lifestyles, pointed out that home could no longer be seen as a single, fixed place. Instead, he predicted, people would increasingly attach the emotional qualities of "home" to wherever they happened to be at the time. What Toffler failed to foresee was that for Pluggies technology itself has been molded into an intellectual shelter that overarches any physical landscape.

In the past, the home was a symbol of warmth and comfort, a place to spend leisure time and pursue hobbies. The splintering of traditional family life due to divorce, single parenthood, and unmarried coupledom, combined with the home's new status as an electronic amusement park and office, has transformed the image of home. To Pluggies the home is primarily one big enclosed electrical outlet. One need look no farther than recent fiction to find evidence of this new domestic scene: "Now they lived through machines, they were addicted to machines. . . . There were not enough plugs," David Leavitt writes in his 1988 novel *Equal Affections*, describing the electronic dependencies of a pair of gay lawyers. Leavitt goes on to reveal that throughout the couple's house, "The outlets were stuffed with extenders; the extenders were stuffed with extension cords; wires tangled like matted hair under desks, cabinets, beneath the sofa. Electricity hummed through the house even when everything was turned off, wires connecting to other wires, other machines. . . ."

This ever-present web of cords, cables, and connectors serves as a more meaningful (if abstract) home symbol for those hard-core Pluggies who attach greater emotional significance to function than to environment. Thus, the portability of computers, fax machines, phones, television sets, CD players, and other travel gadgets lets them take their "home" on the road in a very real sense.

Pluggies can wrap up their wire web and take it on planes, trains, and gondolas from Venice to Disneyland, at the same time finding shelter within the invisible, humming home of electricity that serves to distance them from the rigors of human relations. Pluggies on the road may be forced to deal with other passengers, desk clerks, and waiters, but once basic arrangements and details have been dispensed with, Pluggies can then retreat into their private world of bits and bytes.

Thus preserved from the anxieties of the outside world, Pluggies can move through their entire lives via a series of invisible networks. Indeed, today's Pluggies could well spawn an entire generation of self-created, self-sufficient, self-absorbed agoraphobes, confined to an electronic house of their own making. Nearly all of life's pleasures, as well as its bare necessities, now can be imported into the home at the touch of a button or through do-it-yourself kits. Children can sit down at their own starter computers (with their own mini-workstation furniture) and study most of the same subjects they learn in school. And when they get bored with their studies, the kids can always switch on an animated football game or World War I dogfight. The only way to get into trouble is to fool around with Dad's "MacPlaymate," a computer-generated dreamgirl who persuades the user to undress her and then make love to her on-screen (this program comes complete with a panic button so an employee can trade in the graphic graphics for a fake spreadsheet in case the boss walks in).

Since man cannot live by sex alone, some restaurants in New York and Los Angeles now fax their menus daily to regular customers, who need only check off their order and fax it back for pick up or delivery later that day. To work off that rich meal, compact home exercise machines and videos (booming since Jane Fonda kicked off the aerobic tape mania in the early 1980s) keep Pluggies from looking like piggies. For a more human touch, the yellow pages are filled with personal trainers who will come to a client's home or office and put her or him through the paces personally. As for inner fitness, dozens of relaxation and subliminal health tapes can be popped into the VCR for hours of serene ocean scenes interspersed with secret whispers to quit smoking and give up french fries. Even Hollywood's New Age sage is getting into the act: "Shirley MacLaine's Inner Workout" videotape ($29.95) arrived on the market in early 1989 with promises of inner peace through relaxation and "self-reduction."

If meditation doesn't make you feel better, there's a plethora of home medical kits on the market that can test for pregnancy, fertility, high blood pressure, diabetes, colon cancer, and (coming soon) even AIDS. Nor are doctors the only professionals losing business to the closet culture; lawyers are being replaced by do-it-yourself divorce and will kits. CPAs are being superseded by simple accounting and tax-filing software, and psychologists are being displaced by computerized Freuds and Jungs.

Summing it all up is a system called "Prodigy." With it, users can order in groceries, read horoscopes, and exchange electronic mail with Gene Siskel, Howard Cosell, and Sylvia Porter (all of whom have columns on the network). Simplicity is the key to Prodigy. When logged on (via modem and a password), the user sees graphics depicting a city. If he wants to go shopping, he tells the computer to go to the mall, where he can "explore" several floors of shops, catalog listings, and other purchasing venues. Placing an order is as simple as pressing a button and typing in a credit card number.

Developed jointly by Sears and IBM, Prodigy is leading the race to put a computer network in every home; incredibly inexpensive by industry standards ($9.95 a month, and the phone calls are usually local), it is also the first service to dish up advertising along with information. Adding a new and prophetic twist to an old theme, a Prodigy financial network listing proclaims, "American Express: Don't Stay Home Without It."

It has not, however, been all smooth sailing. Even for the most technically accomplished Pluggie, information overload can be a threat. "In our enthusiasm to exercise our new machinery, we create unnecessary anxiety; the new-toy syndrome operates with telecommunications equipment as much as with Tinkertoys," Richard Saul Wurman writes in his 1988 book *Information Anxiety*.

The reaction to this anxiety, Wurman says, is that people have begun to turn this technological overkill against its own purpose, using it to block the very communications the machines ostensibly were purchased to facilitate. "Where once we were excited by the prospect of new information and welcomed those devices, such as the telegraph, the telephone, and the radio, that brought us closer to the world, now we have begun to use technology to screen our communications," Wurman writes, noting the growing use of telephone-answering machines to screen out callers rather than to take their messages. By literally pulling the plug, Pluggies can use their gadgets to shield themselves from even the most impersonal of human contacts.

The result is a technology that has actually helped turn the clock back by a century or so. Once upon a time most Americans lived in relatively rural isolation. Self-sufficiency was a necessity, not a choice as it is today. Contact beyond the family and a few neighbors was minimal because of distance and smaller population centers. But as advances in transportation and communications technology created a global community, relative distances between even the most remote towns seemed to shrink. Supermarkets, shopping malls, community colleges, and cultural centers that sprang up nationwide brought together a once disassociated population. Now we are on the verge of coming full circle: with even the simplest of errands and tasks being performed by home computers, the fabric of daily social contact will grow thin again.

On January 1, 1987, the *Washington Post*'s annual "In/Out" list proclaimed that "cocooning" (the act of cuddling up at home with loved ones and pets) was in—and partying all night was out. The new age of indoorsmanship was officially sanctioned. Soon to follow were loungewear fashions for haute cocooners and down-filled sleeping bags designed with the couch, not the campsite, in mind. By 1988 the airwaves were offering soft-drink commercials depicting couples pointedly staying home for the evening and a television game show (featuring nothing but questions about television) entitled "Couch Potatoes." A jaunty 1980s label for those who sit around all day like immobile lumps of complex carbohydrates, munching junk food and flicking channels, the Couch Potato image became a high-concept marketing idea: cuddly lounge spud dolls appeared on shelves in time for the 1988 Christmas season.

The society that fled indoors under the blind, benevolent watch of the Reagan administration has now postdated its reasoning, reinstating the virtues of the tucked-away hearth and home as an excuse for shutting out the troubled world on the other side of the "Welcome" mat. Safe within their own electronic world, Pluggies can revel in their self-image as the modern, closeted embodiment of the great domestic dream—as American as microwaved apple pie and video baseball. The portrait of the happy new family at home is now complete with Dad on the word processor, Mom at the food processor, and the kids glued to their joysticks.

Robert B. Reich

A CULTURE OF PAPER TIGERS

"When the capital development of a country be-
comes a by-product of the activities of a casino, the job is likely
to be ill-done," John Maynard Keynes wrote in 1936. A half-
century later, Keynes's fear seems just as warranted as it was
during the Great Depression. That it does is a sign of how
thoroughly the culture of the new American paper entrepreneur
came to dominate the American economy of the 1980s. Paper
entrepreneurialism not only reflects how we do business, it
reflects how we think about business.

Robert B. Reich teaches business and public policy at the John
F. Kennedy School of Government at Harvard University. Formerly director of policy planning for the Federal Trade Commission,
he is the author of *The Next American Frontier* and, most recently,
The Resurgent Liberal and Other Unfashionable Prophesies.

As recently as 1974, it was not this way. In that year an economic turning point, of sorts, occurred. The International Nickel Company decided to buy up enough shares in the Electric Storage Battery Company to gain control over the board of directors of Electric Storage and thus allow International Nickel to effectively run the company. The managers of Electric Storage Battery did not want International Nickel to run the company, because they didn't believe that International Nickel could do a very good job of it, and they didn't want to lose their own jobs. They thus regarded International Nickel's act as hostile, as it in fact was—the first in a long and not-so-distinguished line of unfriendly initiatives.

Before International Nickel did this dirty deed, Wall Street had viewed such aggression as unseemly, if not unethical. One didn't just *take over* a company. A company was its managers and employees, its trademark and reputation. These attributes could not be purchased *against its will*, or so it was assumed. Besides, there was no reason for such shenanigans. The American economy, then run along more gentlemanly lines, had grown quite large, and at a rapid clip, without stooping to such behavior.

Then Wall Street's other shoe fell. In 1975 the Securities and Exchange Commission decreed that commissions paid on stock transactions were no longer to be based on fixed rates but were to be negotiable. Henceforth, brokers' commissions were to be subject to the free market, to ungentlemanly competition! Within a year, revenues in Wall Street brokerage houses plunged $600 million. This was no time for squeamishness. Forget the niceties. The Street had to forage for new sources of earnings, and hostile takeovers looked like just the place to start.

The supply of investment bankers, as it were, created its own demand. There were twelve hostile takeovers of $1 billion or more in the remainder of the 1970s; between 1981 and 1984 there were forty-five. Then came the leveraged buyouts, culminating in the last days of the Reagan administration, appropriately enough, with the $25 billion buyout of RJR-Nabisco. In 1978 mergers and acquisitions accounted for less than 5 percent of the profits of Wall Street brokerage houses. By 1988 the "M&A business," as it was affectionately called on the Street, accounted for more than 50 percent of their profits.

The Art of the Deal

And profitable it has been. Over the decade, the average incomes of paper entrepreneurs grew 21 percent, compared with a 7 percent rise in the incomes of everyone else. The demand for paper entrepreneurs, in turn, generated more of a supply. Between 1977 and 1987 employment in the securities industry doubled—increasing by an average of 10 percent a year, compared with average yearly job growth of 1.9 percent in the rest of the economy. The stock market crash of October 19, 1987, slowed things down a bit. For several months there were poignant stories of $200,000-a-year investment bankers suddenly forced to sell their East Side duplexes. But within a year, the forward thrust of the M&A business was restored. By the end of 1988 one quarter of all new private-sector jobs in New York City and more than a third of all its new office space were devoted to paper professionals engaged in rearranging assets.

Deal-making has proved particularly lucrative because every time industrial assets are rearranged, paper professionals earn money. The larger and more complex the escapade, the more money they earn. If they handle the legal complexities, they are paid according to the amount of time they put in. If they manage the financial niceties, they are paid a small percentage of the deal. Thus there has emerged a strong interest in doing deals.

With good reason. Paper entrepreneurs not only do the deals but also advise their clients (corporate directors, chief executives, pension-fund managers) about when and whether such deals should be done. Like doctors and automobile mechanics, who occupy equally enviable positions both of advising about the need for their services and supplying the services, paper entrepreneurs have discovered that there is no necessary limit to the amount of service they can urge upon their customers and thereupon provide. Deals thus have become more plentiful and larger.

More plentiful: In 1960 an average of three million shares of stock were traded daily on the New York Stock Exchange. During the entire year, some 12 percent of the listed shares were exchanged and, on average, held eight years before being resold. During an average day in 1988, by contrast, 200 million shares exchanged hands. For the year as a whole, 95 percent of the listed shares were traded, and most remained with their owners for only a few hours. The dollar value of trading in stock index options and futures—bets on how bundles of stocks will move— was five times that of the trades in shares of stock.

Larger: The RJR-Nabisco deal of 1988 generated close to $1 billion in paper-entrepreneurial fees. Like the obscure services listed on hospital bills and automobile repair receipts, those that made up this sum were not self-evident: some $200 million for what was called a "buyout fee"; $400 million for "junk-bond underwriting and bank commitment." "Merger and advisory fees" added another $150 million. The prospective sales of the food and tobacco businesses would earn investment bankers an additional $100 million. The platoon of lawyers and legal advisers reaped at least $50 million.

Deal-making also has created abundant work for lawyers, especially when deals turn sour. Texaco and Pennzoil feuded over Getty Oil Company for almost three years. By the end, Texaco had paid over $60 million to lawyers; Pennzoil, $400 million.

Should the economy suddenly fall into recession or worse, no matter. By the close of the 1980s, paper entrepreneurs were preparing to make money on the pending collapse. Investment banks had already amassed funds for "deleveraged buyouts," the purpose of which would be to do the reverse of what had been done during boom times—this time, reduce the debt load and increase the shares of stock. It was happily anticipated that the bonds of newly bankrupt companies could be purchased for a small fraction of their face values and new shares issued to the remaining creditors. The newly reorganized company could then be sold for a fat profit.

Obscene Profits, Obscure Activity
Through all this, the historic relationship between product and paper has been turned upside down. Investment bankers no longer think of themselves as working for the corporations with which they do business. Corporations now exist for the investment bankers, who openly put them into play, buy and sell stock in them, initiate takeovers and leveraged buyouts. Whole departments of investment banks scan corporate America for businesses ripe for the plucking. It is as if doctors and auto mechanics went house to house instructing the occupants on what they must do to avoid death or breakdown and then ripped them and their cars apart to make the prescribed repairs.

Investment banks are replacing the publicly held industrial corporations as the largest and most powerful economic institutions in America. In 1987 Drexel Burnham Lambert, Wall Street's fastest-growing company, posted earnings of over $1.5 billion, putting it right up there with Xerox and the Monsanto Company. After purchasing RJR-Nabisco, the firm of Kohlberg, Kravis, and Roberts controlled companies with total revenues of $50 billion, transforming KKR into the fifth-largest industrial company in the United States.

Twenty-five years ago the titans of American industry were chief executive officers of major industrial corporations. Today, as in the late nineteenth century, they are investment bankers. Each of the partners of KKR earns about $70 million a year. (One wing of the Metropolitan Museum of Art is named after its benefactor, Henry Kravis.) Michael Milken, of Drexel Burnham, earned, we now know, $550 million in 1988, a sum that exceeded the total amount spent by the United States in the search for a cure for AIDS. Rarely have so few earned so much for doing so little. Never have so few exercised so much power over how the slices of the American pie are rearranged.

The language through which this economic transformation has been accomplished is colorful and childlike, featuring "golden parachutes," payments of "greenmail," "white knights," and poison pills of all hues. The bright colors mask darker realities, calling into question the purpose of the American corporation in the latter decades of the twentieth century. For at least fifty years it had been assumed that public ownership of stocks assured that America's major corporations were well managed and that public trading in such stocks guaranteed that investors received fair value. No longer.

Golden parachutes are nothing more than generous severance payments, often totaling large multiples of an executive's annual salary and bonus, which are awarded—the parachute opens automatically, as it were—when the takeover becomes successful. The proferred justification is dubious: such insurance is thought essential to preserve the executive's impartial judgment about hostile takeover bids. Without the parachute, so the argument goes, the executive would be tempted to fight the takeover even if it were in the best interests of the stockholders. The logic suggests that the only way stockholders can trust corporate executives not to feather their nests at the stockholders' expense is to provide them a prefeathered nest at the stockholders' expense.

Greenmail is ransom, paid to those who are trying to take over the company, to get them to stop offering the company's stockholders high prices for their stock. The ransom is paid by corporate executives and directors, who presumably would lose their jobs if the predator succeeded. The ransom money comes ultimately from the same stockholders who are being courted by the predator. The justifications for greenmail are equally suspect: executives and directors argue that predators don't understand the business and, once in control, would diminish its value. Alternatively they argue that the stockholders don't know how much their stock is *really* worth, and they are being duped by the low bids of predators. Either way, the logic suggests that the current executives and directors are doing a superb job, and only they are fit to judge how superb.

White knights, poison pills, and further exotica also help incumbent management ward off unfriendly predators. By the late 1980s, managers who sensed the possibility of a hostile takeover employed a technique known as the "leveraged buyout." The financial complexities were dazzling, but the underlying principle was straightforward. The corporate managers borrow money, often at high interest rates, to buy up their company's stock. These loans are backed by the company's assets. The managers who now own the company thereupon make it more valuable, either by increasing its productivity or by selling off its divisions. They thus make a bundle. With high leverage, small improvements in operating performance can dramatically increase the value of a tiny equity base.

Here again, the proferred justification is oddly inconsistent with our inherited notions about the function and purpose of the corporation. The argument is that once managers' wealth is tied up in the company, they will become more efficient and improve the firm's performance; that is, managers who own their company work harder and better. But this logic suggests that the same managers have been grossly deficient in the past, failing to act in the stockholders' best interests.

All of these asset-rearranging techniques require the ubiquitous skills of accountants and lawyers. A new field of consultancy has grown up in recent years, euphemistically deemed "earnings management," which consists of the strategic use of accounting conventions—redistributing income from good years to bad, recognizing profits in advance of sales, and similar innovations. The leading edge of American jurisprudence is found in such fields as securities and tax law, where piles of arcane pleadings and truckloads of depositions now inundate our courtrooms and preoccupy squadrons of lawyers, overworked clerks, and despairing judges.

Is This Necessary?

Apologists of such antics argue that they are justified by economic fundamentals. (When you hear an argument based on "economic fundamentals," you would be wise to place a hand firmly over your wallet and keep it there until the perpetrator has moved on.) Faced with the alternatives of investing in new plants, equipment, or research (risky propositions whose payoffs are likely to be in the distant future), or of distributing the earnings to shareholders (who are immediately taxed on such largesse), corporate managers instead see considerable attraction in snapping up profitable well-run companies with established market positions—even their own. They speak of wondrous gains from "synergy," the dynamic effects of pooled management upon what were formerly independent firms, making the whole greater than the sum of the parts. They wax with equal enthusiasm over the gains to be had from disassembling and selling off piecemeal such parts, thus making the sum of the parts greater than the whole. And through it all, they exhibit faith—endless faith, indomitable faith—in the hidden, *potential* value of the assets being purchased, relative to the price they currently fetch on the stock market.

Most of this is nonsense or worse. The record of the 1970s and 1980s is dismally clear. Acquiring companies rarely have done well for their stockholders. Despite all the claims for synergy, there is little evidence to suggest that mergers have on the average enhanced the basic profitability of merging enterprises. The subsequent rush to dismember suggests, in fact, the reverse.

A case in point. R. J. Reynolds, the giant tobacco company, merged with Nabisco, the giant food processor, in 1985. The merger was then hailed as brilliant strategy, through which the tobacco company would diversify into foods. Just three years later, the newly merged company became the object of a mammoth contest between armies of investment bankers pledging billions of dollars for the privilege of breaking it up once again.

Defenders of such escapades also claim that asset-rearranging is no mere speculative game but a means by which the financial market ensures that resources are available for new enterprise. Close examination belies this comforting view. Wall Street's dynamism has little to do with the financing of new commercial venture. During most of the 1980s, new issues of common stock averaged only about 1 percent of the total stock outstanding. Ninety-nine percent of Wall Street's exuberance pertained to shares of stock already in circulation, which became objects of titillating rumor. Portfolio managers frantically bid against one another to take advantage of small upticks or downblips in this vast casino, betting pension funds or mutual funds in which Americans had placed their savings. In effect, most Americans unknowingly were engaged in continuous bidding against one another (and, if their money was entrusted to more than one fund manager, as was often the case, against themselves). It was exactly as if we had all crowded into Vegas for a long binge.

A third justification is often heard of late: takeovers are necessary in order to wake incumbent managers from their stupor. By this view, proper entrepreneurialism is a form of anti-septic, washing away encrusted layers of managerial bureaucracy.

Undoubtedly, American business needs a good housecleaning. But the question is whether hostile takeovers are the most efficient means. There are other, far less debilitating remedies, like competition for markets. Were the antitrust laws enforced against mergers that reduce competition—such as General Foods' recent acquisition of Kraft—managers would have to stay on their toes in order to preserve their company's market share. Product competition is a healthy antiseptic for cleaning away encrusted management. Takeovers are more like defoliants.

The American economy as a whole has not benefited demonstrably from these paper activities. Since the mid-1970s, when most of this began, productivity gains have slowed. Average real wages (controlled for inflation) have stagnated. Average stock prices have barely risen. And only the public-relations office of the United States Chamber of Commerce would contend that Ameri-can firms have stayed competitive with those of Japan, West

Germany, South Korea, and other places around the globe where, incidentally, hostile takeovers and leveraged buyouts rarely, if ever, occur.

Problems with the Paper Economy

I do not want to suggest that all efforts directed at rearranging corporate assets are necessarily wasteful. To the extent that they allocate capital more efficiently to where it can be most productive or smooth out what would otherwise be sudden changes in supply and demand, they make our economy perform better. But what has happened over the last decade has been counterproductive rather than productive. Even by the cynical standards of the 1980s, the new paper entrepreneurs of Wall Street have given greed a bad name.

In one memorable scene of Oliver Stone's 1987 film *Wall Street*, Gordon Gekko, a corporate raider played by Michael Douglas, takes the microphone at the annual meeting of Teldar Paper, a company he is trying to acquire. America has become a second-rate power, Gekko tells the Teldar shareholders. He cites the nation's trade imbalance and loss of industry. Greed, he says, is all we have left. But greed, he continues, is good. It is what makes America a great place to live. It keeps the system going. Gekko is depicted as a Wall Street villain, but his real-life counterparts, the Ivan Boeskys and Michael Milkens, have neither behaved nor sounded very differently from him. In the end, their legacy cannot be separated from the following problems in America's economy:

Myopia: Improvements in productivity often depend on investment strategies geared to the long term. Productivity gains come gradually. Research aimed at developing fundamentally new technologies is apt to go slowly, yielding little or no profit for many years. The development of the internal combustion engine, electronics, xerography, and semiconductors each depended on a quarter-century or more of trial and error. Commercialization often requires the development of large production facilities, distribution and sales networks, and quality-control systems. All this demands a willingness to invest now for greater returns in a distant future.

But paper entrepreneurs typically require that investments pay off in the short term at the expense of greater yields later on. General Electric's costly acquisition of RCA, for example, resulted in less research for both. In 1987 General Electric cut its research spending by 8 percent. Under new management, RCA's famed David Sarnoff Research Center, for decades an incubator of television technology, slashed its staff by 25 percent. Or consider Borg-Warner, another company specializing in high technology. After a fierce takeover battle in the 1980s, the firm gutted its research laboratory. A recent study undertaken by the National Science Foundation concludes that takeovers and leveraged buyouts have accounted for a substantial slowing of America's research and development.

Truncated vision is due, in part, to the necessity of repaying huge loans used to finance such asset rearrangements. Nothing so focuses the corporate mind as threat of bankruptcy. Yet this is not a complete explanation. Asset rearrangers also have changed the pattern of stock ownership in ways that emphasize immediate gain. Not long ago, the majority of stock on our exchanges was owned by individuals, many of whom remained with their companies for years. It was not unusual for such an investor to take a mildly proprietary interest in how his or her company was doing and what it was planning to do. Today 70 percent of corporate stock is bought and sold by professional portfolio managers of mutual funds, pension funds, and insurance companies. These managers must do more than invest for the future—they must also attract and keep clients. So they are under pressure to demonstrate the short-term earnings that potential clients demand. In the search for quick profits, they move in and out of large positions with little regard for the strengths of the underlying enterprise. Securities analysts and brokers likewise hope to show profits by correctly guessing the short-term fluctuation of price-earning multiples instead of the long-term potential for growth.

On the management side, the motivation is similar. The average corporate chief executive may have an even smaller stake in future growth than the average stockholder. The frenetic movement of corporate assets engenders a similar shifting of managerial talent. Top executives are fired, or they are lured to other newly rearranged corporations. They feel no loyalty to their present companies, which, after all, are regarded by directors and stockholders as little more than collections of financial assets. Thus the average term of office for today's chief executive officers is only four years.

Wasted talent: Asset rearranging also harms productivity by using up the energies of some of our most talented citizens. Paper entrepreneurs now embody the nation's most original economic thinking and energetic wheeling and dealing. The result is a "brain drain" from product to paper. Today's corporate executives spend an increasing portion of their days fending off takeovers, finding companies to acquire, and responding to depositions in lawsuits. Most of our top corporate executives are trained in law and finance—in contrast to three decades ago, when most were trained in marketing, engineering, and sales.

Our best minds are increasingly drawn to the pie-dividing professions of law, finance, and accounting and away from pie-enlarging professions like engineering and science. While graduate programs in law and accounting are booming, engineering and science programs are foundering—again in contrast to other industrialized nations. The most sought-after jobs among business school graduates continue to be in finance and consulting, where the specialty is the shuffling of corporate assets. Out of a recent graduating class of 721 at the Harvard Business School, a grand total of seven reported that they had gone on to start ventures of their own. "Independence" to today's business graduate means working for McKinsey instead of for General Motors.

Opportunism: The money required to rearrange industrial assets—

to mount hostile takeovers, to defend against hostile takeovers, to return a company to private ownership by repurchasing the publicly owned shares of stock—typically is borrowed. As has been suggested, high leverage creates extraordinary opportunities for profit. But it also creates substantial danger should the economy sputter and interest payments be missed. This was, after all, the lesson we were supposed to have learned in the 1920s, when America last went on a speculative spree: there are few adventures more thrilling than gambling in the stock market with someone else's money and few more dangerous to the overall economy.

Corporate debt in the 1980s has reached alarming proportions. Twenty-five years ago, the average American corporation paid sixteen cents of every dollar of pretax earnings in interest on its debt. In the 1970s, it was 33 cents. Since 1980, the average large corporation has been paying more than 50 cents of every dollar of pretax earnings in interest. The Brookings Institution, not known for its alarmist rhetoric, undertook to examine the effects on corporate America of a recession similar in severity to that which rocked the nation in 1974 and 1975. The Brookings computer simulation revealed that, with the levels of debt prevailing in the late 1980s, one in ten American firms would succumb to bankruptcy.

Such fragility marks the triumph of private greed over social rationality. It may be in the self-interest of a lone paper entrepreneur to bet a giant American corporation against the odds. If he wins, he earns a fortune. If he loses, most of the loss is borne by those who lent him the money; and he can always make another bet. Eventually he will win big. But if all paper entrepreneurs behave similarly, the entire economy is bet against the odds. This is precisely what has occurred.

Divisiveness: An economy based on asset rearranging has a final disadvantage. It tends to invite zero-sum games, in which one group's gain is another's loss. As those engaged in rearranging the slices of the pie become more numerous and far more wealthy than those dedicated to enlarging the pie, social tranquility is threatened. Trust declines. As trust declines, the pie may actually shrink.

There are signs that this vicious spiral has begun, as each corporate player seeks to preserve its standard of living by expropriating a portion of the declining wealth of another group. Corporate raiders expropriate the wealth of employees by forcing them to agree to lower wages and then passing the savings on to the new stockholders. Corporate borrowers utilizing high-yield ("junk") bonds expropriate the wealth of other bondholders, and of employees, by suddenly subjecting the entire enterprise to greater risk. Executives expropriate the wealth of stockholders by paying greenmail to would-be acquirers or by undertaking a leveraged buyout and then reselling the company at a higher price. Investors expropriate other investors' wealth by trading on inside information.

The result is an economy ruled by the cynical values of takeover artists like Asher B. Edelman, whose course at the Columbia School of Business—in which he offered a $100,000 reward to any student who found a company he could acquire— was called "Corporate Raiding—The Art of War." Worse still, especially for workers in dying industries like auto and steel, it is an economy in which the victors' pyrrhic sense of triumph is not very different from that of the T-shirt slogan that became so popular in the days following the stock market crash of 1987, "Whoever dies with the most toys wins."

Throughout the world we are witnessing the triumph of capitalism over centrally planned economies. In Eastern Europe as well as the Soviet Union, risk-taking and initiative are increasingly seen as better stimuli to growth than directives from the top. How sad then that America, the nation that became a model for the social benefits of capitalism, should end the 1980s contradicting its own history and succumbing to the zeal of a group of entrepreneurs more intent on rearranging paper than on creating real value.

Henry Louis Gates, Jr.

BLACKNESS WITHOUT BLOOD

The question of color takes up much space in these pages, but the question of color, especially in this country, operates to hide the graver questions of the self.

—James Baldwin, 1961

...blood, darky, Tar Baby, Kaffir, shine...moor, blackamoor, Jim Crow, spook...quadroon, meriney, red bone, high yellow...Mammy, porch monkey, home, homeboy, George...

Henry Louis Gates, Jr., is currently editing the *Complete Works of Zora Neale Hurston* and Oxford University Press's Schomburg Library of Nineteenth-Century Black Women Writers. His own books include *The Signifying Monkey* and *Figures in Black*. He is W. E. B. Du Bois Professor of Literature at Cornell University.

spearchucker, schwarze, Leroy, Smokey . . . mouli, buck, Ethio-
pian, brother, sistah. . . .

—Trey Ellis, 1989

I had forgotten the incident completely, until I read Trey Ellis's essay, "Remember My Name," in a recent issue of the *Village Voice* (June 13, 1989). But there, in the middle of an italicized list of the by-names of "the race" ("the race" or "our people" being the terms my parents used in polite or reverential discourse, "jigaboo" or "nigger" more commonly used in anger, jest, or pure disgust) it was: "George." Now the events of that very brief exchange return to mind so vividly that I wonder why I had forgotten it.

My father and I were walking home at dusk from his second job. He "moonlighted" as a janitor in the evenings for the telephone company. Every day but Saturday, he would come home at 3:30 from his regular job at the paper mill, wash up, eat supper, then at 4:30 head downtown to his second job. He used to make jokes frequently about a union official who moonlighted. I never got the joke, but he and his friends thought it was hilarious. All I knew was that my family always ate well, that my brother and I had new clothes to wear, and that all of the white people in Piedmont, West Virginia, treated my parents with an odd mixture of resentment and respect that even we understood at the time had something directly to do with a small but certain measure of financial security.

He had left a little early that evening because I was with him and I had to be in bed early. I could not have been more than five or six, and we had stopped off at the Cut-Rate Drug Store (where no black person in town but my father could sit down to eat, and eat off real plates with real silverware) so that I could buy some caramel ice cream, two scoops in a wafer cone, please, which I was busy licking when Mr. Wilson walked by.

Mr. Wilson was a very quiet white man, whose stony, brooding, silent manner seemed designed to scare off any overtures of friendship, even from white people. He was Irish, as was one-third of our village (another third being Italian), the more affluent among whom sent their children to "Catholic School" across the bridge in Maryland. He had white straight hair, like my Uncle Joe, whom he uncannily resembled, and he carried a black worn metal lunch pail, the kind that Riley carried on the television show. My father always spoke to him, and for reasons that we never did understand, he always spoke to my father.

"Hello, Mr. Wilson," I heard my father say.

"Hello, George."

I stopped licking my ice cream cone, and asked my Dad in a loud voice why Mr. Wilson had called him "George."

"Doesn't he know your name, Daddy? Why don't you tell him your name? Your name isn't George."

For a moment I tried to think of who Mr. Wilson was mixing Pop up with. But we didn't have any Georges among the colored people in Piedmont; nor were there colored Georges living in the neighboring towns and working at the mill.

"Tell him your name, Daddy."

"He knows my name, boy," my father said after a long pause. "He calls all colored people George."

A long silence ensued. It was "one of those things," as my Mom would put it. Even then, that early, I knew when I was in the presence of "one of those things," one of those things that provided a glimpse, through a rent curtain, at another world that we could not affect but that affected us. There would be a painful moment of silence, and you would wait for it to give way to a discussion of a black superstar such as Sugar Ray or Jackie Robinson.

"Nobody hits better in a clutch than Jackie Robinson."

"That's right. Nobody."

I never again looked Mr. Wilson in the eye.

But I loved the names that we gave ourselves when no white people were around. And I have to confess that I have never really cared too much about what we called ourselves publicly, except when my generation was fighting the elders for the legitimacy of the word "black" as our common, public name. "I'd rather they called me 'nigger,'" my Uncle Raymond would say again and again. "I can't *stand* the way they say the word *black*. And, by the way," he would conclude, his dark brown eyes flashing as he looked with utter disgust at my tentative Afro, "when are you going to get that nappy shit *cut*?"

There was enough in our public name to make a whole generation of Negroes rail against our efforts to legitimize, to naturalize, the word "black." Once we were black, I thought, we would be free, inside at least, and maybe from inside we would project a freedom outside of ourselves. "Free your mind," the slogan went, "and your behind will follow." Still, I value those all too rare, precious moments when someone "slips," in the warmth and comfort of intimacy, and says the dreaded words: "Was he colored?"

I knew that there was power in our name, enough power that the prospect frightened my maternal uncles. To open the "Personal Statement" for my Yale admission application in 1968, I had settled upon the following: "My grandfather was colored, my father is Negro, and I am black." (If that doesn't grab them, I thought, then nothing will.) I wonder if my daughters, nine years hence, will adapt the line, identifying themselves as "I am an African American." Perhaps they'll be Africans by then, or even feisty rapper-dappers. Perhaps, by that time, the most radical act of naming will be a return to "colored."

I began to learn about the meanings of blackness—or at least how to give voice to what I had experienced—when I went off to Yale. The class of 1973 was the first at Yale to include a "large" contingent of Afro-Americans, the name we quickly and comfortably seized upon at New Haven. Like many of us in those years, I gravitated to courses in Afro-American studies, at least one per semester, despite the fact that I was pre-med, like almost all the other black kids at Yale—that is, until the ranks were devastated by organic chemistry. (The law was the most common substitute.) The college campus, then, was a refuge from explicit racism, freeing us to read and write about our "racial" selves, to organize for recruitment of minority students and faculty, and to demand the constitutional rights of the Black Panther party for self-defense—an action that led, at New Haven at least, to a full-fledged strike in April of 1970, two weeks before Nixon and Kissinger invaded Cambodia. The campus was our sanctuary, where we could be as black as the ace of spades and nobody seemed to mind.

Today the white college campus is a rather different place. Black studies, where it has survived—and it has survived only at those campuses where *someone* believed enough in its academic integrity to insist upon a sound academic foundation—is entering its third decade. More black faculty members are tenured than ever before, despite the fact that only eight hundred or so black students took the doctorate in 1986, and fully half of these were in education. Yet for all the gains that have been made, racial tensions on college campuses appear to be on the rise, with a monitoring group finding incidents reported at over 175 colleges since the 1986–87 academic year (and this is just counting the ones that made the papers). The dream of the university as a haven of racial equity, as an ultimate realm beyond the veil, has not been realized. Racism on our college campuses has become a palpable, ugly thing.

Even I—despite a highly visible presence as a faculty member at Cornell—have found it necessary to cross the street, hum a tune, or smile, when confronting a lone white woman in a campus building or on the Commons late at night. (Once a white coed even felt it necessary to spring from an elevator that I was about to enter, in the very building where my department was housed.) Nor can I help but feel some humiliation as I try to put a white person at ease in a dark place on campus at night, coming from nowhere, confronting that certain look of panic in their eyes, trying to think grand thoughts like Du Bois but—for the life of me—looking to them like Willie Horton. Grinning, singing, scratching my head, I have felt like Steppin Fetchit with a Ph.D. So much for Yale; so much for Cambridge.

*

The meanings of blackness are vastly more complex, I suspect, than they ever have been before in our American past. But how to explain? I have often imagined encountering the ghost of the great Du Bois, riding on the shoulders of the Spirit of Blackness.

"Young man," he'd say, "what has happened in my absence? Have things changed?"

"Well, sir," I'd respond, "your alma mater, Fair Harvard, has a black studies department, a Du Bois Research Center, and even a Du Bois Professor of History. Your old friend, Thurgood Marshall, sits like a minotaur as an associate justice on the Supreme Court. Martin Luther King's birthday is a *federal* holiday, and a black man you did not know won several Democratic presidential primaries last year. Black women novelists adorn the *New York Times* best-seller lists, and the number one television show in the country is a situation comedy concerning the lives and times of a refined Afro-American obstetrician and his lovely wife, who is a senior partner in a Wall Street law firm. Sammy Davis, Jr.'s second autobiography has been widely—"

"Young man, I have come a long way. Do not trifle with the Weary Traveler."

"I would not think of it, sir. I revere you, sir, why, I even—"

"How many of them had to die? How many of our own? Did Nkrumah and Azikwe send troops? Did a nuclear holocaust bring them to their senses? When Shirley Graham and I set sail for Ghana, I pronounced all hope for our patient people doomed."

"No, sir," I would respond. "The gates of segregation fell rather quickly after 1965. A new middle class defined itself, a talented tenth, the cultured few, who, somehow, slipped through the cracks."

"Then the preservation of the material base proved to be more important than the primal xenophobia that we had posited?"

"That's about it, Doctor. But regular Negroes still catch hell. In fact, the ranks of the black underclass have never been larger."

I imagine the great man would heave a sigh, as the Spirit of Blackness galloped away.

From 1831, if not before, to 1965, an ideology of desegregation, of "civil rights," prevailed among our thinkers. Abolitionists, Reconstructors, neoabolitionists, all shared one common belief: that if we could only use the legislature and the judiciary to create and interpret the laws of desegregation and access, all else would follow. As it turns out, it was vastly easier to dismantle the petty forms of apartheid in this country (housing, marriage, hotels, and restaurants) than anyone could have possibly believed it would be, *without* affecting the larger patterns of inequality. In fact, the economic structure has not changed one jot, in any fundamental sense, except that black adult and teenage unemployment is much higher now than it has been in my lifetime. Considering the out-of-wedlock birthrate, the high school drop-out rate, and the unemployment figures, the "two nations" predicted by the Kerner Commission in 1968 may be upon us. And the conscious manipulation of our public image, by writers, filmmakers, and artists, which many of us *still* seem to think will bring freedom, has had very little impact in palliating our structural social problems. What's the most popular television program in South Africa? The "Cosby Show." Why not?

Ideology, paradoxically, was impoverished when we needed it most, during the civil rights movement of the early 1960s. Unable to theorize what Cornel West calls "the racial problematic," unwilling (with very few exceptions) to theorize class, and scarcely able even to contemplate the theorizing of the curious compound effect of class-cum-race, we have—since the day after the signing of the Civil Rights act of 1965—utterly lacked any instrumentality of ideological analysis, beyond the attempts of the Black Power and Black Aesthetic movements, to *invert* the signification of "blackness" itself. Recognizing that what had passed for "the human," or "the universal," was in fact white essentialism, we substituted one sort of essentialism (that of "blackness") for another. That, we learned quickly enough, was just not enough. But it led the way to a gestural politics captivated by fetishes and feel-bad rhetoric. The ultimate sign of our sheer powerlessness is all of the attention that we have given to declaring the birth of the African American, and pronouncing the Black Self dead. Don't we have anything better to do?

Now, I myself happen to like African American, especially because I am, as a scholar, an Africanist as well as an African-Americanist. Certainly the cultural continuities among African, Caribbean, and Black American cultures cannot be denied. (The irony is that we often thought of ourselves as "African" until late into the nineteenth century. The death of the African was declared by the Park school of sociology in the first quarter of this century, which thought that the hyphenated ethnicity of the Negro American would prove to be ultimately liberating.) But so tame and unthreatening is a politics centered on onomastics that even the *New York Times,* in a major editorial, declared its support of this movement.

> If Mr. Jackson is right and blacks now prefer to be called African-Americans, it is a sign not just of their maturity but of the nation's success. . . . Blacks may now feel comfortable enough in their standing as citizens to adopt the family surname: American. And their first name, African, conveys a pride in cultural heritage that all Americans cherish. The late James Baldwin once lamented, "Nobody knows my name." Now everyone does [December 22, 1988].

To which one young black writer, Trey Ellis, responded recently: "When somebody tries to tell me what to call myself in all uses just because they come to some decision at a cocktail party to which I wasn't even invited, my mama raised me to tell them to kiss my black ass" (*Village Voice,* June 13, 1989). As he says, sometimes African American just won't do.

Ellis's amused rejoinder speaks of a very different set of concerns, and made me think of James Baldwin's prediction of the coming of a new generation that would give voice to blackness:

> While the tale of how we suffer, and how we are delighted, and how we may triumph is never new, it always must be heard. There isn't any other to tell, it's the only light we've got in all

this darkness. . . . And this tale, according to that face, that body, those strong hands on those strings, has another aspect in every country, and a new depth in every generation (*The Price of the Ticket*).

In this spirit, Ellis has declared the birth of a "New Black Aesthetic" movement, comprising artists and writers who are middle class, self-confident, and secure with black culture, and not looking over their shoulders at white people, wondering whether or not the Mr. Wilsons of their world will call them George. Ellis sees creative artists such as Spike Lee, Wynton Marsalis, Anthony Davis, August Wilson, Warrington Hudlin, Joan Armatrading, and Lisa and Kelly Jones as representatives of a new generation who, commencing with the publication in 1978 of Toni Morrison's *Song of Solomon* (for Ellis a founding gesture) "no longer need to deny or suppress any part of our complicated and sometimes contradictory cultural baggage to please either white people or black. The culturally mulatto *Cosby* girls are equally as black as a black teenage welfare mother" ("The New Black Aesthetic," *Before Columbus Review*, May 14, 1989). And Ellis is right: something quite new is afoot in African-American letters.

In a recent *New York Times* review of Maxine Hong Kingston's new novel, Le Anne Schreiber remarks: "Wittman Ah Singh can't be Chinese even if he wants to be. . . . He is American, as American as Jack Kerouac or James Baldwin or Allen Ginsberg. . . ." I remember a time, not so very long ago, when almost no one would have thought of James Baldwin as typifying the "American." I think that even James Baldwin would have been surprised. Certainly since 1950, the meanings of blackness, as manifested in the literary tradition, have come full circle.

Consider the holy male trinity of the black tradition: Wright, Ellison, and Baldwin. For Richard Wright, "the color curtain" —as he titled a book on the Bandung Conference in 1955 when "the Third World" was born—was something to be rent asunder by something he vaguely called the "Enlightenment." (It never occurred to Wright, apparently, that the sublime gains in intellection in the Enlightenment took place simultaneously with the slave trade in African human beings, which generated an unprecedented degree of wealth and an unprecedentedly large leisure and intellectual class.) Wright was hardly sentimental about Black Africa and the Third World—he actually told the first Conference of Negro-African Writers and Artists in Paris in 1956 that colonialism had been "liberating, since it smashed old traditions and destroyed old gods, freeing Africans from the 'rot' of their past," their "irrational past" (James Baldwin, *Nobody Knows My Name*). Despite the audacity of this claim, however, Wright saw himself as chosen "in some way to inject into the American consciousness" a cognizance of "other people's mores or national habits" ("I Choose Exile," unpublished essay). Wright claimed that he was "split": "I'm black. I'm a man of the West. . . . I see and understand the non- or anti-Western point of view. . . ." But, Wright confesses, "when I look out upon the vast stretches of this earth inhabited by brown, black and yellow men . . . my reactions and attitudes are those of the West" (*White Man, Listen!*). Wright never had clearer insight into himself, although his unrelentingly critical view of Third World cultures will certainly not make him required reading among those of us bent upon decentering the canon.

James Baldwin, who parodied Wright's 1956 speech in *Nobody Knows My Name*, concluded that "this was, perhaps, a tactless way of phrasing a debatable idea. . . ." Blackness, for Baldwin, was a sign, a sign that signified through the salvation of the "gospel impulse," as Craig Werner characterizes it, seen in his refusal "to create demons, to simplify the other in a way that would inevitably force him to simplify himself. . . . The gospel impulse—its refusal to accept oppositional thought; its complex sense of presence; its belief in salvation—sounds in Baldwin's voice no matter what his particular vocabulary at a particular moment" (Craig Werner, "James Baldwin: Politics and the Gospel Impulse," *New Politics* [Winter 1989]). Blackness, if it would be anything, stood as the saving grace of both white *and* black America.

Ralph Ellison, ever the trickster, felt it incumbent upon him to show that blackness was a metaphor for the human condition, and yet to do so through a faithful adherence to its particularity. Nowhere is this idea rendered more brilliantly than in his sermon "The Blackness of Blackness," the tradition's classic critique of blackness as an essence:

"Brothers and sisters, my text this morning is the 'Blackness of Blackness.'"

And a congregation of voices answered: "That blackness is most black, brother, most black . . ."

"In the beginning . . ."

"At the very start," they cried.

". . . there was blackness . . ."

"Preach it . . ."

". . . and the sun . . ."

"The sun, Lawd . . ."

". . . was bloody red . . ."

"Red . . ."

"Now black is . . ." the preacher shouted.

"Bloody . . ."

"I said black is . . ."

"Preach it, brother . . ."

". . . an' black ain't . . ."

"Red, Lawd, red: He said it's red!"

"Amen, brother . . ."

"Black will git you . . ."

"Yes, it will . . ."

". . . an' black won't . . ."

"Naw, it won't!"

"It do . . ."

"It do, Lawd . . ."

". . . an' it don't."

"Hallelujah . . ."

"It'll put you, glory, glory, Oh my Lawd, in the WHALE'S
BELLY."
   "Preach it, dear brother..."
   "...an' make you tempt..."
   "Good God a-mighty!"
   "Old aunt Nelly!"
   "Black will make you..."
   "Black..."
   "...or black will un-make you."
   "Ain't it the truth, Lawd?"

(Ellison, *Invisible Man*)

Ellison parodies the idea that blackness can underwrite a meta-
physics or even a negative theology; that it can exist outside and
independent of its representation.

And it is out of this discursive melee that so much contemporary
African-American literature has developed.

The range of representations of the meanings of blackness
among the post–*Song of Solomon* (1978) era of black writing can
be characterized—for the sake of convenience—by the works of
C. Eric Lincoln (*The Avenue, Clayton City*), Trey Ellis's manifes-
to "The New Black Aesthetic," and Toni Morrison's *Beloved*, in
many ways the ur-text of the African-American experience.

Each of these writers epitomizes the points of a post–Black
Aesthetic triangle, made up of the realistic representation of
black vernacular culture: the attempt to preserve it for a younger
generation (Lincoln), the critique through parody of the essentialism of the Black Aesthetic (Ellis), and the transcendence of the
ultimate horror of the black past—slavery—through myth and the
supernatural (Morrison).

The first chapter of Eric Lincoln's first novel, *The Avenue,
Clayton City* (1988), contains an extended re-creation of the
African-American ritual of signifying, which is also known as
"talking that talk," "the dozens," "nasty talk," and so on. To
render the dozens in such wonderful detail, of course, is a crucial

manner of preserving it in the written cultural memory of African Americans. This important impulse to preserve (by recording) the vernacular links Lincoln's work directly to that of Zora Neale Hurston. Following the depiction of the ritual exchange, the narrator of the novel analyzes its import in the following way:

> Guts shook his head sadly as he could hear the unmistakable repartee of the dirty dozens above the clapping and the loud laughter which always somehow seemed to be louder and somehow more pitiful whenever they were talkin' that talk. Two quick-tongued contestants were already hacking away at each other's family tree, prodded on to ever more colorful and drastic allegations by the third-party agitators whose job it was to keep the verbal skirmish at high heat.
>
> "Hey, man, your daddy's so funny he'd make a three-dollar bill look real!"
>
> "Yeah! And your mama's so ugly that when she saw her reflection in the millpond, she thought it was a turtle an' jumped in an' tried to catch it!"
>
> "That ain't nothin'. If your A'nt Letty was in a beauty contest with a buffalo and a bulldog, she'd be second runner-up."
>
> "Around the bend came the L&N, an' it was loaded down with your mammy's men!"
>
> "Well, your mammy's in the po'house; your daddy's in the jail. An' your sister's on the corner tryin' to work up a sale!"
>
> "I'm gon' tell you 'bout *your* sister. She wears so many flour sack drawers she flapjacks twice a day!"
>
> "Yeah! An' you-all eat so many black-eyed peas 'til if your mama had a baby, she'd have to shell it!"
>
> "I hear that when your daddy opens his lunch box, all he finds in it is two air sandwiches an' a long drink of water!"
>
> "The first time your daddy went to church they buried him!"
>
> "Yeah. Now when God made Adam, He made him quick, but when God made your daddy, it made Him sick!"
>
> "You better watch out. You know I don't play no dozens!"

"If you don't play, just lay dead an' pat your foot while me and your mama play!"

As Guts neared the circle of revelers, he could see a tall, skinny youth of light complexion moving around in a tight circle, cutting some kind of step to the handclap rhythm of nine or ten other boys gathered under the light. It was Finis Lee Jackson, Mamie Jackson's boy who dropped out of the Academy school to work for Mr. Bimbo loading rags and scrap iron down by the railroad. Guts couldn't hear what Finis Lee was saying, but he guessed it must have been nasty or the crowd wouldn't be whooping and hollering like they were. And he knew that as soon as Finis got through, somebody else would step into the ring and the show would go on. But he never did have a chance to find out what nastiness Finis was up to because somebody spotted him leaving the Flame and put the word out.

"Ol' Creeper comin'! Cool it."

The clapping stopped. There was a long moment of silence, and then Finis Lee, determined not to forfeit his time in the ring, took on a pious look like a Methodist preacher and intoned:

> Amazin' grace, how sweet the sound
> It done saved a wreck like me. . . .

"A-man! A-man!" came a chorus of responses liberally interposed with sniggles and suppressed whoops.

"Evening, Mr. Gallimore," one of the boys said as Guts shuffled on toward the circle.

"Don't be tryin' to 'good evening' me," Guts said, looking at nobody in particular. "An' ain't no use to try to git so holy all of a sudden an' mess up no church song jest because you see me comin'. I know what you been up to. I heard you talkin' that ol' nasty talk. It's jest a sin an' a shame before Jesus in His heaven. That's what it is!"

"That's right, Mr. Gallimore. You sho' right. I been tryin' to tell these ol' nasty-talkin' boys to shape up an' get on the ball!"

It was Nero Banks, one of the younger boys who had only recently begun to hang out under the light.

Without bothering to even search him out in the crowd, Guts warned, "Boy, don't you play with me. I know who you is, an' I'm old enough to be your daddy twice if I wanna be, an' I don't take no sass. If you ain't got no respect for grown folks, try to have a little bit for yourself. That's the reason colored folks like you don't never git nowhere. You spend your time tryin' to impress a no-good passel of nasty-talkin' niggers an' you end up bein' jest like them—nasty an' good-for-nothin'-but-trouble!"

The circle gave way, and Guts Gallimore shuffled on up The Avenue to his wife, Rosie, and his hot tub to soak his feet and pray for a call to preach. But other calls echoed after him through the hot and steamy darkness.

"That's right, Mr. Gallimore! You're right 'til you're left, an' when you're left, right don't make no difference."

"Good night, Guts. Don't let your meat loaf, your gravy might curdle!"

"So long, Mr. Gallimore, 'cause so short can't cut no mustard."

Trey Ellis, whose first novel, *Platitudes*, is a satire on contemporary black cultural politics, is an heir of Ishmael Reed, the tradition's great satirist. Ellis describes the relation of what he calls "The New Black Aesthetic" (NBA) to the black nationalism of the sixties, engaged as it is in the necessary task of critique and revision:

Yet ironically, a telltale sign of the work of the NBA is our parodying of the black nationalist movement: Eddie Murphy, 26, and his old *Saturday Night Live* character, prison poet Tyrone Green, with his hilariously awful angry black poem. "Cill [sic] My Landlord," ("See his dog Do he bite?"); fellow Black Packer Keenan Wayans' upcoming blaxploitation parody *I'ma Get You Sucka!*; playwright George Wolfe, and his parodies of both "A Raisin in the Sun" and "For Colored

Girls..." in his hit play "The Colored Museum" ("Enter Walter-Lee-Beau-Willie-Jones.... His brow is heavy from 300 years of oppression"); filmmaker Reginald Hudlin, 25, and his sacrilegious *Reggie's World of Soul* with its fake commercial for a back scratcher, spatula and toilet bowl brush all with black clenched fists for their handle ends; and Lisa Jones' character Clean Mama King who is available for both sit-ins and film walk-ons. There is now such a strong and vast body of great black work that the corny or mediocre doesn't need to be coddled. NBA artists aren't afraid to publicly flout the official, positivist black party line.

This generation, Ellis continues, cares less about what white people think than any other in the history of Africans in this country. "The New Black Aesthetic says you just have to *be* natural, you don't necessarily have to *wear* one."

Ellis dates the beginning of this cultural movement with the publication of *Song of Solomon* in 1978. Morrison's blend of magical realism and African-American mythology proved compelling: This brilliantly rendered book was an overnight bestseller. Her greatest artistic achievement, however, and most controversial, is her most recent novel, *Beloved*, which won the 1988 Pulitzer Prize for Fiction.

In *Beloved*, Morrison has found a language that gives voice to the unspeakable horror and terror of the black past, our enslavement in the New World. Indeed, the novel is an allegorical representation of this very unspeakability. It is one of the few treatments of slavery that escapes the pitfalls of *kitsch*. Toni Morrison's genius is that she has found a language by which to thematize this very unspeakability of slavery.

Everybody knew what she was called, but nobody knew her name. Disremembered and unaccounted for, she cannot be lost because no one is looking for her, and even if they were, how can they call her if they don't know her name? Although she has claim, she is not claimed. In the place where long grass opens, the girl who waited to be loved and cry shame erupts into her separate parts, to make it easy for the chewing laughter to swallow her all away.

It was not a story to pass on.

They forgot her like a bad dream. After they made up their tales, shaped and decorated them, those that saw her that day on the porch quickly and deliberately forgot her. It took longer for those who had spoken to her, lived with her, fallen in love with her, to forget, until they realized they couldn't remember or repeat a single thing she said, and began to believe that, other than what they themselves were thinking, she hadn't said anything at all. So, in the end, they forgot her too. Remembering seemed unwise. They never knew where or why she crouched, or whose was the underwater face she needed like that. Where the memory of the smile under her chin might have been and was not, a latch latched and lichen attached its apple-green bloom to the metal. What made her think her fingernails could open locks the rain rained on?

It was not a story to pass on.

Only by stepping outside of the limitations of realism and entering a realm of myth could Morrison, a century after its abolition, give a voice to the silence of enslavement.

For these writers, in their various ways, the challenge of the black creative intelligence is no longer to *posit* blackness, as it was in the Black Arts movement of the sixties, but to render it. Their goal seems to be to create a fiction *beyond* the colorline, one that takes the blackness of the culture for granted, as a springboard to write about those human emotions that we share with everyone else, and that we have always shared with each other, when no white people are around. They seem intent, paradoxically, in escaping the very banality of blackness that we encountered in so much Black Arts poetry, by *assuming* it as a legitimate ground for the creation of art.

To declare that race is a trope, however, is not to deny its palpable force in the life of every African American who tries to function every day in a still very racist America. In the face of

Anthony Appiah's and my own critique of what we might think of as "black essentialism," Houston Baker demands that we remember what we might characterize as the "taxi fallacy."

Houston, Anthony, and I emerge from the splendid isolation of the Schomburg Library, and stand together on the corner of 135th Street and Malcolm X Boulevard attempting to hail a taxi to return to the Yale Club. With the taxis shooting by us as if we did not exist, Anthony and I cry out in perplexity: "But sir, it's only a trope."

If only that's *all* it was.

My father, who recently enjoyed his seventy-sixth birthday, and I attended a basketball game at Duke this past winter. It wasn't just any game; it was "the" game with North Carolina, the ultimate rivalry in American basketball competition. At a crucial juncture of the game, one of the overly avid Duke fans bellowing in our section of the auditorium called J. R. Reid, the Carolina center, "rubber lips."

"Did you hear what he said?" I asked my father, who wears *two* hearing aids.

"I heard it. Ignore it, boy."

"I can't, Pop," I replied. Then, loud-talking all the way, I informed the crowd, while ostensibly talking only to my father, that we'd come too far to put up with shit like this, that Martin Luther King didn't die in vain, and we won't tolerate this kind of racism again, etc., etc., etc. Then I stood up and told the guy not to say those words ever again.

You could have cut the silence in our section of that auditorium with a knife. After a long silence, my Dad leaned over and whispered to me, "Nigger, is you *crazy*? We am in de Souf." We both burst into laughter.

Even in the South, though, the intrusion of race into our lives usually takes more benign forms. One day my wife and father came to lunch at the National Humanities Center in Research Triangle Park, North Carolina, where I'm currently a fellow. The following day, the only black member of the staff cornered me and said that the kitchen staff had a bet, and that I was the only person who could resolve it. Shoot, I said. "Okay," he said. "The bet is that your Daddy is Mediterranean—Greek or Eyetalian, and your wife is High Yellow." "No," I said, "it's the other way around; my Dad is black; my wife is white."

"Oh, yeah," he said, after a long pause, looking at me through the eyes of the race when one of us is being "sadiddy," or telling some kind of racial lie. "You know, *brother*," he said to me in a low but pointed whisper, "we black people got ways to *tell* these things, you know." Then he looked at me to see if I was ready to confess the truth. Indeterminacy had come home to greet me.

What, finally, is the meaning of blackness for my generation of African-American scholars? I think that many of us are trying to work, rather self-consciously, within the tradition. It has taken white administrators far too long to realize that the recruitment of black faculty members is vastly easier at those institutions with the strongest black studies departments, or at least with the strongest representation of other black faculty. Why? I think the reason for this is that many of us wish to be a part of a community, of something "larger" than ourselves, escaping the splendid isolation of our studies. What can be lonelier than research, except perhaps the terror of the blank page (or computer screen)? Few of us—and I mean *very* few—wish to be the "only one" in town. I want my own children to grow up in the home of intellectuals, but with black middle-class values as common to them as the air they breathe. This I cannot achieve alone. I seek out, eagerly, the company of other African-American academics who have paid their dues, who understand the costs, and the pleasures, of achievement, who care about "the race," and who are determined to leave a legacy of self-defense against racism in all of its pernicious forms.

Part of this effort to achieve a sense of community is understanding that our generation of scholars is just an extension of other generations, of "many thousands gone." We are no smarter than they; we are just a bit more fortunate, in some ways, the accident of birth enabling us to teach at "white" research institutions, when two generations before we would have been teaching at black schools, overworked and underfunded. Most of us define ourselves as extensions of the tradition of scholarship and academic excellence epitomized by figures such as J. Saunders Redding, John Hope Franklin, and St. Clair Drake, merely to list a few names. But how are we *different* from them?

A few months ago I heard Cornel West deliver a memorial lecture in honor of James Snead, a brilliant literary critic who died of cancer recently at the age of thirty-five. Snead graduated valedictorian of his class at Exeter, then summa cum laude at Yale. Fluent in German, he wrote his Scholar of the House "essay" on the uses of repetition in Thomas Mann and William Faulkner. (Actually, this "essay" amounted to some six hundred pages, and the appendices were written in German.) He was also a jazz pianist and composer and worked as an investment banker in West Germany, after he took the Ph.D. in English literature at the University of Cambridge. Snead was a remarkable man.

West, near the end of his memorial lecture, told his audience that he had been discussing Snead's life and times with St. Clair Drake, as Drake lay in bed in a hospital recovering from a mild stroke that he had experienced on a flight from San Francisco to Princeton where Drake was to lecture. When West met the plane at the airport, he rushed Drake to the hospital, and sat with him through much of the weekend.

West told Drake how Snead was, yes, a solid race man, how he loved the tradition, and wrote about it, but that his real goal was to redefine *American studies* from the vantage point of African-American concepts and principles. For Snead, taking the black mountaintop was not enough; he wanted the entire mountain range. "There is much about Dr. Snead that I can understand," Drake told West. "But then again," he concluded, "there is something about his enterprise that is quite unlike ours." Our next move within the academy, our next gesture, is to redefine the whole, simultaneously institutionalizing African-American studies. The idea that African-American culture was exclusively a thing apart, separate from the whole, having no influence on the shape and shaping of American culture, is a racialist fiction. There can be no doubt that the successful attempts to "decenter" the canon stem in part from the impact that black studies programs have had upon traditional notions of the "teachable," upon what, properly, constitutes the universe of knowledge that the well-educated should know. For us, and for the students that we train, the complex meaning of blackness is a vision of America, a refracted image in the American looking-glass.

Snead's project, and Ellis's—the project of a new generation of writers and scholars—is about transcending the I-got-mine parochialism of a desperate era. It looks beyond that overworked masterplot of victims and victimizers so carefully scripted in the cultural dominant, beyond the paranoid dream of cultural autarky, and beyond the seductive ensolacements of nationalism. Their story—and it is a new story—is about elective affinities, unburdened by an ideology of descent; it speaks of blackness without blood. And this *is* a story to pass on.

Herman Schwartz

CIVIL RIGHTS AND
THE REAGAN COURT

It took all of Ronald Reagan's eight years. But it now appears that he achieved one of his major goals: hastening an end to the Second Reconstruction in America. Reagan not only succeeded in reducing the protection of specific laws; he transformed the federal judiciary, once the foremost champion of individual rights, into a threat to those laws.

The key to this transformation was the Reagan appointments to the Supreme Court. Along with Nixon appointee William H. Rehnquist, whom Reagan elevated to chief justice, and conserva-

Herman Schwartz, Professor of Law at American University in Washington, D.C., is editor of *The Burger Years* and author of *Packing the Courts*. He writes regularly for *The Nation* and has participated in many civil rights and civil liberties cases.

tive Kennedy appointee Byron White, the Reagan justices—Sandra Day O'Connor, Antonin Scalia, and Anthony Kennedy—have consistently voted together to strike at civil rights laws adopted for minorities, women, and the disabled.

Affirmative Action

The Court's approach to affirmative action is the best illustration of this change. Affirmative action has troubled the Court since it first faced the issue in 1974 in a case involving preferential admissions to a state law school. There, the Court avoided the issue by dismissing the case on procedural grounds. Four years later, it could duck the problem no longer, and in the landmark *Regents of the University of California v. Bakke* (1978), it gave a constitutional green light to race-preferential plans in admittance to state-run higher education so long as the plans did not involve fixed quotas. There was no majority decision, as the Court splintered three ways in a 4-4-1 division. Because he was the decisive swing vote—as in so many cases during his time on the Court—Justice Lewis F. Powell, the conservative Virginia Democrat appointed by Nixon, would set the governing rules for legally acceptable affirmative action in *Bakke* and a series of sharply divided Supreme Court decisions over the next ten years.

A full majority was available the following year, however, in *United Steelworkers v. Weber* (1979), when a 5-2 vote of the Court upheld a private employer's affirmative action plan against a challenge under Title VII of the Civil Rights Act of 1964, which bans discrimination in employment. The following year, in *Fullilove v. Klutznick*, six justices upheld a federal government plan to require states to set aside 10 percent of their contracts for minority business on construction financed by the federal government. All the justices who voted to uphold the plan, including Chief Justice Warren Burger as well as Justices Powell and White, made a point of commenting on the sad history of racial discrimination in the construction industry.

By 1981 affirmative action seemed solidly established. Many

employers, universities, and state governments had become accustomed to it. Some even saw affirmative action as a positive benefit. As a Bank of America executive observed, "We want to ensure a work force that reflects the diversity of the markets that we serve." Hundreds of thousands of plans in various industries were established, and minorities and women were able to make sizeable gains. At the Kaiser plant in Gramercy, Louisiana, the site of the *Weber* case, the number of minority craft workers jumped from five to fifty-six (today they are almost 20 percent of the total). Supreme Court rulings in other civil rights settings, particularly those making it easier for minorities and women to win job discrimination suits, added to the force of *Weber*. In order to forestall suits or settle them, employers adopted affirmative action on their own.

Reagan, Ed Meese, and Bradford Reynolds changed all that, despite the fact that in the 1980s the strong initial complaints against affirmative action, especially by Jewish groups fearing the revival of the kinds of quotas once used to exclude Jews from higher education, quieted down. From its first days in office, the Reagan administration targeted affirmative action. Professing devotion to "color blindness"—a devotion that developed only when the possibility arose that whites might be affected by color consciousness—the administration launched a full-scale attack against civil rights statutes. Most of its efforts failed. It was continually rebuffed by Congress, and, more often than not, the Supreme Court upheld affirmative action plans except when white employees were laid off in favor of minority workers with less seniority.

Reagan and Meese had a complete triumph in one respect, however. They reshaped the federal judiciary in general and the Supreme Court in particular. Despite the Robert Bork defeat, when Anthony Kennedy took his seat on the High Court in February 1989, it finally became the Reagan court.

The first ominous sign appeared two months later when Kennedy joined the four other conservatives in ordering a reconsideration of an important 1976 civil rights decision. That was just a signal, however, for the reconsideration order itself did not actually decide anything. The case of *Richmond v. J. Croson and Co.* the following year did, however, and in both style and substance the Court's decision revealed such a cold indifference to the continuing plight of minorities that Justice O'Connor, who wrote the Court's opinion, felt impelled to protest that the majority did not think that "government bodies need no longer preoccupy themselves with rectifying racial injustice."

The facts in the case were these: In 1983, the Richmond City Council, seeing that blacks had almost never gotten any city contracts, voted to require prime contractors on city contracts to set aside at least 30 percent of their contract dollar amount for minority business enterprises. Waivers were available if the goal could not be met. The plan, which was modeled on the federal plan approved in *Fullilove*, was designed to last for five years, but after the plan had been in operation a few months, a white prime contractor, who had lost a contract for plumbing fixtures in a Richmond city jail, challenged the city.

In a 6-3 decision the Court struck down the Richmond plan. Writing for the majority, Justice O'Connor declared that as a matter of fundamental constitutional law, official action for minorities to help make up for some of the disadvantages resulting from centuries of oppression would be viewed by the Court with the same hostile skepticism—in constitutional terms "strict scrutiny" —as prejudiced and racist actions against minorities. She then set down conditions for a constitutionally acceptable program so stringent that few such plans will ever pass legal muster.

In her opinion O'Connor also had to explain away the *Fullilove* decision, which was the model for the Richmond plan. She did so by resorting to some constitutional history to distinguish between federal and state power. According to her, the Fourteenth Amendment was adopted in order to prevent the states not only from doing bad things to blacks but from doing good things for them that might adversely affect whites. "Section 1 of the Fourteenth Amendment stemmed from a distrust of state legislative enactments based on race," she wrote in the decision that led a bitter

Justice Thurgood Marshall to protest that this "turns the Amendments on their heads. . . . Nothing whatever in the legislative history of either the Fourteenth Amendment or the Civil Rights Acts remotely suggests that the States are foreclosed from furthering the fundamental purposes of equal opportunity to which the Amendment and those Acts are addressed."

The *Croson* decision also exposed the meretriciousness of one of the Reagan justices' most frequently proclaimed loyalties. Since coming onto the Court, O'Connor has been a vociferous defender of localism and states' rights. She and the Reagan conservatives have continually proclaimed their allegiance to judicial restraint, repeatedly attacking liberals for not showing proper deference to the popularly elected branches of government. But the virtues of localism and of judicial restraint were conveniently forgotten in *Croson* when it came to protecting white contractors. Suddenly the decision of a local city council no longer mattered. Instead, for O'Connor, the plan adopted by a 5-4 black majority of the Richmond City Council was an exercise of blatantly racial politics by blacks that justified especially close scrutiny by the courts.

Rough as it was, the Court's assault on affirmative action in *Croson* did not satisfy the two newest Reagan appointees. Both Scalia and Kennedy condemned all race-preferential programs, insisting instead that the only acceptable approach is one that limits preferences to identifiable victims of specific discrimination.

Victims' Rights

But proving you are a victim of discrimination is no easy task before the Reagan court. In the past, discrimination victims could rely on the Supreme Court's 1971 ruling in *Griggs v. Duke Power*. There, Chief Justice Warren Burger, speaking for a unanimous Court, ruled that once employees show that an employer's ostensibly neutral employment practices result in a grossly disproportionate disparity between the minorities in the workforce and those in the pool from which that force is drawn, the employees win unless the employer can show that the practices are justified by business necessity. One of the many benefits of this decision was that it forced employers to examine and discard many tests and requirements that they had long used unthinkingly. Such qualifications as high school diplomas for janitors and height requirements for police, which had excluded many minorities and women, often turned out to be unnecessary.

The difficulty and expense of defending these cases after *Griggs* led many employers to settle or to adopt affirmative action plans voluntarily. They anticipated that such plans would not only take care of the discrimination charge by minorities and women but, if court-approved, would also protect them against so-called "reverse discrimination" suits by white male workers.

In *Ward's Cove Packing Co. v. Atonio* (1989), the Reagan Court changed this balance by requiring employees to prove that their employer is *not* justified in using an employment practice that results in disproportionately few minorities being hired. The decision, which overturned eighteen years of law, is contrary to normal notions of who has to prove what in a suit. It is extremely difficult to establish that an employment practice is not justified, for the employer has most of the evidence about why he or she chose a job selection procedure. It is hard for an employee to get access to that information, and if the plaintiff is an applicant who was turned down for a job, he or she is even less likely to know about the business in question.

The Reagan Court did not stop here, however. The same day that the Court issued *Ward's Cove*, in *Martin v. Wilks* it hit at challenges to employment discrimination from the other end. Many employers, facing a long, drawn-out suit, choose to settle and accept a court-approved consent order, often involving the establishment of an affirmative action plan. Hearings are held to give interested parties a chance to be heard on the fairness of the deal, and if it is approved, this has usually meant that the matter is closed. Those who could have come into the suit and didn't choose to can rarely mount an effective challenge later.

Or so it was before the Court's decision in *Martin v. Wilks*. There the five conservatives, led by Rehnquist, ruled that white firefighters who could have come into the Birmingham suit when it was being litigated but chose not to could challenge it as much as ten years after the plan went into effect, and even later. The decision overrode decisions of almost all the federal appellate courts going back to 1980. As a result, employers considering settlement will now have another strong reason not to. Not only has their litigation position been immensely strengthened by *Ward's Cove*, but even if they decide to settle, they will not gain their other goal, which is to be protected against suits by nonminority employees.

The Court's patience was much shorter, however, when it was women or minorities who delayed in suing. In *Lorance v. A.T.&T. Technologies, Inc.*, decided a week after *Martin v. Wilks*, the Court threw out the case of several women who had tried to challenge a seniority system for being deliberately discriminatory. When the system was first adopted in 1979, the women were not harmed by it. Not surprisingly, they did not choose to file a difficult and expensive lawsuit against something that had not yet hurt them. But when in 1982 the new seniority system began to result in their demotion, they promptly sued. "Too late," said the Court. The women should have sued when the system was first instituted, even though they were not affected by it until three years later. To allow the suit, said Justice Scalia, "would disrupt . . . valid reliance interests," something he and the majority were quite willing to tolerate in the *Martin* case, where white males delayed nearly ten years before suing.

Original Intent

These decisions follow from a heads-I-win, tails-you-lose approach to legislative and constitutional intent. Shortly after Edwin Meese became attorney general in 1985, he told the American Bar Association that the "original meaning of constitutional provisions and statutes [is] the only reliable guide for judgment" by judges. Where individual rights based on constitutional provisions are to be considered, Meese went on to insist, the framers' original intention was the sole legitimate basis for constitutional analysis.

"Original intent" is, however, a particularly unreliable guide for determining the scope of constitutional rights about discrimination and equality under the Civil War Amendments. Even the foremost advocate of "original intent," Robert Bork, once conceded, "History ... tells us much too little about the specific intentions of the men who framed, adopted, and ratified the great clauses." Also, we are a nation with a racist and sexist history, and the history of the Fourteenth Amendment prohibiting discrimination by the states is clouded by ideas long since discredited. In the original debate over the Fourteenth Amendment, what comes through is a resistance to any kind of racial mixing and an acceptance of segregation. As the late legal historian Alexander Bickel concluded, "[T]he Amendment as originally understood, was meant to apply neither to jury service nor suffrage, nor antimiscegenation statutes, nor segregation." The same Congress that adopted the Amendment appropriated money for segregated schools in the District of Columbia.

If anything, the attitude underlying *Plessy v. Ferguson* (1896), where the Supreme Court gave its stamp of approval to segregation, is closer to the "original intent" of the framers of the Fourteenth Amendment in the 1860s than was *Brown v. Board of Education* (1954). And so far as the constitutional rights to equal treatment of women are concerned, a good indication of the mid-nineteenth-century attitude is Justice Joseph Bradley's comment in an 1873 decision upholding Illinois's authority to deny women the right to practice law. Just five years after the Fourteenth Amendment was ratified, Justice Bradley observed, "The paramount destiny and mission of woman are to fulfill the noble and benign offices of wife and mother. That is the law of the Creator."

With statutory rights, however, the matter is quite different. There has usually been no dispute over the proposition that, as

Chief Judge Patricia Wald of the Court of Appeals in Washington, D.C., wrote recently, it is the business of the judge to "try and enforce...[statutes] as Congress meant them to be enforced." Congressional legislative history is usually available in the form of committee reports and debates, often deliberately created in order to help courts interpret a statute. Congress and others in fact consider committee reports to be the official legislative commentary on a law, and the reports are prepared and approved with that in mind.

Conservatives have turned the matter upside down. They advocate original intent for constitutional questions, where it really doesn't have much of a place, but urge the opposite on statutory questions. Justice Scalia, the most aggressive and imaginative of the new conservative justices, has argued in speeches and opinions that the search for the legislative intent of a statute is unwise and unwarranted. "Asking what the legislators intended...is quite the wrong question," he said some years ago. Legislative history and other such sources of congressional intent should be ignored. According to Scalia, a statute should be read "not on the basis of which meaning can be shown to have been understood by a larger handful of the Members of Congress; but rather on the basis of which meaning is...most in accord with context and ordinary usage." Scalia has, in fact, frequently shown his scorn for the legislative branches, Congress, and the state legislatures, and his approach has given the Reagan justices a free hand in developing their notions of "context and ordinary usage."

What this selective approach to history means in practice may be seen with particular vividness in two cases decided on the same day in the closing weeks of the 1988–89 Supreme Court term: *Patterson v. McClean Credit Union*, which dealt with the 1866 Civil Rights Act, and *Dellmuth v. Muth*, which ruled out suits against states in federal court under the Education of the Handicapped Act.

Patterson v. McClean Credit Union is the case in which Justice Kennedy first showed where he stood on civil rights issues. There he voted to reconsider *Runyon v. McCrary* (1976), a 7-2 decision that, following a decision in a housing case eight years earlier, ruled that the 1866 Civil Rights Act prohibited discrimination in all private contracts. Many Supreme Court decisions and over one hundred lower court cases had relied on these decisions, and they were an important part of the civil rights structure. *Patterson* itself dealt with whether the 1866 act banned racial harassment on the job, and nobody in the case even questioned the correctness of *Runyon*. The 5-4 decision to reconsider that decision in April 1988, after *Patterson* has already been argued, sent shock waves through the civil rights community.

In response, an avalanche of briefs supporting the *Runyon* decision, including a bipartisan brief from sixty-six senators and 118 members of Congress, descended on the Court, and the conservatives quickly backed off. Kennedy wrote their opinion.

First, Kennedy grudgingly reaffirmed *Runyon*, but just on the basis of precedent, without commenting on its correctness. He then weakened the Act significantly by reading it as not protecting against racial harassment on the job or job promotion—unless the promotion involved "an opportunity for a new and distinct relationship between the employer and employee." For his statutory interpretations, Kennedy relied on his own reading of the phrase "make and enforce" a contract and his conception of how the 1866 Civil Rights Act meshed with the 1964 Civil Rights Act despite the hundred-year difference in their enactment dates. No precedent or other authority was invoked by Kennedy, and the legislative history cited by Justice Brennan showing that Congress intended an expansive reading to "make and enforce" was simply ignored.

Kennedy also wrote for the Court in the *Dellmuth* case. In that decision, he and the conservative majority refused to allow a handicapped student to recover damages from the State of Pennsylvania for violating the Education of the Handicapped Act (EHA). When Congress enacted the EHA in 1975, Kennedy said, it did not comply with a Supreme Court ruling that, if Congress wants to subject the state to damage suits, it must do so not only clearly (which it had) but explicitly in the text of the statute. The catch is that this requirement was not imposed by the Court until 1985 and, as the four dissenters complained, "could have [been] anticipated only with the aid of a particularly effective crystal ball." Dismissed by the majority as irrelevant were what Kennedy conceded were strong indications by Congress that the states were indeed to be held liable in such damage cases.

Back to the Future

The consequences of this onslaught are already apparent. Less than three months after these decisions, the *Wall Street Journal* reported that at least thirteen racial harassment cases brought under the 1866 Civil Rights Act had been dismissed since *Patterson*. Lawyers are turning down employment discrimination cases because they are too costly to litigate and almost impossible to win. According to lawyers for the NAACP Legal Defense and Education Fund, Inc., the Court's decisions have made it "difficult to bring a case; far more difficult to settle a case; difficult to decide to settle a case."

The result is a situation reminiscent of a century ago when, in an 1883 decision that drew an angry dissent from the first Justice John Harlan, the Supreme Court held that "there must be some stage in the progress of [the former slave's] elevation when he . . . ceases to be the special favorite of the laws." That ruling led to decades of discrimination and segregation, as Congress, the High Court, and the nation turned their backs on the First Reconstruction. Blacks are certainly not as helpless today as the ex-slaves were a century ago, and national attitudes are also very different. But the consequences of racism remain, and even without a Bensonhurst or a Howard Beach, America cannot afford to abandon the Second Reconstruction that the Supreme Court initiated in 1954 with its *Brown* decision.

To all this, the Reagan court seems oblivious. In *Croson*, O'Connor found it necessary to protest that the majority did not "view racial discrimination as largely a phenomenon of the past." In *Patterson*, Kennedy insisted that "neither our words nor our decisions should be interpreted as signalling one inch of retreat from Congress's policy to forbid discrimination in the private, as well as the public, sphere." Perhaps not. But for the black plaintiffs in those cases, such words are hardly consoling. What they point up is that the only kinds of racial injustices the Reagan court now finds worth rectifying are instances of demonstrably intentional prejudice aimed at individuals. That is better than nothing, but given the persistence of deeply entrenched racism and sexism, it is grossly inadequate.

A hostile federal judiciary led by the Supreme Court can only be counteracted by state and national legislation if we are to avoid a quick end to the Second Reconstruction. But as recent history shows, getting such legislation passed, especially by Congress, is difficult and time consuming. Whether enough political muscle can be mustered is uncertain. If it cannot, what is certain is that the future for minorities, women, and all who have been hurt by discrimination will be bleak—even by 1980s standards.

Sean Wilentz

THE TRIALS OF TELEVANGELISM

In 1987, at the outset of the PTL ("Praise the Lord")
scandal, the Reverend Jimmy Swaggart solemnly announced that
"the gospel of Jesus Christ has never sunk to such a level as it
has today." Never mind the Inquisition: it had taken Jim and
Tammy Faye Bakker to drag Christianity to the very depths of
depravity. Nobody could have guessed that a year later it would
be the Reverend Jimmy's turn to cry, once his sexual carryings-
on came to light. We may never know if Swaggart's denunciation

Sean Wilentz is Professor of History at Princeton University
and author of *Chants Democratic: New York City and the Rise of
the American Working Class, 1788–1850*. He writes regularly
for the *New Republic*, *Dissent*, and the *Village Voice*. He is at
work on a book about the origins of democracy in America.

of the Bakkers projected his still-secret guilt upon a pair of vulnerable rivals. What is clear is that Swaggart's disgrace (and the Bakkers'), along with Pat Robertson's cranky presidential crusade in 1988, made a mockery of what was supposed to be the great awakening of conservative evangelicalism. Rarely in modern times has a movement of such reputed magnitude self-destructed so suddenly.

Yet, as with everything connected to evangelical politics, appearances were deceiving. Although the evangelical right failed to turn itself into a successful Christian party (or fully convert the GOP), it nonetheless changed the nation's cultural and political life during the 1980s. The key to this change lies in the career of Jerry Falwell. Before he disbanded the Moral Majority and beat a strategic retreat to his church and university in Lynchburg, Virginia, Falwell gave the country a sense of what it would be like to have an American mullah. During most of the Reagan years, Falwell seemed to be everywhere at once—standing up for Star Wars, denouncing sodomy, fighting secular humanism, and urging patriotic Americans to buy all the Kruggerands they could afford.

Born in 1933 to a pious, dutiful homemaker and a successful Lynchburg bootlegger-businessman ruined by drink, Falwell was less the dour backwoods Bible thumper than a middle-class striver. He studied for two years to become an engineer before receiving God's call and transferring to a fundamentalist Bible college. Although loyal to fundamentalist doctrine, he also encouraged his congregation to compete successfully in the race of life. "Lessons in worldly success," Frances FitzGerald has called his early sermons, "how-to-do-it manuals in the mainstream tradition of Billy Graham and Norman Vincent Peale."

Falwell's Lynchburg congregation consisted not of the amorphous rural classes, so commonly invoked as the mainstay of postwar fundamentalism, but of city people, many of them on the way up, with hardscrabble rural backgrounds. They had come to Lynchburg with the arrival of major national corporations during the 1950s, and they formed the boundary of a rapidly growing middle class. With his methods of "saturation evangelism"—equal parts Christian stewardship and relentless door-to-door salesmanship— Falwell reached out to these people and built his Thomas Road Baptist Church into one of the largest "super churches" in the nation. By the early 1970s it had a splendid new sanctuary, a Christian academy and elementary school, a syndicated television ministry, a rehabilitation center for alcoholics, and a membership of thousands. If not quite of the mainstream secular world, Falwell and his congregation were certainly in it in a way their parents and grandparents never were.

The trouble was the world was rapidly changing in ways that deeply wounded fundamentalist sensibilities. Just as they began to climb out from behind the walls of social inferiority and cultural isolation, fundamentalists felt attacked on all sides. For many, the 1962 and 1963 Supreme Court decisions banning prayer in public schools were the first of these troubling changes. For Falwell, the decisive challenge was the civil rights movement.

In 1965, at the time of the Selma marches, Falwell used his pulpit to blast activist clergymen, especially Martin Luther King, Jr., for getting mixed up in politics and ignoring their duties as servants of Jesus Christ. Four months later, when a band of civil rights demonstrators targeted his church for nonviolent protests, they were evicted and arrested. Twenty years later, Falwell called these events a personal turning point: first, because they began a spiritual journey that led him to reject his racism (he now calls the civil rights workers of the 1960s "courageous"); second, because they taught him that religion and politics need not be kept separate. But in the 1960s no such calming perspective was possible. Fundamentalists like Falwell, who believed in a doctrine of pietistic withdrawal, had their backs to the wall. Their continued abstention from politics meant acquiescing to the elimination of structures of white supremacy that were deeply embedded in Southern fundamentalist life. As it happened, the crisis atmosphere abated in Lynchburg over the next few years. Falwell and his congregation found ways to make their peace with civil rights while preserving their church as an overwhelmingly white community.

But by the 1970s the sense of frustration and panic returned. Falwell has cited the 1973 *Roe v. Wade* ruling as his moment of awakening. So too for others who wound up in the Moral Majority. From that moment on, opposition to abortion became a key element in the rise of evangelical political fervor. Abortion did not stand alone, however. Other developments also fed the simmering revolt. There was the duplicity of Watergate, the disgrace of America's defeat in Vietnam, the waning of patriotic anticommunism, the gay rights movement, Jimmy Carter's "betrayal" of his evangelical heritage once in office, and a shaky economy, as seen in the ascendancy of OPEC.

Earlier generations of fundamentalists might have been able to distance themselves from such changes, shrug their shoulders, and wait for the Second Coming. But Falwell and untold thousands were already too much in the world for that. Every day they witnessed horrifying spectacles of libertinism, permissiveness, and disorder. Unless something was done, "the Enemy"—Falwell's term for the forces of Satan—would destroy America and prevent it from being the providential nation that would help usher in the millennium.

Television became the critical instrument in this perception of the world, and in Falwell's hands it would also be the critical instrument in rallying the faithful. At the outset, what became known as televangelism was a natural continuation of the older evangelical radio ministries (one of which, Charles Fuller's "Old Fashioned Revival Hour," Falwell credits for his conversion). Emboldened by a 1960 FCC directive allowing paid religious broadcasts to be considered part of the public-service programming required of all affiliates, Falwell and other ministers expanded their outreach, taking advantage of the latest breakthroughs in video technology. By 1971 more than three hundred stations carried Falwell's services from Thomas Road Baptist Church.

There were, of course, problems with this success. A television ministry threatened to undercut the fiercely independent communal autonomy that had long been a pillar of American evangelical Protestantism. An electronic church whose "congregants" tuned in to Falwell was a financial threat to local churches. It might even undermine the traditional subordination of a preacher to his own congregation. A successful television preacher could have a huge audience and at the same time minimal pastoral obligations. If he chose, he could simply turn church government over to the little oligarchy surrounding him.

Better than most, Falwell was able to finesse these problems. He did, after all, have his Thomas Road Church (administered by a close-knit group of local advisers). He approached religion, including televised religion, as a growth industry with room for everyone. On the one occasion when his pastoral leadership and personal integrity came under serious question—a 1973 SEC investigation involving improper bond issues—Falwell was able to plead inexperience and save face. Rarely, however, was it necessary for him to make excuses. He quickly learned to apply his masterful door-to-door hucksterism to the airwaves, raising millions of dollars while cultivating an appealing image.

The image was crucial. Although viewed by liberals as a loudmouth bullyboy, Falwell came as close as someone in the conservative fundamentalist fold could to a generic pan-Protestantism. He was most emphatically not a charismatic or holiness ranter. There was no faith healing or talking in tongues at Thomas Road Baptist. In his tasteful, postmodern colonial church, Falwell rarely raised his voice for long. His delivery, if not particularly stirring, was recognizably avuncular and down-to-earth. The whole operation strove for a touch of class. Aware of the importance of tradition in his native Virginia, Falwell even modeled his church's buildings on Thomas Jefferson's architectural designs. There was something safe and reassuring about his broadcasts. To an uninitiated viewer, it all might have looked like nothing more than, well . . . church. One had to listen awhile to catch Falwell's message.

At the heart of the nation's problems, Falwell declared—the

main cause of America's loss of prestige, the decline of patriotism, and the triumph of pervasive liberalism—was a moral rot that derived from the breakdown of sexual rules and of the "traditional family." It was not the first time that American religion and politics had become entangled with profound changes in sexual norms. The evangelical outbursts of the 1820s and 1830s helped legitimate the very model of bourgeois family life and domestic bliss that Falwell and others mythologize as the biblically inspired nuclear unit established for eternity. The fundamentalist uprisings of the 1920s involved a reaction against the New Woman and against the alleged effeminacy of the liberal, modern man whom Billy Sunday called "a wishy-washy sissified sort of galoot that let everybody make a doormat out of him."

Falwell tapped into the deeply sexualized anxieties that followed from the social upheavals of the last twenty years. These anxieties didn't just involve fears of androgyny and male lust; they entailed elemental distinctions between order and chaos, cleanliness and pollution. For Falwell and other fundamentalists, as well as millions of Americans, the qualities of maleness and femaleness are not malleable. They are divinely ordered essences, "intimately woven," as Falwell wrote in 1980, "in the overall fabric of personality."

Fully mature persons are either completely masculine or completely feminine, qualities that Falwell attaches to his long-suffering mother and his tragically doomed father, as well as to his own "Christian marriage." At Thomas Road Baptist, these distinctions are reinforced less in the liturgy (though Falwell always projects a beefy ex-jock presence) than in the visual imagery of Falwell's sermons. On one occasion, Falwell instructed his congregation to reject the prevailing depiction of Jesus Christ as a meek, diaphanous hippie-type with long hair and a billowing robe: "Christ wasn't effeminate. . . . The man who lived on this earth was a man with muscles. . . . Christ was a he-man!"

Yet everywhere they looked in the late 1960s and 1970s, Falwell and his congregation saw a mainstream culture hell-bent

on androgyny (and with it the destruction of the American family
and the loss of national virility). Worse still, they saw politicians
going along with it all. One day the sissified galoots in Washington were proposing constitutional amendments that would force
Christian women to be drafted for combat duty. The next day they
were touting legislation that would make homosexuals a legally
protected minority, thereby thrusting perverts on unwilling Christian employers and school boards.

Male lust, the flip side of androgyny, showed its face everywhere from the porno houses to the divorce courts. More important, the calls for equality by ERA feminists, pro-choice groups,
and other proponents of women's rights promised to let men
evade their responsibilities, prey upon women's bodies, and deny
women the legal and moral protections they deserved. A hideous
vision unfolded before fundamentalists' eyes: sexual and mental
abuse of women and children, babies slain in their mothers'
wombs—all in the name of sexual freedoms that did more to
oppress women than to liberate them.

By the end of the 1970s, the cumulative effects of fundamentalism's encounters with the postwar world had raised the possibility of launching a conservative Christian crusade around moral
and sexual issues unlike any seen for half a century. It took
secular right-wing organizers like Paul Weyrich to suggest the
contours (and the name) for the Moral Majority and complete
Falwell's entry into politics. But Falwell also proved himself an
enormously capable organizer.

Very quickly the Moral Majority, along with its sibling organizations, the Christian Voice and the Religious Roundtable, attracted
attention, raised planeloads of money, and added conservative
Protestants to the election rolls. Exact figures are hard to come
by, but estimates put the number of voters registered by the
Moral Majority and the other religious groups at two million. The
new vote was solidly behind the man who endorsed the evangelical revolt, Ronald Reagan. In 1976 two-thirds of the combined
evangelical-fundamentalist vote went to the born-again Jimmy

Carter. Eight years later, the Reagan-Bush ticket garnered an astounding 81 percent.

The payback for this loyalty was a combination of rhetorical support for the fundamentalist cause and the appointment of friendly federal officials, especially in the courts. It will take future historians to determine just how much of a role Falwell and his friends played in Reagan appointments to the bench, but by the end of the 1980s, they certainly had every reason to be pleased with the results.

Within the churches, meanwhile, Falwell's activities bolstered the fundamentalists' efforts to recapture the leadership of various major fellowships. The most dramatic and wrenching shift came within the Southern Baptist Convention (SBC), the largest Protestant fellowship in the United States. By 1980 fundamentalist conservatives, spearheaded by Bailey Smith, had taken command of the SBC's national offices and done all they could to root out moderate influences. Fundamentalist and charismatic precepts also began to seep into mainline churches and the popular culture. By mid-decade it was common for rock-ribbed Presbyterians to sing evangelical hymns (not in the approved hymnal), to touch and squeeze each other, to attend workshops on *glossolalia*. Even athletics were now affected by religion. It seemed impossible to watch a sporting event without hearing the winner credit his or her victory to a personal relationship with Jesus Christ.

Falwell's rise also contributed to the literal-minded, absolutist temper that permeated public discussion in the 1980s. We must be careful here about grouping him with others who came on the public scene with moral and cultural prescriptions. The Moral Majority emerged from a very different part of the forest than the pop Platonism of Allan Bloom or the curdled feminism of Women Against Pornography. Where they converged was in their willingness to take words or symbols (the Bible, long hair, dirty pictures) as a transparent text with a meaning that would impel people to act, either for good or ill. America, awash in bad symbols, had to exorcize the devil behind them—be he Nietzsche,

Larry Flynt, or Satan himself—and bring back good standards and good symbols. By the mid-1980s American discourse was full of in-your-face affirmations about duty, flag, and family—no questions asked.

But as far as consolidating a national political base and changing America's views on other important issues, Falwell's achievement is much cloudier. In some respects the right-wing evangelicals had their most startling electoral impact in 1978, before the Moral Majority, when they helped defeat a number of prominent congressional liberals. In 1982, despite some mild boasts by Falwell, the religious right made little difference in the congressional vote nation-wide. In some states Moral Majority chapters gained control of seats on local school boards and Republican committees, but generally they failed to capture the political machinery. By 1985 candidates discovered that direct endorsement by political evangelicals could lead to a net loss in votes. On the national level the Reagan White House kept up its rhetorical support of the Moral Majority (and made the necessary appointments), but fairly quickly backed away from the evangelical legislative program.

Explanations abound for why the Moral Majority so soon reached the limits of its power. Most of these center on specific aspects of Falwell's fundamentalist background—which, for all his aspirations to ecumenicism, he could never quite shake. His mounting belligerence, for example, shaped as it was by his Manichean faith, violated what the sociologist James Davison Hunter calls an "ethic of civility" in American politics, a shared unspoken scruple that compels people not only to tolerate others' beliefs but to be tolerable to others. In Falwell's case his television mask turned him into the kind of "hot" personality that leaves the public cold.

The Moral Majority's organizational structure also displayed some of the weaknesses of Falwell's fundamentalist background. Although Falwell claimed that his organization represented a broad spectrum of conservative Protestants, Jews, and Roman Catholics, its foundations were far narrower. In actuality the whole operation resembled a national fundamentalist parachurch with its base in the local congregations. This organization helped the group grow quickly (by 1981 there were an estimated 400,000 Moral Majoritarians), but it also hindered any coordinated effort on political issues outside of presidential elections. It disguised the unevenness of the Moral Majority's development state by state, all but ensuring that Falwell would be continually embarrassed by the outrageousness of an independent spokesman or chapter.

The notion that there really was an absolute moral majority in the country that thought the same way Falwell did and was ready to fight for its vision also turned out to be a myth. Although polls showed that a large number of Americans—perhaps one-third—said they supported all of Falwell's key positions on homosexuality, school prayer, abortion, and the "traditional family," they also showed that the rest held to more liberal positions. Even evangelical Christians hardly formed a moral and political bloc. As Falwell himself admitted, some of the sharpest attacks on him came from such bastions of determined ultrafundamentalist separatism as the Fundamentalist Baptist Fellowship and Bob Jones University.

In the end, though, it was Falwell's politics that evoked the most negative reactions—the widespread suspicion, even among conservative believers, that he and the evangelical right represented a dark, antidemocratic strain in modern American politics. Being called a fascist, a bigot, and a warmonger clearly stung Falwell, and he has devoted a good deal of energy to settling scores with the liberal press for allegedly misrepresenting his views. No doubt he was prejudged in some quarters. But his political pronouncements did often slide off the edge of Christian moralism, "free enterprise" economics, and hard-line anticommunism into tropes reminiscent of the right-wing zealots of the 1930s and the McCarthyites of the 1950s. The irony is that some of his nastiest rhetoric accompanied his early efforts to make his movement more pluralistic.

When Falwell began his crusade, he underestimated the importance of grounding it in one of the great shibboleths of postwar

American life—the "Judeo-Christian tradition" that supposedly forms the nation's ethical foundation. As Mark Silk detailed in an illuminating little book, *Spiritual Politics*, Judeo-Christianity emerged after 1945 as the latest in a series of American adhesional faiths—an attempt to provide everyone with a common religious cause and a "quasi-spiritual alliance to the religiously impartial state." Falwell was not blind to such ecumenicism. Early on, he said nice things about Israel, which, to many people's surprise, turned out to be perfectly consistent with his fundamentalist beliefs. (Israel plays a significant and heroic role in fundamentalist eschatology, as derived from the Book of Ezekiel.) But like other fundamentalists, Falwell still believed America had been founded "by godly men upon godly principles to be a Christian nation."

A storm of protest, particularly from Jews, forced Falwell to reshape himself into an unswerving advocate of Judeo-Christian pluralism. But who then was "the Enemy"? Back in the 1950s both liberal and conservative Judeo-Christians thought they knew the answer. "The Enemy" was godless totalitarianism, specifically international communism, including its American adherents and fellow travelers. By the 1980s, however, domestic anti-communism was an inauspicious rallying point for building a broad consensus on moral conservatism. So the religious began talking about a new enemy—secular humanism.

Until 1970, only a few thousand Americans had even heard of the secular humanists, that hearty little band of atheists and world-government types. Conservatives might have missed them altogether if Justice Hugo Black, in a celebrated 1961 decision, hadn't mentioned secular humanism, along with Buddhism, Taoism, and Ethical Culture, as one of several atheistic religions to be guaranteed full First Amendment rights. By 1980 fundamentalists like Falwell's colleague Tim LaHaye had picked up the term and invested it with conspiratorial powers—the many-horned beast of modern liberalism, with its pornography, homosexuality, feminism, and big government. Here a line could be drawn, not between Christian and non-Christian, but between Judeo-Christianity and "the Enemy," secular humanism. And here a new political line could also be drawn between the Judeo-Christians who acknowledged that the United States had been founded on Holy Writ and the heathen who did not.

The invention of secular humanism helped Falwell and the Moral Majority open lines of communication to politically important conservative and neoconservative Jews. But demonizing secular humanism also had disastrous costs. The term was so capacious as to suggest that everyone from Thomas Jefferson to Madonna shared the same basic beliefs. Most of secular humanism's presumed tenets—the vaunting of personal freedom, the toleration of different personal beliefs—were so deeply enshrined in American culture that it was hard for most Americans to see where they ran afoul of basic American principles. The actions undertaken by pious conservatives to uproot secular humanism in the schools—notably the suit that led to a 1987 decision barring forty-four "secular humanist" texts from Alabama public schools— seemed at odds with Falwell's announced opposition to censorship. Such actions also raised a dilemma. If secular humanism was, indeed, a religion, why shouldn't it enjoy the same rights and privileges that conservative evangelicals claimed for themselves?

The more Falwell and his allies tried to build a coalition atop their fundamentalist following, the more they confirmed that they were out of touch with the prevailing ideas about democracy. In 1984 the historian Martin Marty concluded that the fundamentalists could succeed on their own terms only in the event of an utter political and economic collapse, leading to "a state religion, compulsory in character, authoritarian in tone, and 'traditional' in outlook." How much of this Falwell understood at the time is unclear. In the mid-1980s, he did, however, begin to soften his public posture.

In 1980, for example, Falwell appeared sympathetic to banning all homosexuals from public-school teaching, but later he insisted he would not abridge their right to teach "as long as they don't use the classroom to promote homosexuality as an alternative lifestyle." Similarly, he kept repeating that abortion is murder but added that abortions are permissible in cases of rape or incest. Falwell even took pride in the fact that his Liberty University trained men and women for professional careers, thus raising the question of what his idea of the "traditional" family and the "traditional" wife now meant.

During Reagan's second term Falwell could still launch into fire-and-brimstone oratory. "Satan had mobilized his own forces," he reflected in his 1987 autobiography, "to destroy America by negating the Judeo-Christian ethic." But the jeremiads now came in passing. So beholden to White House friends had Falwell become that well before the 1988 campaign he endorsed George Bush, a man who had waffled on the abortion issue and who, for all his protestations about being born again, couldn't seem to get straight the simplest biblical reference. The result is a situation that has enraged fundamentalist purists, who in 1988 cast their lot with Pat Robertson's campaign.

Falwell and his followers are in some ways better off than they were when he began the Moral Majority. Falwell ended the decade with more dignity than virtually all the other high-profile televangelists. He is now free to devote himself to institution building (in particular to his dream of turning Liberty University into a fundamentalist Notre Dame), knowing that the new conservative Supreme Court may yet overturn *Roe v. Wade* and that he has secured for fundamentalist believers a national respectability that was unimaginable twenty years ago.

But he has failed to secure the long-term political initiative. In 1989, politicians who had supported Falwellian and New Right positions on abortion stammered and stumbled, surprised by the public's reaction to the *Webster* decision. Growing portions of the Republican party now predict a political disaster unless the party finally loses its identification with the religious right.

It is one thing to affect the nation's cultural tone, quite another to translate that into enduring political power. Jerry Falwell had to learn this lesson the hard way. While he was learning it, he contributed mightily to the political dreariness of the Reaganite Gilded Age and won his share of victories. We are only beginning to recover.

William Adams

VIETNAM SCREEN WARS

The Reagan era has bequeathed to us much, including, ironically, a new version of the materialist theory of the politics of culture. The essential claim of this theory is seductively simple: cultural expression reproduces, through all the appropriate "mediations," the topography of social life. In the current version of this theory, the conservative political and social forces of the 1980s have defined the contours of its mass culture. To look in on the movies or television is to see darkly the social foundations of Reaganism: the reaffirmation of "traditional values" (the family, patriotism, work), the resuscitation of anticom-

William Adams is assistant to the president of Wesleyan University. His essays have appeared in the *Georgia Review*, the *Antioch Review*, and *Dissent*. He is at work on a book about the films of the Vietnam War.

munism, fetishes of the marketplace, the attack on alternative lifestyles.

The equation is tempting, especially in the case of one of the more notable cultural bequests of the decade: the films of the Vietnam War. For in the iconography of Reaganism, Vietnam was the protean symbol of all that had gone wrong in American life. Much more than an isolated event or disaster of foreign policy, the war was, and still remains, the great metaphor in the neoconservative lexicon for the 1960s, and thus for the rebellion, disorder, anti-Americanism, and flabbiness that era loosed among us.

It was not, significantly, until the full bloom of Reaganism that the Vietnam War became an acceptable subject for film. *Platoon* (1986), the epitome of the 1980s Vietnam film, was closely preceded or followed by nearly a dozen major productions. And as if to seal the legitimacy of the war as a subject for popular treatment, network television gave us two series, *China Beach* and *Tour of Duty*. From painful taboo to cultural icon, the Vietnam War had suddenly become a rich source of popular fictions, a story we could not hear repeated often enough.

It is convenient, then, to assume that the sudden appearance of "the Vietnam War film" on the cultural scene is linked to the conservative agenda, or at least to expect that the infant genre will reproduce the original political conflicts: hawks against doves, cold warriors against new leftists, *The Green Berets* (1968) against *Apocalypse Now* (1979). But neither expectation fits well with the stories most of these films tell. A closer look at the recent Vietnam films reveals instead a tangle of impulses: self-criticism and reaffirmation, toughness and sentimentality.

Depicting a "Bad" War

The trail of paradox begins with the fact that the better part of the genre builds upon the assumption that Vietnam was the model of a bad war. Francis Ford Coppola's *Gardens of*

Stone (1987) is emblematic in this regard. The only film to date that deals seriously with professional military characters and institutions, *Gardens of Stone* records the frustration and confusion produced when the Vietnam soldier's experience is pressed against traditional forms of patriotic loyalty and heroism. Clell Hazard (James Cann), the old war horse, veteran of World War II and Korea, paragon of military honor and virtue, describes the war as "bad judgment... a screw up." Hazard's surrogate son, Jackie Willow, confesses a similar sort of confusion in a letter from Vietnam shortly before his death. "All my life...," he writes, "I knew... I'd live and die in the Army. Just something I knew. But after this... I don't know anymore." The criticism is painfully inchoate, but its dramatic pitch and function are clear. From the perspective of tradition, both cinematic and political, the Vietnam War was profoundly subversive. It undermined a powerful set of expectations concerning the virtues of heroism and patriotism and the practices that nurture them.

Those same expectations are at issue in director Oliver Stone's second voyage into Vietnam, *Born on the Fourth of July* (1990), which explores at length the youthful image of heroism that Ron Kovic carries with him into the Marines, Vietnam, and finally the humiliation of postwar life in the 1970s. As the title of the film so blatantly announces, Kovic's formative experience is the boyish, sentimental, gleaming patriotism of small-town America of the 1950s. All that comes after—the ordeal of combat, the physical anguish of wounds and rehabilitation, the torment of paralysis and social estrangement—is bitterly measured against the background of that seductive fantasy of martial and civic virtue.

In the films focused on the combat story—*Platoon, Full Metal Jacket* (1987), *Hamburger Hill* (1987), HBO's *War Stories* (1987), *Bat 21* (1988)—irony takes the form of an implacable futility. "We just go back and forth blowin' the shit out of each other for hills nobody wanted," says one of the characters in *War Stories*. This image is reproduced quite literally in the exhausting and operatic *Hamburger Hill*, a story based on a real and very bloody operation in the Central Highlands of Vietnam in 1968. Focusing on a few days in the life of an infantry platoon, the film follows the doomed cast in its horrifying assaults on entrenched North Vietnamese soldiers, a process that consumes most of the principal characters.

Everyone knows, of course, that the source of such futility is not geography. "We been up and down this same terrain before," says one of the grunts in *Hamburger Hill:* "For what?" The question underscores the absence of political logic and purpose, the fundamental aimlessness of the war. Oliver Stone's *Platoon* produces this sense of aimlessness in its photographic technique and narrative structure. *Platoon* plants the viewer in the dense immediacy of the jungle, forbidding a larger tactical or strategic view. The plot unfolds within similarly restricted perspectives. The ultimate horizon of meaning is the tiny platoon. It is a world rich in private and intimate experience and knowledge, but stunningly short of political, historical, or cultural references. The enemy, seen only in fleeting moments, is essentially unavailable and mysterious. The Vietnamese civilian population is predictably "inscrutable," alternately the object of vengeful violence and missionary concern. The characters in *Platoon* eschew ideology and indeed political language of any kind, as if it were impossible to bridge the gap between the brutal realities of the war and the abstract understandings—geopolitics, anticommunism, containment—given to frame it. In the vision of *Platoon*, the war in Vietnam is a conflict that will not be made sense of.

For those who do not die of it, the lesson in irony is completed on coming home to a society violently divided over the war and indifferent, or downright hostile, to its participants. This means not only no heroes' welcome, a master theme in all coming-home films, but that the heroes themselves are exiles in their own land. The characters in *Hamburger Hill* muse bitterly over the now legendary story of returning soldiers being greeted by bands of shit-slinging antiwar protesters. Real or imagined, such rejection is typically answered by withdrawal. The hero of *Birdy* (1985) retreats into a mute fantasy world while caged in the mental ward of a military hospital. In *Distant Thunder* (1988), Mark Libby

(John Lithgow), the nervous and introverted hero, retreats to a wild veterans community in the Washington mountains where he and several war buddies live as hostages to their own memories.

The more recent *Jackknife* (1989), the first film of distant retrospection in the Vietnam genre, ties together the separate moments of the ironic cycle in the friendship between two veterans, still struggling, after some twenty years, to come to terms with their memories and one another. With the exception of several brief flashbacks, the story unwinds in the present. But it hinges on two crucial moments in the past: a single battle in Vietnam, where both Megs (Robert De Niro) and Davey (Ed Harris) are wounded, and the earlier time in Davey's life when he was the star of the football team, the idol of his classmates, the quintessential all-American boy.

Jackknife explores the disjunction between these moments. As a Vietnam vet, Davey is a disaster. Alcoholic, withdrawn, and bitter, he cannot find his way back to the war, and thus to the root of his rage. Near the end of the film, Davey finds his way back to his high school and stares drunkenly into the trophy case where his exploits are memorialized. The real mystery, his gaze announces, is how one from such favored origins could have strayed so far from the path of promise, especially since that path followed the prescribed route of heroism and patriotic virtue.

There is a deep and sometimes comic bitterness that issues from these reversals. The characters in *Hamburger Hill* resort to a kind of dark stoicism: "Don't mean nothin," they chant, "not a thing." Shifting the object and scale of such anger, the hero of one of HBO's *War Stories* ("The Mine") muses over his imminent death: "God's just been fuckin' with me, now he's through." Secular or metaphysical, political or personal, this bitterness signals the deeper pathos that is by now characteristic of the Vietnam soldier's story.

A Country Coming Apart

The profound political anxiety that rumbles about in these films is that the long episode in Vietnam has somehow subverted the assumptions that define our culture. In the few unflinchingly conservative Vietnam films of the 1980s—*Rambo: First Blood Part II* (1984), *Uncommon Valor* (1983), and the rabid *Hanoi Hilton* (1987)—the allegorical significance of the war is revealed as a crisis of national will. Vietnam was that moment in history when we questioned our own innocence. Here the line to the politics of Reaganism is unmistakable. Our deepest problem in Vietnam, these films suggest, was our own nervous self-regard. But for the most part, the drama of lost innocence figures very differently. The deeper worry of the majority of these films, good and bad alike, is that the old story of American goodness was fatally subverted in Vietnam. And not by some implacable Fate or malevolent Other but through internal, self-generated, self-destructive disorders.

Unlike many World War II films, where the experience of combat creates or intensifies social solidarity, the Vietnam stories are haunted by images and episodes of disintegration. *Hamburger Hill* documents a series of dangerous confrontations between members of the platoon it follows. The conflicts are racial and social, as well as personal, but consistently connected to the miserable futility of the lives the grunts have in common. In *Platoon*, Chris Taylor (Charlie Sheen) concludes his own experience of the war with the striking summary: "We didn't fight the enemy in Vietnam, we fought ourselves." The remark describes the dangerous conflict in Taylor's platoon. But it is also intended as commentary on the aimlessness of the war. Since there was no obvious sustaining logic to the conflict, no enemy in the conventional sense, we turned the guns—in bitterness, regret, self-contempt—on ourselves.

The theme of political disintegration emerges most dramatically in the suspicion, nearly universal in Vietnam films, of official elites. The combat films—*Hamburger Hill, Platoon, Bat 21, War Stories*—cast a steadily jaundiced eye toward the officer corps, the most available incarnation of authority. The dangerously energetic young lieutenant, often compromised by his class background as well as martial enthusiasm, is an almost requisite figure in combat stories. So, too, are insensitive "higher authorities" who issue the dangerous and often incomprehensible orders that compound the miseries of combat.

The POW/MIA subgenre mentioned above (*Rambo: First Blood Part II, Uncommon Valor, Hanoi Hilton*) chew rather morosely on a bitter and powerfully reactionary sense of betrayal by the highest political authorities. "Will we be allowed to win this time?" Johnny Rambo asks before his first redemptive voyage into postwar North Vietnam. *Hamburger Hill* aims its rage at liberal politicians, journalists, and college students, all compromised by their class connections and antiwar sympathies. Less conservative narratives refocus these complaints but grapple nonetheless with corrupt and corrupting officialdom. Adrian Cronauer (Robin Williams), the sardonic disk-jockey hero of the darkly comic *Good Morning, Vietnam* (1987), directs his wit at the alternately inept and malicious American war machine. Stanley Kubrick's *Full Metal Jacket* (1987) sustains the bitterly satirical characterizations of civilian and military authorities characteristic of his earlier works, *Paths of Glory* and *Dr. Strangelove*. The allegorical intent in all of this is unmistakable: the Vietnam War was finally our civil war, a story of collective as well as local disintegrations, a struggle inside the American mind and body politic.

The problem of lost innocence is also rendered psychologically. The treatment of violence in Vietnam films of the 1980s is instructive in this sense. Brutality and brutalization are almost inescapable subjects in stories dealing with war, but in the case of Vietnam they have taken a peculiarly reflective turn. In addition to the violence that lurks "out there" in the mysterious force of the enemy, there is also the violence that lurks in the heart of the ordinary combat soldier.

This subject is for the most part broached in the form of the ritual passage of the young soldier into the fraternal order of combat. Jackie Willow, the young and doomed hero of *Gardens of Stone*, hankers after the day he will win the Combat Infantry Man's Badge, the sign of the battle-initiated. "And when it's my time . . . if that's the only decoration they bury me with . . . well, I'll rest in peace." Rafterman, the Marine photographer in *Full Metal Jacket*, brutally rephrases Willow's naive longing: "I want to get into the shit," he tells Joker (Matthew Modine), the film's cynical and irrepressible hero. The same sort of desire preoccupies the central figure of the first episode of HBO's *War Stories*, a clerk in Vietnam who wants nothing more than to see some action. He, too, gets his wish, with the predictably ironic conclusion that his first shots fired in anger are his last.

But it is Oliver Stone's *Platoon* that pushes such preoccupations furthest. Like the figures just mentioned, Chris Taylor, the film's hero, is a romantic, eager to learn about himself and the world through the ordeals of warfare. He does, though not in the way he anticipates. For the truly dangerous conflict that Taylor must endure is not the struggle with the enemy but the struggle between his immediate superiors, Sergeants Barnes and Elias, symbols of sheer destructiveness on the one hand and a binding humanity on the other. Taylor's personal education ends with the discovery that the battle between Barnes and Elias is really a battle within himself. The seat of chaos is not out there, in "the other." It is, Taylor learns, in the recesses of one's own soul. The coda of *Platoon*—"We didn't fight the enemy in Vietnam, we fought ourselves"—here takes on still further allegorical significance. The powerful conflicts in the body politic let loose by the war are rooted somehow in the destructive urges of the collective psyche.

This vague but alluring notion of internal chaos, both personal and collective, appears with striking consistency in a number of films that have appeared since *Platoon*. *Distant Thunder*, the latest version of the postwar readjustment narrative, is the story of Mark Libby's struggle to leave a small community of veterans living in the mountains of Washington and return to the world he has abandoned. As numerous episodes in the story suggest, Mark's essential problem is that he cannot control the aggressive impulses he learned in the war. He thus has no choice but to live as an outcast, the savagery of his surroundings mimicking the wildness of his impulses.

A similar psychology is represented by Megs (Robert De Niro) in *Jackknife*. Although invested with warmth and genuine humanity, there is also a dangerous, unpredictable rage in Megs. We see it first when his buddy Davey, desperately resisting Megs's missionary impulses, demands to see Megs's hands. The knuckles and wrists bear multiple scars, remnants of his many encounters with panes of glass. When he finally succumbs, momentarily, to his own demands near the film's conclusion, we know that in Megs, too, there is a reservoir of violent energy, closely connected to the war and contained only with great vigilance.

Anxiety over the internal rage and violence that surfaced in the war, and perhaps explains it, does not always appear in the form of violent wishes, acts, or memories. It also takes shape in the symbolics of sexuality, specifically in ubiquitous, almost obligatory, references to prostitution. *Platoon* is silent on this matter, but nearly all other "in-country" films feature the rituals of whoring. The HBO *War Stories* episode "The Pass" takes place entirely inside the sort of makeshift bar and whorehouse that typically surrounded base camps in Vietnam. *Hamburger Hill* features two extended sequences in similar terrain and *Full Metal Jacket* chooses to fuse the two moments in its portrayal of the Tet offensive. A large part of *Good Morning, Vietnam* takes place in "Jimmy Wah's Bar," an archetypal Saigon strip-joint where almost any sort of pleasure can be had for ten bucks.

This ubiquity suggests that the whorehouse-bar-strip-joint is not just another place in the war but the source of a potent thematic message. *Off Limits* (1988), a military detective story set in Saigon during the war, comes closest to deliberately articulating this message. Like any good detective story, *Off Limits* takes place in a setting of corruption and disease. In this case the scene is a very dark version of Saigon, a den of "... gangsters, cowboys, refugees, deserters, druggies, insects, black marketeers." Here the standard location is enhanced by a peculiar narrative twist. *Off Limits* is the story of the multiple murders of Vietnamese prostitutes, murders committed, as we learn in the opening scene, by a high-ranking American officer. This flashy symbolism is complemented throughout the film by passages that carefully connect the American presence in Vietnam with prostitution. "I no talk GIs," a Vietnamese whore tells one of the investigators during an official interrogation. "GIs kill my brothers, make fuck-things my sisters. They have big party Vietnam."

One of the not so hidden themes here is that the war itself was a collective violation, perhaps a criminal endeavor, in the psychological if not the legal sense of the word. The possibility was first raised in *Apocalypse Now*. "What are the charges?" the dazed and drunken Captain Willard asks the military policemen who bring him his orders in the opening scene of the film. It is a beautifully formed question, repeated in various ways throughout the film. The renegade Colonel Kurtz is consistently portrayed as a criminal. And the distinction between his individual transgressions and the normal business of the war are deliberately obscured. "Charging a man with murder in this place is like giving speeding tickets at the Indy 500," Willard muses. Kurtz is the individual analogue of the American war machine, the same craft a bit further upstream.

More recent films of Vietnam advance related suggestions. *The Killing Fields* (1985) passionately dissects the cool and abstract logic of national interest that permitted the United States to bomb and support a coup in Cambodia, illegal actions that helped unleash the Khmer Rouge. Other films insist upon a more literal connection between criminality and violent desire. "This war ain't about freedom, it's about pussy," says a wisecracking Marine in *Full Metal Jacket*. It is an alarmingly precise and provocative statement. In the absence of legitimating ends, the destructive passions of war turned in Vietnam into a riot of private, and potentially criminal, desires. Vietnam became an imaginary psychic and physical landscape where all sorts of normally forbidden impulses were given sudden freedom.

The preoccupation with anarchic desire is given its fullest expression in Brian de Palma's *Casualties of War* (1989), a film based upon a U.S. Army court-martial and a subsequent essay that appeared in the *New Yorker* in the late 1960s. De Palma's script follows the abduction, rape, and murder of a young Vietnamese girl by a squad of American infantry soldiers, and the efforts of one GI to defy and bring to justice the perpetrators. While the film attempts to ground this disaster in the dehumanizing violence of the war, here, too, the narrative impulse is finally moral and allegorical. While his comrades descend into bestiality, the principal character struggles, not quite successfully, to comprehend and repulse the Evil that surrounds him. The difficulty of that struggle is determined in large measure by the fact that the menace he confronts is not associated with some malevolent Other. It emerges instead from the intimate and once familiar confines of his own world.

The display of such passions, as well as the particular events releasing them, have a good deal to do with the intrinsic fascination of the stories. The fascination is in part voyeuristic. Like a good horror story, the Vietnam War is an intriguing subject for cinematic representation because of the brutal excess it contains. But this superficial intrigue is mixed with a more serious and complicated enthrallment. What is so disturbing in the Vietnam story is that it subverts the traditional narrative framework of American history and identity. The shapes of virtuous missionaries, liberators, anticommunists, to cite a few of the mythical figures in which we have invested cultural capital, are for the most part glaringly absent from the films of Vietnam. What has taken their place is irony, images of disintegration, and fitful meditations on violence, desire, and inner demons.

The Wilderness Metaphor

What complicates this picture is that most of its horror is delivered in familiar and finally reassuring garb. This domestication is achieved in part through the symbolism of setting. In *Distant Thunder*, Mark Libby's memories of the war, and the destructive impulses it left him with, are continuously counterposed to the natural setting of his community in exile. To rejoin the family, society, the world is to come out of the woods, to choose the civil over the natural. This opposition is repeated throughout the genre: most obviously, perhaps, in the equation of Vietnam with the jungle, a savage and mysterious habitat where equally savage and mysterious passions come to be exercised. "Never get out of the boat," Willard nervously reminds himself in *Apocalypse Now* as he drifts deeper into the primeval green. Such fear is clearly etched into the mood of all the 1980s Vietnam combat films. *Platoon* develops this code through a claustrophobic cinematography, burying the camera in the close and oppressive surroundings of "the boonies." Most of *Hamburger Hill* takes place in the mud and tangled undergrowth of "the hill," a place of Dantesque proportions in its slimy and gruesome detail.

The symbolic association of Vietnam with a savage natural landscape continues even when the setting is urban and cosmo-politan. *Off Limits* and *Good Morning, Vietnam* take place in Saigon. But their Saigon is a special kind of urban landscape. Like the generic town in the Western, it is marginal civilization, still defined by the vast and dangerous Nature that surrounds it. Symbolically, at least, such proximity explains why the city is so regularly portrayed as the scene of gambling, prostitution, drugs. Cinematic Saigon is the frontier town in Asian drag, site of marginality and perversion, the border of the civilized world.

The familiar figure here is of course "the wilderness," a quintessentially American narrative setting, which takes, in the case of Vietnam, an exotic and mysterious form. Like the original wilderness, cinematic Vietnam is the kind of place where mythi-cal forces do battle for souls. And it is also a place where fear and fascination are mixed in almost equal measure. If the wilderness is finally to be tamed, it is not without a certain risk that one will "go native" in the process, or regret in the end that one did not.

But taming is nonetheless the name of the game, in Westerns

as well as narratives about the war, and a number of recent films have given us interesting variations of the domesticating sequence. *Off Limits* employs the conventions of the detective genre to this end. The demonic forces loosed in the world are temporarily brought to bay by the hero-detectives, Sergeants McGriff (Willem Dafoe) and Alababy (Gregory Hines), the standard bearers of order in a Saigon filled with pimps, druggies, gamblers, and deserters. The same is true for the plot of *Distant Thunder*, which returns the wild veteran to the domestic orders of fatherhood and marriage by taming his aggressive impulses.

What is distinctive about this scenario in the case of the Vietnam narratives is that the work of civilizing and domesticating is only rarely directed outward, toward some uncivilized "Other" who haunts the wilds. Consistent with the reflective and psychological turn of these films, the savage has migrated within. The agents of disorder in *Apocalypse Now*, *Off Limits*, *Birdy*, *Distant Thunder*, *Full Metal Jacket*, *Platoon*, and *The Killing Fields* are all Americans or American institutions, and the taming of them is finally a matter of collective self-discipline.

Warped and Appealing Heroes

It is not simply the mythical resonance of setting that makes many of the Vietnam stories familiar. Like their less ambiguous World War II predecessors, the narratives of Vietnam supply us with a stock of attractive heroes. The difference is that the Vietnam genre departs wildly from the traditional standards of attractiveness. "I fuck nuclear waste" trumpets Blaster, an appealingly demented character in *Uncommon Valor* during a moment of happy machismo. We are a long way here from John Wayne and Audie Murphy, even in this otherwise conservatively congenial film. But we are closer than might at first be thought to some archetypal and oddly reassuring conceptions of civic and martial virtue.

Such virtue must appear from the outset in very antiheroic form. For just as Vietnam will not bear the narratives of just causes, it will not support the normal troupe of heroes performing the usual heroic deeds. Since the deeds are so often heinous and so disconnected from satisfying purposes, the hero is himself bound to be scarred. Like Mark Libby in *Distant Thunder,* the central figures in all the coming-home dramas are psychologically and morally stained. Their stories consist largely of the purgative cleansing of their souls. The combat stories—*Platoon, Full Metal Jacket, War Stories, Hamburger Hill*—document the violent histories from which such blemishes emerge.

Indeed, the antihero of these narratives is typically outside the normal boundaries of society, an outlaw and rebel. Chris Taylor of *Platoon* murders his platoon sergeant, while Mark Libby in *Distant Thunder* literally lives outside the boundaries of the civilized world. Being good detectives, McGriff and Alababy in *Off Limits* are also figures of the edges, part criminal, part saint. Even the cartoon-like Johnny Rambo is portrayed as an outlaw, a figure of the margins looking in on the normal routines of American life.

Where such estrangement is not literal, it is at least psychological. In *Full Metal Jacket,* Private Joker is set apart from the world around him by his sardonic vision. Adrian Cronauer of *Good Morning, Vietnam* is a less virulent and threatening version of Joker, and similarly estranged from the official world. Even politically muted films like *Gardens of Stone* or *Bat 21* or the flaccid *Tour of Duty* contain clear signals that their heroes are in some important ways different, offbeat, and unable to fit into conventional social patterns.

But although the antihero from the Vietnam War, unlike his straighter predecessors, does not occupy the moral center of things, he remains a compelling figure. Indeed, Vietnam has become in our filmmakers' imaginations a macabre sort of romantic voyage, a testing journey in physical space and the moral geography of the soul. *Platoon* opens with a large troop plane disgorging the young, would-be hero on the steamy runway of distant Vietnam, a prototypical scene repeated or implied in various forms in *Hamburger Hill, Good Morning, Vietnam,* and

Full Metal Jacket. There are journeys within journeys, too. *Bat 21* literally drops its hero into the inferno of war, as the ubiquitous helicopter does with infantry soldiers in most of the combat stories.

Like more traditional romantic voyages, these journeys are extended ordeals, trials of character and virtue. But in the case of Vietnam, the trial has taken on a special quality. For this war was a journey into not only physical danger but the special torments of a conflict that carried no sustaining logic and that was only briefly supported by the society that organized and financed it.

In the peculiar logic of Vietnam reminiscence, it is this moral ambiguity that supplies the antihero with much of his sentimental and romantic power. The cinematic veteran of Vietnam is distinguished from the rest of us by his passage through an ordeal both physical and existential.

The political logic of antiheroism begins to appear in the darkly demotic sense of fraternity that shines through this abuse. "We all no-good dumb niggers on this hill," says Doc, the impassioned black medic in *Hamburger Hill*. The phrase is marvelously supple. "The hill" educates its victims in democratic virtue through collective oppression and a deeper recognition of human likeness. The egalitarian impulse is also registered in unabashedly populist sentiments, and in this respect the Vietnam films follow more closely the prescriptive formula of the World War II film: wars are fought by common men. Chris Taylor in *Platoon* describes his comrades as "salt of the earth types," a view elaborated in great detail, and with more than a little enthusiasm, throughout the genre. *Hamburger Hill* is full of such types, presented in the appropriate ethnic and racial mix. *Gardens of Stone* and *Off Limits* feature the common man in military dress: the senior enlisted corps, black and white, of the U.S. Army. Robert De Niro's Megs in *Jackknife* is an earthy and compelling blend of quiet tenderness and buried violence etched against the gritty background of a working-class neighborhood in Meriden, Connecticut.

Behind such displays of populist enthusiasm, and quietly reinforcing it, is a steady drone of class resentment. The characters in *Hamburger Hill* comment relentlessly on the college students who escaped their fate, while *Gardens of Stone* paints a disparaging portrait of the officer corps. *Off Limits* goes even further in this direction. The high-ranking American officer murdering prostitutes turns out to be a bitter noncommissioned officer dressed up in the uniform of an army colonel. Like some wayward character of Genet's, his violence is revenge on the status he has always wanted.

Similar goals are achieved in the authority-bashing so pronounced throughout the genre. It is difficult in these films to find anyone with positive thoughts about any form of authority, military or civilian. Just as they resent the social inequalities implicit in their experience of the war, the working-class or underclass figures who typically occupy the foreground of Vietnam films are contemptuous of power as part and parcel of their democratic character.

It is significant, however, that such contempt never leads to open rebellion. Indeed, the critical, ironic energy of most of these films is typically constrained by a notion of civic discipline sustained by a muted, abstract, but profound patriotism. This patriotism is most clear in the final stages of the antihero's journey. After making countless references to the futility of the war, and repeatedly acknowledging its destructive consequences, Clell Hazard, the hero of *Gardens of Stone*, decides to return to Vietnam. His logic is in part professional. The war, after all, is "family business," and Clell is bound to play the old warrior's role of guide, protector, teacher. But there is also a more general sense of political obligation lurking in Hazard's professionalism. The same sort of commitment is characteristic of the grunts in *Hamburger Hill* and *Platoon*, who complain steadily about the stupidity of it all but in the end do what they are told. Extending this conclusion to the homefront, postwar dramas like *Birdy*, *Distant Thunder*, and *Jackknife* define their veterans as victims of moral theft: they completed their end of the bargain, but America did not.

The fulfillment of civic obligation and the abstract and sentimental patriotism in which it is rooted take us to the very heart of the charisma of the antihero. A good bit of the pathos the cinematic "Vietnam veteran" has come to embody, and thus a good deal of his sentimental and box office appeal, is due to the fact that he did what he was asked to do *in spite of it all.* The veteran is not merely a victim of miscalculation, stupidity, corruption, or betrayal, to note the range of implicit "explanations" for the Vietnam debacle in these films. He is a victim who remains tethered to the polity, and thus to the victimizer, in the midst of his pain: he is the exemplar, in the inverted logic of this *mythos,* of the ultimate political sacrifice.

The last of the major Vietnam films of the decade, *Casualties of War* and *Born on the Fourth of July,* complete this urge to recover and rehabilitate. The final scene of Oliver Stone's sentimental rendering of Ron Kovic's biography is nothing less than a delayed reentry fantasy, the hero come home at last to the center of the polity that has so abused him. Here is Kovic, the survivor now of both the war and the antiwar movement, waiting in his wheelchair to appear before the Democratic National Convention. It does not matter that we do not know how Kovic came to become political or how he came to be a figure of interest to the Democratic party (there was surely a story there, but Stone does not tell it). What is offered instead is a pure moment of symbolic reincorporation, the crippled warrior recognized at last by the society that had so recently scorned him.

In the case of de Palma's far grimmer tale, the domesticating note is struck not so much in the structure of the narrative as in the film's casting. The survivor and moral subject of this bloody tale is Michael J. Fox, the funny, sweet star of the television sitcom *Family Ties* and, more lately, of Steven Spielberg's suburbanized *Back to the Future* fantasies. *Casualties of War* is a very hard film to watch, not simply because of the brutality and relentless doom of its plot, but because Michael J. Fox seems out of character as the confused infantryman who struggles to find his ethical bearings in the face of the moral cataclysm. Indeed, Fox at times seems like nothing so much as a good suburban high school kid who has wandered by accident onto the set of *A Touch of Evil*. But this displacement, so awkward in the heart of the film, functions in an oddly reassuring way in the long run. It is the actor/character Fox, and the iconic values he has come to embody, that finally prevail in *Casualties of War*, and in so doing allow a familiar, domesticating presence to soften the film's corrosive implications.

The Americanization of a Symbol

The considerable interest aroused by the Vietnam War films of the 1980s is closely connected to their strangely paradoxical vision, at once so alienated from yet dependent upon the traditional cultural landscape. There is corrosive energy at work in most of the cinematic renderings of Vietnam produced in this decade, but there is also a subtle form of compensation. As the stage for antiheroic romance, cinematic Vietnam extends to the war an arc of symbolism integral to our own mythical history and mind. And this, in turn, makes possible the release of equally congenial cultural values: equality, pluralism, individualism; the suspicion of authority and power surrounded and softened by a vague and sentimental patriotism. In spite of all the pain, something like "the American character" endures in the darkly charismatic, inverted heroes who suffered and ultimately survived the war.

Things could be much worse, of course, for the very problems that make some kind of salutary meaning necessary also ensure that whatever affirmations these stories have to offer, they cannot reproduce (the Reagan era notwithstanding) the political consciousness that preceded the event they retell. No matter how desperate our urge to domesticate the war or locate within its darkness some form of compensatory light, we will only with great difficulty be able soon to reengage the narrative that broadly defined the pre-Vietnam American world, the United States as "the great locomotive," in Dean Acheson's famous metaphor, "puffing away to pull the rest of the world into civilization." What derails that mighty image is mythic Vietnam, a place of inner demons as well as nervous satisfactions.

Debora Silverman

CHINA, BLOOMIE'S, AND THE MET

In September 1980 Bloomingdale's announced it had "unleashed the largest merchandising venture ever in the history of the store" by transporting the riches of China to New York. Advertisements declared that now consumers could travel to China without a passport. Embark on the journey to the East Side, urged the ads in the *New York Times*; in Bloomingdale's one can experience the "sights, sounds, smells and scents of

Debora Silverman is Associate Professor of History at the University of California at Los Angeles. She is the author of *Selling Culture: Bloomingdale's, Diana Vreeland, and the New Aristocracy of Taste in Reagan's America* and *Art Nouveau in Fin-de-Siecle France: Politics, Psychology, and Style*. She is at work on an interpretive biography of Vincent Van Gogh.

China." The entire premises of the Lexington Avenue store were transformed into a vision of an opulent, hieratic China, land of emperors, mystery, and dazzling artisans feeding the emperors' relentless needs for magnificence. The outside of Bloomingdale's was bedecked with the banners representing the ancient Chinese martial arts: sabers and their exquisitely crafted blade cases. Inside the store's capacious halls, numerous veneered black and red screens were erected, turning the open space into a multiplicity of small, intimate compartments resembling a maze of shiny black boxes. Here the glistening "baubles, bangles, and

Bloomingdale's China ad, 1980.

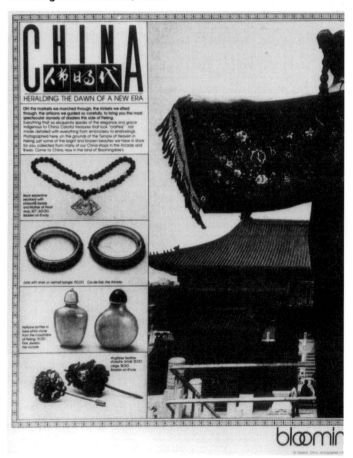

bedazzling things" of China, as they were called, were displayed. Among the varied objects bombarding the spectator-buyer with their shimmering surfaces were gold and jade bracelets, cinnabar bowls and plates, multicolored woven shawls, coral and garnet boxes, and short jackets and long robes shot through with gold threads, silks, and sequins.

The Chinese imports offered at the re-created Bloomingdale's were presented in the store's display information and in ads in three ways: as timeless, aristocratic, and rare. Each of the three characteristics reflected the peculiar selectivity with which Bloomingdale's marketers fashioned their image of the People's

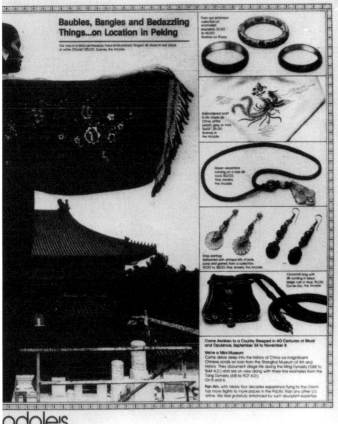

178 · Debora Silverman

Republic. Bloomingdale's China was a prerevolutionary and preindustrial China, whose luxury artisans practiced the traditions, unbroken, of the emperors. It was a civilization construed as particularly gifted in the creation of delicate, artistic objects for intimate pleasures.

The metahistorical quality of Chinese civilization came through in the Bloomingdale's ads celebrating the "country steeped in forty centuries of opulence and ritual," whose "richness, mystery, and romance were barely touched since Marco Polo's journey seven hundred years ago." And in display cases, placards identified the "ancient craft of lacquer" and the "timeless weavers' art." The promotion literature also stressed that Bloomingdale's buyers, who spent months in China looking for merchandise, had performed an invaluable service for the Chinese people. The buyers' "tireless tracking," patient "sifting," and relentless efforts had led to the rediscovery of Chinese craft treasures, hidden from the public in the aftermath of the Cultural Revolution. From the "warehouses, back alleys, and small markets" in China, Bloomingdale's had rescued the essence of Chinese culture and was offering it as booty to gentrified New Yorkers.

Gone were the days when China was inseparable from Maoist uniforms, the monochrome caps and jackets beloved of the 1960s American counterculture. The uniformity of Mao's blues was replaced by the extravagant irregularity of ancient nobilities. The imperial tone was set by the sabers adorning the outer walls of the store. Inside, store placards promised the "most spectacular dynasty of dazzlers this side of Peking." The dynastic dazzlers included woven rugs, "prerevolutionary pieces, each and every one"; coats and robes modeled on the magnificent handmade robes worn by the emperors; cloisonné jewelry that reproduced the styles of the Ch'ing dynasty; cinnabar tableware and boxes advertised as originally made for palace use; and objects like the "Double Happiness Ginger Jar," Bloomingdale's "reproduction of a T'ang dynasty treasure."

The packaging of China as timeless and aristocratic was

complemented by the theme of its special devotion to the rare and hand-crafted. The artifacts for sale at the Chinese Bloomingdale's were consistently presented as "precious and original." Display shelves in the store were filled with "hand-painted porcelain underglaze bowls," "hand-carved cinnabar coasters," and "handwoven rugs," whose "rare and original" qualities could be found "exclusively at Bloomingdale's." These craft objects and a multitude of others—"each one a work of art"—testified to what Bloomingdale's promoters called the special Chinese "concern for utmost quality and artistic merit."

Bloomingdale's glorification of China in the guise of a timeless, aristocratic civilization dedicated to the handicrafts revealed two fundamental contradictions. First, the dazzling artifacts from the People's Republic were not authentic vessels of ancient mysteries but rather the simulated products of a shrewd business alliance between the Bloomingdale's managers and the Communist Chinese government. Indeed, the Chinese imports were the first fruits of a new commercial agreement between the United States and China, which Bloomingdale's was among the first to cash in on. Eager to increase its exports abroad, China signed a 1979 trade agreement with the United States in which the Chinese offered to manufacture consumer and luxury items in China to the desired specifications of the American client.

A peculiar paradox enabled the Communist Chinese to cooperate with the center of consumer capitalism. In 1979 and 1980 China embarked on a new program, the "four modernizations," to help stimulate its much-needed economic development. The "four modernizations" included science, technology, industry, and technical education, which government officials stated would also provide the required components for a "new decade of socialist construction." As in other times in its history, China proposed to pave the roads of modern construction with the proceeds from the sale of its feudal heritage. Since the time of Marco Polo, China had struck a bargain with the West, ransoming off the rich, exotic artifacts of its imperial culture in exchange for the tools of modernization. In 1980 China was again eager to

Selling "bloomies" and China.

"export its cultural legacy," which had been prohibited under Mao as the domain of the "four olds" (language, art, customs, and clothes). The profits from the Bloomingdale's sales of simulated noble China would be used to pay the advisers from the Conoco, Fluor, and American Steel corporations that the Chinese had invited to help with their communist goal of the "four modernizations."

Bloomingdale's acted quickly on the new United States–China trade agreement and set to work establishing ties with Chinese craft manufacturers who would fill their orders. The items commissioned were designed by Bloomingdale's artists in New York, who projected their fantasies of the opulent, mysterious empire and ordered accordingly. This, then, was the origin of the "authentic" Chinese imports, envisioned in New York by Bloomingdale's designers and then custom-made in China with labels stating in both English and Chinese, "Made in China for Bloomingdale's." Thus Bloomingdale's image of China was fashioned on the basis of a double artifice: the objects that captured the "essence" of China were themselves first sketched out on Lexington Avenue, and then they were made in China exclusively for Bloomingdale's in manufactories set up especially for American export.

Bloomingdale's explicitly celebrated its own responsibility for creating China in its image. A *New Yorker* cartoon that showed Chinese factory managers stating that they had "to wait for Bloomingdale's instructions to begin production'" was used by the store in its own ad campaign to illustrate its "newest

"Before we decide on our next expansion of the people's industry, shouldn't we check with Bloomingdale's?"

Drawing by Stevenson; © 1980 The New Yorker Magazine, Inc.

expansion in China." Other ads credited Bloomingdale's own buyers for ensuring the standards and quality of Chinese products. One claimed that the beautiful handmade Chinese sweaters knit for Bloomingdale's were "developed one-on-one with the Chinese . . . to our standards, our American taste, with the Chinese attentiveness to quality and detail." Another rhapsodized, "Oh, the artisans we guided so carefully to bring you . . . everything that so eloquently speaks of the elegance and grace indigenous to China." And a third explained that the Bloomingdale's representatives on location in Beijing made sure that the Chinese objects "looked crafted, not made."

The second contradiction intrinsic to the presentation of China at Bloomingdale's emerged in relation to the "handmade" and "original" qualities attached to the merchandise. During the previous ten years Bloomingdale's had participated in a more general marketing movement, the arrival of the hand-crafted item in the department store. In the nineteenth century, when the department store was born, it was perceived as the enemy of the handmade item. In Zola's *Au Bonheur des Dames*, for example, the department store is presented as a ruthless, voracious monster, whose commitment to volume and fast turnover signaled the death of the small retail shop and the individual artisans who supplied it. In America, since the late 1970s, this assumption of a life-and-death struggle between the big department store and the individual artisan has been dramatically altered. Department stores have welcomed the craftsman, reflecting and expressing Americans' attraction to the signed, individually rendered item. This absorption of the artisanal into the centers of consumer emporiums marks the ultimate reversal of the 1960s back-to-nature, back-to-the-homemade-crafts impulse. If the production of handmade use objects once expressed cultural rebellion, now department stores offer signed, individually crafted items, from chocolate to underwear, as purchasers' status symbols.

Bloomingdale's handicraft China was part of this broader change in merchandising over the past decade. The China show clarified a contradiction underlying the general trend of promoting "original" craft items in the department store. For although the Chinese plates, robes, coats, and jewelry at "Bloomie's" were surrounded by placards proclaiming their "rare," "original," and "handcrafted" character, the number and variety of items suggested their very lack of uniqueness. How could scores of rugs and bins overflowing with cloisonné stickpins be seen as "each and every one a work of art"? Although the items were at least partly handmade, they were hardly the fruits of a single, patient, and skilled artisan who worked as had those under imperial tutelage. The Bloomingdale's China wares had a claim on being handmade in that they were not made by machines. But the craft objects imported from China were produced at human assembly lines, where massive orders for hand-painted fans, bowls, plates, and clothes were filled by intense division of labor and specialization. The "timeless artisans" who supplied Bloomingdale's shelves and racks worked at repetitive, painstaking tasks in which scores of skilled laborers contributed a monotonous small part in the creation of a single craft product.

If their production by sweated craft labor belied the handmade character of the Chinese items, their supposed "rare" and "unique" qualities were subverted by their very plethora. Bloomingdale's tried very hard to envelop the many objects on display in a distinction suggested by their history and lineage. Thus, as we have seen, scores of "Double Happiness Ginger Jars" were associated with the dynasty of their origin, and other items were labeled as reproductions of statues and relics of religious shrines. Yet the Bloomingdale's China spectator was assaulted by the sheer volume of the items and soon became anesthetized, as in all department stores, by the number and variety of the objects for sale. The stated sacred and imperial legacies of the objects dissolved in the kingdom of the commodity. The tags on the Chinese items leveled them into a single category, that of price. All the proclamations of distinction, of noble heritage, and of ritual use collapsed; underwear with "Made in China" labels, cinnabar coasters, miniature horse sculptures modeled on those of the emperors, and reprocessed imperial robes—all blurred into one mesmerizing imperative: How much does it cost?

China at the Metropolitan Museum, 1980

No sooner had the Bloomingdale's China project begun to wind down than a new celebration of China as the crucible of luxury, aristocracy, and rare artistic crafts was born. In December 1980 the Metropolitan Museum of Art opened an exhibition at its Costume Institute, "The Manchu Dragon: Costumes of China, the Ch'ing Dynasty, 1644–1912." Organized and installed by Diana Vreeland and her assistants, the Met show displayed magnificent Chinese imperial robes. The robes were not suspended in cases as in other costume exhibits; they were draped on mannequins' bodies and set in rooms reproducing the palace and temple settings in which the robes were originally worn. In this way Vreeland aspired to transport the viewer into the authentic atmosphere of Chinese imperial culture. Protected for centuries in China behind the walls of the emperors' quarters, the "Forbidden City," the opulence, refinement, and delicacy of what Vreeland called "the land of jade" were now exposed to public view.

Significantly, in the months before the Met show opened, many of the same precious Chinese robes to be exhibited at the Met had been on display at Bloomingdale's, where a special museum had been established for the duration of the China sales campaign. The Metropolitan exhibition was on the surface very different from the Bloomingdale's project. At the department store the real Chinese robes had been difficult to distinguish from the panoply of reproductions offered for sale in close proximity; the Met show focused only on the rare, authentic robes, lifting them out of the marketplace into the citadel of scholarship, connoisseurship, and historical explication. Yet despite the presumed difference between the consumerist and high cultural versions of China, the 1980 Met museum show shared the themes and selectivity of the Bloomingdale's packaging of China. The theme of the Met exhibition was the celebration of China as a timeless, aristocratic culture devoted to artistic crafts. And the ethos of the Metropolitan's curator, Diana Vreeland, was closer to a marketing strategy than to the task of historical education. The Metropolitan's Chinese robes show emerged as a perfect pendant to the Bloomingdale's presentation of China preceding it; it projected fantasies of wealth, power, and leisure attached to an ancient imperial civilization and displayed them in the form of a fashion show.

The Met exhibition extended Bloomingdale's vision of China as a timeless world "steeped in forty centuries of ritual and opulence." The costume show covered the entire span of the Manchu reign, a period of almost three hundred years. Historical specificity was entirely lacking in the exhibition displays; the only guiding principle was the emphasis on the long reign of luxury and opulence signified by the rulers' magnificent clothes and elegant furniture. The exhibit lacked basic information to enable the viewer to differentiate the various rulers and their historical contexts. The tags on the artifacts identified the robes, the materials out of which they were made, and their historical provenance, usually generalized as the "Ch'ing dynasty," which thus placed it somewhere between the seventeenth and twentieth centuries.

The aristocratic and artisanal character of the Bloomingdale's China show also reappeared as the organizing themes at the Met. The exquisitely crafted stuffs of the emperors filled the Met halls with the original "dynastic dazzlers" celebrated in simulated form at Bloomie's. Lacquer screens, carved jade jewelry, celadon porcelains, pen quills and inkstands studded with precious stones, ivory and cinnabar miniature sculptures carved into women's hair combs—these were some of the objects crafted to the standards of the rulers. In the center of one of the exhibition halls, Vreeland re-created a royal boudoir, framed by a carved-wood pagoda top and bright red silk linens across the bed. The emperors' presence was felt throughout the shimmering surfaces of their multicolored robes and in the costumes worn by their wives and concubines. In one tiny corner near the imperial boudoir appeared a glimpse of the China beyond the ruler. A "Chinese coolie" was displayed, standing on a stepped platform, dressed entirely in a simple white shroud and hat. The white simplicity of the designated coolie contrasted sharply to the breathtaking colors of the imperial clothes and interiors by which it was quickly overwhelmed.

Like the contradictions in the Bloomingdale's project, the Met's presentation of China as timeless, aristocratic, and artisanal was subverted by the visibility of very timely elements in the exhibition. The attempt to reconstitute Chinese court life and clothes was mired in a thick layer of Western fantasy, specifically the fantasy of the fashion show designer and promoter. The influence of Diana Vreeland brought about the suspension of the normal categories of scholarly accuracy, historical erudition, and artistic connoisseurship with which museum shows are normally mounted. Vreeland approached the Chinese robes with the declaration, "I'm looking for the most farfetched perfection . . . and I'm terrible at facts. But I always have an idea. If you have an idea, you're well ahead!" The artifacts of Chinese civilization were

Summer robe of state for a high-ranking court official. The Metropolitan Museum of Art, Rogers Fund, 1964 (64.214).

subjected to the antihistorical drama of a woman who had invented the "composite photo" for shock effect.

The quintessentially Vreelandian perspective imposed on Chinese civilization emerged at the Met show in two ways. The first was in the use of mannequins. Immediately on entering the gallery, the spectator was thrown into a bizarre underworld closer to the more extreme pages of *Vogue* than to Chinese imperial courts. In a dimly lit room, one heard high-pitched ancient Chinese music, and one's senses were assaulted by a very powerful smell. Vreeland had drenched the room in a fragrance that she explained as capturing the essence of China—her friend Yves Saint Laurent's new perfume, called Opium. Opium may have been the essence of China to Vreeland, but, as Orville Schell reminds us, the drug had been originally imported into China by Western merchants in the eighteenth and nineteenth centuries, where, in contravention of Chinese law, they had traded the drug "at enormous profit for silk, tea, and silver." Opium, Schell continues, had been the traditional source of conflict between China and the West, for it epitomized the unequal and humiliating character of foreign treaties and actions. The 1980 Saint Laurent Opium fragrance drenching the Ch'ing dynasty Chinese emperors' robes re-created the historical license of Western misappropriation of China and added a startling new irony to the record of Western representations of the East. The sights of China immediately greeted the viewer who had just recovered from the sounds and smells. In a long row stood, in varying languorous poses, ten female mannequins bedecked in court robes and ceremonial costumes. The mannequins had elongated features, especially marked in their face, hands, ears, and feet. Tall and ungainly, the "Chinese" mannequins in costume had faces painted in different color schemes—brown, pink, yellow, red, and black. Their pointy faces and ears gave them the strange look of Mister Spock in "Star Trek." Whatever their origin, the mannequins embodied an extension of the pages of an elite fashion magazine rather than representative types who might have worn Chinese courtly vestments.

The triumph of fashion illusionism over Chinese history appeared in a second way. The labeling of the objects in the show focused exclusively on their exquisite surfaces. Not only was explanation of historical provenance missing, but the exhibit labels offered no sense of the meaning and function of the Chinese robes and decorative arts within their national context. The labels delineated, in great detail, the richness and variety of the materials that went into the creation of the robes and other court costumes. This strategy resembled the descriptions used at fashion shows, where the dress paraded is complemented by the stated explanation of its contents. At the Met's China show the spectator was endlessly bombarded with tags stating "embroidered wool tabby, highlighted with gold silk threads and brocaded velvet"; "informal suit, silk damask topped with sequined scarf," and so forth. In all the labels, the anachronistic jargon of fashion talk like "informal suits," "at-home wear," and "summer dress" was matched by an obsessive attentiveness to the expensive materials quite clearly visible on the surface of the imperial garments.

At the time of the Chinese robes exhibition, reviewers like

Rita Reif commented that "there was more fantasy than fact in these displays." Reif went on to note one glaring inaccuracy in the show, which altered the meaning and function of the imperial robes: they were not worn for public display but for private worship. Reif remarked that the magnificent robes were always worn underneath a long, plain overcoat; only the borders of the brightly colored robes were ever visible on the emperor. In addition, Reif indicated that Vreeland had mixed and matched Chinese raiment indiscriminately. Never would a Chinese wife or courtesan of the emperor have worn an "outfit" like the ones created by Vreeland. Reif claimed that the mannequins displayed the "layered look" of the 1970s fashion designers rather than the style of any Chinese historical period.

There was another visible distortion in the Met's China show, which sapped the Chinese robes of their primary significance and function. The essence of the Chinese robe was not on its surface but in the deep symbolic meaning that it expressed. The Chinese robes operated in a cosmological system where all material objects were redolent with meaning. Not only wool tabby and gold thread adorned the emperor's robes, but symbols of his authority and of his place in a sacred hierarchy binding the gods and their earthly representatives. The imperial robes had as their insignia the five-fingered dragon, a symbol exclusively reserved for the ruler. The emperor's robe was a microcosm of the heavenly macrocosm; all types of natural forces were splayed across the robe—fire and water, sky and air—summarizing all of creation on the body of the emperor. Encased in the robe, the ruler's body symbolized the axis and his head the apex of the universe. Rigid codes governed the symbolism of all garments, and each person in the Chinese social system, from bureaucrat and palace guard to scholar and soldier, had a particular outer sign to mark his rank. Thus, the clothes at the Met show all originally expressed the membership of their bearer in a caste system, and the signs and designs on the outer garb were emblems of position in the hierarchy of man and nature. In Diana Vreeland's hands, the links between surface, symbol, meaning,

Court robe for an empress. The Metropolitan Museum of Art, Gift of Robert E. Tod, 1929 (29.36).

and social function so central to the Chinese imperial garments were eliminated. The "Empress of Clothes" pressed the Chinese artifacts into the service of a new fad for gilded and glossy outfits befitting a new American cult of visible wealth and power.

The devotees of Diana Vreeland and the contemporary cult of opulence surfaced at a grand celebration at the Met two weeks before the opening of the Chinese robes exhibition. On the evening of December 8, 1980, the Council of Fashion Designers sponsored a lavish gala to greet the show and pay tribute to its artificer, Vreeland. The *New York Times* characterized the christening party as "Fashion's Big Night at the Met." Seven hundred people paid $300 apiece to dine on the obligatory coquilles Saint-Jacques and fillet of beef, to watch Chinese fireworks, and to get an exclusive preview of the show.

The designers sponsoring the Chinese evening at the Met were longtime associates of Diana Vreeland, among them Yves Saint Laurent, Bill Blass, Oscar de la Renta, Adolfo, and Halston. Led by Blass, they created a party theme à la chinoise to capture the "proper air of mystery" intrinsic to China. The Met's Great Hall and dining area were transformed into a "Red Palace." Red carpets graced all the floors of the party chambers, which were lit from above by red spotlights. The grand reflecting pool around which the dinner guests sat was surrounded by huge banners hung from the ceiling. The tables were laid with black tablecloths and red napkins, and enlivened by red glazed vases filled with yellow lilies and sprays of quince. The ironic overtones of such a "red China" seemed to bother no one; the fashion council created its version to echo the luxury and exoticism captured in the exhibition's dazzling displays.

According to all reports, the splendor of China soon paled when compared with the lavish opulence exhibited by the party's American participants. "Fashion's big night at the Met" used China as a backdrop; the real show was in the array of new clothes designed by the party's sponsors and paraded on the partygoers. A new line of costumes was launched at the Met— "luxurious dresses" that "overshadowed the grandeur of the imperial robes." Stately Nancy Kissinger arrived in an original by Adolfo, the exclusive designer who was busy preparing Nancy Reagan's first inaugural suit. Diana Vreeland wore a shimmering gold jacket set off by a black skirt. Two representatives from Bonwit Teller's in "glittering dresses" promoted the sumptuous look of the new season's fashions. A Bloomingdale's executive arrived at the party in a multicolored, embroidered Chinese robe.

The Met party and its glorification of aristocratic Chinese culture coincided with President-Elect and Mrs. Reagan's December 1980 trip to New York, where they were joined at private dinners by fashion moguls Bill Blass and Oscar de al Renta. Nancy Reagan collected Chinese porcelains and lacquer tables, and revealed that her initial project as First Lady would be the redecoration of the White House private quarters to accommodate her exquisite Chinese decorative pieces. Two weeks after the Met party, the *New York Times Magazine* devoted its cover story to Françoise and Oscar de la Renta. Splashed across the Sunday magazine was a huge color photo of the rich and elegant designer couple, she in a blazing gold tunic and a collar six strands thick with pearls, he in a sleek black suit. The article, by Francesca

Stanfill, was titled "Living Well Is Still the Best Revenge." Stanfill celebrated the "rarefied taste" and powerful wealth of the couple, "distinguished," she stated, by their "sense of luxury" and the fact that "they have no fear of ostentation, nor are they inhibited by the pressure of discretion that often characterizes those with old fortunes." The fortune of Dominican-born Oscar de la Renta (né Renta) had been made in the mid-1970s, "not by shrewd marketing or even avant-garde designing, but by an unerring taste, and, to a great extent, a familiarity with his affluent clientele." De la Renta's specialty was extravagance, which usually took the form of massive ruffles attached to flamboyant skirts and evening gowns. While these luxury fashions had been the preserve of a small coterie of the wealthy for a decade, a new clientele and public presence now focused on the de la Rentas.

Stanfill associated the de la Rentas with a shift in American high society, a shift she predicted would be expressed in the Reagan White House. She identified the de la Rentas as part of a "new professional elite": "the very rich, the very powerful," the representatives of "current talent and current fame." This elite, according to Stanfill, was different from previous ones. This was no "leisure jet set," nor a society filled with bearers of old money and old family names. The de la Rentas were at the center of a "phalanx" of the "working upper-crust," a nouveau riche group that represented the fusion of society with big business. Fashion designers were a central part of this new elite, as managers of international licensing empires and as media celebrities binding their products to their personal identities. This was a group marked by "the energy, incentive, fearlessness, and aggressiveness of the ambitious." Vreeland was identified in the article as another figure in this new elite: "Now everything is power and money and how to use them both," Vreeland declared.

Stanfill went on to describe how the de la Rentas cloaked their ambition in elegant, opulent surroundings in a series of country and city residences whose overstuffed, cozy interiors were filled with refined luxury items. Françoise de la Renta, renowned for her talents as a decorator, arranged her rooms as "sybaritic backdrops" for her weekly salons; "masses of Rothschild lilies, flocked red velvet walls edged in *faux marbre*, silk upholstered Second Empire chairs, mother-of-pearl cabinets, windows swagged in heavy, fringed silk": these were some of the vessels of the de la Rentas' ineffable taste. Françoise told the *Times* reporter that she had developed her style as a decorator by studying great works of French literature, especially Balzac. "One thing that is very noticeable in Balzac is the *demimondaine*." She smiles. "One can learn a hell of a lot from the *demimondaine*."

The use of the motto "Living well is the best revenge" in relation to the unchecked pursuit of wealth, as symbolized by the de la Rentas, has undergone a telling transformation. A Spanish proverb, the phrase originated as a statement of philosophical resignation to fate: God was cruel, the world was difficult and painful, and one had to bear it with the understanding of an individual's limited power to control it. The motto was popularized in America through its association with the F. Scott Fitzgerald circle in the 1920s. Gerald Murphy, an American expatriate in France who socialized with the Fitzgeralds and Ernest Hemingway, invoked the saying in the context of the bohemianism, nonconformity, and bitterness that followed the devastation of World War I. Murphy and his coterie proposed a life of license in isolation as a reaction to the shattering of all ideals by the war. In 1980–81, "Living well is the best revenge" had gone from being associated with the anguished withdrawal of postwar hedonists to being tied to the raucous centrality of elite Reagan supporters. Rather than having to do with wreaking revenge on a world that has exposed moral ideals as illusions, the slogan now implied revenge on the poor, who were considered undeserving.

The Reagan Inauguration:
Opulence and Chinoiseries
The inauguration of Ronald Reagan in January 1981 channeled the celebration of luxury, and its presumed historical

The President with Nancy Reagan in chinoiserie.

carriers, from the salons of the New York fashion designers to the chambers of state. The image-makers of aristocratic privilege in clothes and interior design were not only associates of curator Diana Vreeland but friends of Nancy and Ron. And the cult of visible wealth expressed in culture and merchandising was transposed into the policies of social repudiation pursued by the Reagan White House.

The Reagan presidential inaugural festivities trumpeted the arrival of opulence at the highest levels of state. Commentators like R. Williams, Laurence Leamer, and Michael Kinsley noted the "staggering splendor" and coronation tone to the affair. President Reagan requested that invitees don the formal morning "stroller" suit, popular at the time of the Prince of Wales, for the swearing-in ceremony. Nancy Reagan's gowns, gloves, embroidered handbags, hand-sewn shoes, and floor-length minks changed constantly before the eyes of the public. Outfitting Nancy were her longtime friends, designers Bill Blass, Adolfo, and Galanos, who garbed the First Lady in their new concept of the "sybaritic outfit." At one of the gala inaugural events the Reagans and the Bushes were treated to an evening of Hollywood entertainment, taped live for television. Frank Sinatra organized the evening, and the performers' stage was set directly opposite a platform on which four plush winged chairs were arranged. Nancy and Ron looked like the king and queen observing their many jesters; Mrs. Bush sat shimmering in an embroidered Chinese robe.

The Reagan inauguration set the tone for the full-fledged cult of visible luxury and unrestrained flaunting of wealth. The $16 million inaugural extravaganza witnessed the arrival of the millionaire Californians and Hollywood stars in Washington, where they inched their way through a crush of limousines and gorged on endless delicacies. A startling contrast to the rich Reagan revelers was seen in one telling incident, when the Washington city derelicts and bag ladies made their way into Union Station, crashing the party reserved for those who had bought the $1,000 entry tickets. The hungry poor, whom Reagan aides were soon to dub wily cheaters, helped themselves to the "lobster bisque, shrimp merlin, escargots, and vitello alla gaetano" heaped on forty tables. The mingling of the super rich and the street people under the iron-and-glass sheds of Union Station offered a startling juxtapostion of the two worlds.

The dedication of Nancy Reagan to display brought new attention to the elite fashion designers; the *Times* noted in January that "their business is booming, despite the recession." Nancy's cult of snobbism in appearance also legitimized lavish ornamental femininity. Nancy had been, for over twenty years, a "professional lady" who spent her days with Betsy Bloomingdale, Jean Smith, Mary Jane Wick, and Marion Jorgenson on the complex work of maintaining a youthful and elegant appearance. The *New York Times* and other papers indicated that a new kind of woman had arrived in the train of Nancy Reagan and her sumptuous adornments. This was not an eastern woman but a Sunbelt beauty, who "cared about style and did not want to look unobtrusive." She was "upwardly mobile, suburban, with a sensibility founded on buying power and an unabashed appreciation of luxury." Nancy represented this woman's values; she unleashed a new era of style, a style that melded the nouveau riche values of the de la Rentas and Blasses with the rugged individualism of Western entrepreneurs and their wives. "We've worked for this," the wife of a Texas real estate developer at the inaugural ball was quoted as saying. "We're proud and we're not afraid to show it." The sense that hard work should be rewarded was the theme expressed by other women attending the ball. Bedecked in ruffled satin gowns by Blass, de la Renta, and Galanos, and gleaming in egg-shaped rubies, diamonds, ostrich feathers, and ermine capes, these women noted how they were "tired of having to apologize for ourselves." Nancy Reagan provided these women with a "lift": "Now we know it's all right to buy grand clothes again without looking out of place." The *Times* article concluded that in some ways these women were the Cinderella wives of Horatio Alger husbands, who offered visible proof to everyone beneath them on the social scale that "they can do it too."

Vreeland's Allure and Reagan's Political Culture

The "new woman" at the inaugural balls expressed in fashion the ethos of Reagan's politics of rugged, venturesome individualism and its ideology of deserved rewards. From the beginning of his administration, Reagan was relentless in his declaration of the need for a return to the old American values of individual effort and risk-taking, and the upward mobility to follow from both. Reagan justified the inaugural luxury as evidence of the riches that were obtainable in American society through hard work and talent.

Many writers have pointed out the anachronisms and ironies of Reagan's free-enterprise ideology: the rough-and-tough individualist idealized by the rancher-president has little basis in either the marketplace of advanced corporate capitalism or the personal success story of the president himself. The president never liked to work, and he prospered less from individual effort than from a combination of luck, corporate power, and the uncanny ability to please. He got his start in both economic and political life as the "corporate ambassador" for General Electric in the 1950s. He was drafted into gubernatorial politics by millionaire California conservatives Tuttle, Salvatori, and Rubel in 1964. And few members of Reagan's inner circle of friends and advisers—Alfred Bloomingdale, Justin Dart, William French Smith, or Charles Wick—owed their wealth and position to the operations of isolated individuals striving in the free market. Reagan's appeal to ordinary Americans to aspire to freedom, self-reliance, moral rectitude, and individual diligence is a masterful exercise of the "politics of symbolism."

The Reagan politics of theater and of elitist individualism received a striking cultural expression in the work and writings of Diana Vreeland. A few months before the opening of the Met China show Vreeland published a book called *Allure*. The text of *Allure* revealed that Vreeland nourished fantasies not only of opulent nobilities of the past but of cruelty and decadence in the present.

Allure was a mixture of memoirs and oracles from the queen of the elite fashion world, whose taste and sense of style had been nurtured in over thirty years of editing *Vogue* and *Harper's Bazaar*. A large folio volume with huge black-and-white fashion photos interspersed with textual comments by Vreeland, the book collected Vreeland's favorite fashion photographers, from the Baron de Meyer to Irving Penn, and her favorite beautiful women, among them the Vicomtesse de Ribes, Greta Garbo, Evita Perón, Gertrude Stein, Marilyn Monroe, and the Duchess of Windsor. The dust jacket characterized as "by turns witty, sharp, extravagant, and cruel," the "Vreelandian perspective" which took the reader through a "luxurious, gossip-ridden world that DV knows so well."

One clear theme of *Allure* was aristocratic revival and its contemporary aesthetic emulation. Vreeland glorified the "stature," "inner exaltation," "bones," and "strength" of the Duchesse de Gramont, the beauty of Russian noblewoman Princess Yousoupoff, and the visible royalty of Princess Bebar, wife of the last sultan of the Ottoman Empire. Born in France and brought up in England, Mrs. Vreeland (née Diana Hoffman Dalziel) recalled that the coronation of George V in 1911 was a central event in her early life. She loved the "correctness and perfect design" of the horses, carriages, and military men in procession and lamented that such grace "survives today only in the army, the navy, the church, and in royalty." In other places in the book Vreeland hinted at the many members of the upper crust that she knew personally. Invoking no less an authority than Marcel Proust, one of her favorite authors, she passed scathing comments on other people's social backgrounds: she described Maria Callas as "common as mud"; Josephine Baker, the music hall performer, as "a total Parisienne, even though she was a laundress's daughter from St. Louis"; and, in the inverse, Vreeland remarked of Elsa Maxwell that "she looked vulgar; her nose was vulgar. She looks like a cook on her day off... of course, she no doubt had just been dining with a king—always kings!! She had the best taste in people."

Much of Vreeland's book aspired to define the meaning of true "elegance" and "allure." Vreeland acknowledged that aristocracies of the blood were gone; female aristocracies of the spirit could be cultivated through style and taste, manifested in the ineffable qualities of "elegance" and "allure." The meaning of "allure" was ambiguous in Vreeland's account. Allure is "something that *holds* you; it is something around you like a perfume or a scent. It's like memory—it pervades." In another section Vreeland distinguished fashion from elegance. Fashion is transient; "elegance is innate." It is a quality, according to Vreeland, possessed by certain animals, like gazelles, and women like Audrey Hepburn. The clearest definition Vreeland arrived at was "Elegance is refusal."

Vreeland's "witty, sharp, extravagant" tone, and her snobbish celebration of old and new aristocracies, had long been her trademark. In the 1930s, when Mrs. Vreeland began writing for *Harper's Bazaar*, she established a column, "Why Don't You...?"

which amused Depression readers with bits of advice like "Why don't you convert your ermine coat into a bathrobe?" and "Why don't you wash your hair with champagne?" For Vreeland then, as now, all of this was grand posturing and playacting. When and whether she ever had real contact with European royalty and nobility is unclear. According to Jesse Kornbluth, Vreeland never had any formal education to speak of, trained briefly with the Ziegfeld Follies chorus girls as a dancer, and then ran a lingerie shop in London that specialized in black underwear. By her own admission, her world was a stage: "Performance is all I cared about as a child and it's all I care about now." Kornbluth characterized Vreeland as a shrewd individualist and ambitious businesswoman who had to work hard to subsidize her aristocratic affections: "Though fated to be remembered as a high-society fashion oracle, Diana Vreeland has, all these years, been one of our greatest actresses, systematically parading her precariously luxurious life as a way of earning her daily *madeleine.*"

Less amusing and more pernicious themes surfaced in *Allure*, articulated in scathing and sadistic tones, suggesting the underside of the aristocratic revival. Vreeland had a long history of insidious statements, from the time in her 1930s columns that she recommended "Why don't you wear bare knees and long white knitted socks as Unity Mitford does when she takes tea with Hitler at the Carlton in Munich?" In 1980 Diana Vreeland sprinkled *Allure* with her memoirs of the 1930s. At one point she discussed the German spas and chuckled about her German doctor's prediction of mass murder:

> At the Kurhaus, in Freiburg-im-Breisgau, Reed and I would take baths and massages in the Black Forest. Every morning Dr. Govens would apply the Grenz ray to my sinuses. In the coming war they were going to release it and everyone in sight would be dead—they'd tell you all this. "Ooo," I'd say, "I can hardly wait; you Germans are so busy—such busy-bodies!"

Sadism and violence appeared in *Allure*, in the service of Vreeland's commitment to shock. She recounted how she discovered the composite photo for *Vogue* as a capstone to her career objective of not being boring or predictable. "I think laying out a beautiful picture in a beautiful way is a bloody bore. . . . The most boring thing on earth is to be of the world of what you do. That means people only expect from you what they think they'll get. That to me isn't the Big Time." Vreeland claimed that "you've got to blow the picture right across the page and down the side, crop it, cut it in half, do something with it!" Her violent artificing led her to "put arms and legs and everything else together" in a single layout, the composite photo. Faces were always missing from these spreads, which made *Vogue* notorious in the 1960s. Cutting up and mixing body parts of different models on a page, Vreeland declared, "I want arms! I want legs! I want hands!" Another of her innovations for *Vogue* was painting a white model shiny black with shoe polish and studding her eyes, breasts, and arms with diamonds, as testimony to the fact that "there's no place in the world where there's a vein of precious stone that doesn't belong to people of color. And they look so marvelous in jewels. . . . But a true black hand, however black, would have been . . . banal."

Allure depicted the shoe-polish-sprayed model and the dismembered elements of composite fashion photos. It also included a huge five-page insert that Vreeland had commissioned, though it was too barbaric even for *Vogue*. Vreeland thought it would be amusing, and shocking, to photograph an eye-lift operation. *Allure* published this photo spread, which *Vogue* had censored, illustrating with magnified camera lenses all phases of the cutting, lifting, and grafting of the eye skin. Vreeland said these pictures captured the fact that "I adore artifice!"

Diana Vreeland cultivated detachment and disengagement; the meaning and substance of her statements and her photos were always subordinated to the creation of effect, as long as it was not a bore. An omnipotence fantasy ruled these illusions; they were filled with the sense that the world could be shaped and reshaped in the cutting hands and bizarre eyes of its Vreelandian maker.

Vreeland's main message in *Allure*, that "elegance is refusal," had not only sexual but social implications. "We mustn't be afraid of snobbism and absurdity. And we mustn't be afraid of luxury—there are no pictures of poverty here!" she exclaimed. *Allure* was a big seller in 1980, and has been since. In 1982 it received the Annual Rodeo Drive Gala Award in Los Angeles. Along the Beverly Hills street, the home of the exclusive boutiques where Nancy Reagan had shopped for her first inaugural wardrobe, Vreeland's book was displayed in every window, with costly jewels, scarves, shoes, and clothes wrapped around it. DV did talk once about poverty in *Allure*, explaining that when Elsa Maxwell lost all her money, she took it in style—when her piano and furniture were repossessed, she "performed an entire opera" for Vreeland, "slapping it out on those big, fat thighs of hers." Perhaps this was the fantasy of poverty that the Rodeo Drive merchants wished to nurture.

Mark Caldwell

THE LITERATURE OF AIDS

In the 1990s, if the optimists are right and the world is lucky, someone will be able to write the history of AIDS. If the epidemic has peaked by then—and some observers argue that this has already happened—we will still be living out the denouement of a widespread human tragedy. But we will know its scale and when we can expect it to play itself out, even in the absence of a vaccine or completely effective therapy. Then, perhaps, we will be in a position to assess AIDS, to decide how it harmed us, and what, if anything, it taught us.

Right now we know the etiological cause of the disease: HIV,

Mark Caldwell teaches English literature at Fordham University. He writes regularly for the *Village Voice* and the *Philadelphia Inquirer*, among other publications. His most recent book is *The Last Crusade: The War on Consumption, 1862–1954.*

the human immunodeficiency retrovirus. Less surely, we know how HIV leads to the immunosuppression that in turn permits fatal opportunistic infection. We know in a general way how HIV can be spread—sexually, by the sharing of blood products, and from mother to child. But the exact mechanism of the transmission remains elusive (this, by the way, is not new among epidemic diseases; no one has settled how tuberculosis and polio spread). No one knows exactly how many people are now infected with HIV. Nor how fast it is spreading to others. Nor, in the long run, how helpful or harmful drugs like AZT will prove to most of those who take them. It is painful to admit, of course, but the most honest gesture we can make to posterity is to admit that we are at a loss when it comes to answering the ultimate questions about AIDS.

This ignorance may inspire a spirit of future charity toward writing on this subject—and we will surely need one. Although much of what has been written on AIDS may have done some good, most of it, considered on its own merits, is shrill, muddled, tendentious, and overdetermined. Of course, in the middle of a crisis, in the absence of certainty, we naturally settle for what helps at the moment: *bricolage*. But sadly, when it comes to the literature of AIDS, what in the 1980s linked most writers was hyperbole.

Randy Shilts's *And the Band Played On* (1987) remains to date the most widely read and, for better or worse, the most influential mass-market book on AIDS. It is also thoroughly typical of its genre in its taste for melodramatic utterance. Shilts designates Rock Hudson's death from AIDS in 1985 as a watershed, one that converted the earlier panicked silence of the press and broadcast media into relentless publicity. But surely *And the Band Played On* itself accelerated that process and helped, besides, to establish the vocabulary with which popular discussion of AIDS has been conducted ever since.

The book has the merit of demonstrating a point almost no one would now care to dispute: the epidemic could have been stemmed, if not stopped, by early action. In the four years between 1981 (when the first cases were reported) and 1985, AIDS continued to spread in the U.S. From the very beginning of that period, any physician who cared to pay attention to the epidemiological data, in fact any intelligent layman, was in a position to guess—though not, until 1984, to know—that AIDS was a blood-borne and sexually transmitted disease, probably viral in origin. Shilts documents the dithering that afflicted virtually everyone who might have acted to publicize this theory. Scientists and physicians, public health authorities, gay political leaders, and business interests—all are drubbed for not speaking out earlier. Shilts expertly deploys the facts of the widespread tragedy that had emerged by the late 1980s to drown out any sympathy in his reader for the hesitation or denial that in the early 1980s prevented effective action against the disease.

The problem with *And the Band Played On* is the grating emotionalism of its ace-reporter language. It is every bit as riddled with panic and unexamined prejudice as its targets. In his "Notes on Sources," Shilts calls his book a "work of journalism" and disclaims any fictionalization, but he adds that "for purposes of narrative flow, I reconstruct scenes, recount conversations and occasionally attribute observations to people with such phrases as 'he thought' or 'she felt.'" Such references, Shilts vaguely adds, "are drawn from either the research interviews I conducted for the book or from research conducted during my years of covering the AIDS epidemic." Odd journalism indeed if, as Shilts appears to be saying, he has reconstructed other people's thoughts and utterances out of his own experience as a reporter in the field. But that is the tenor of his comment, and it is revealing.

Whatever its documentary basis, *And the Band Played On* adopts, often disastrously, the language of pulp fiction. It presents a series of interwoven vignettes from the lives of doctors, gay men with and without AIDS, activists, and observers, the common thread among which is the overheated Sidney Sheldonesque prose in which their thoughts and actions are described. Here, for example, is Don Francis, the Centers for Disease Control researcher on whose authority much of the epidemiological information of *And the Band Played On* seems to rely:

> The car swerved, jolting Don Francis awake. Francis regained control of his Volvo and continued home. The night before, he had arrived home at 6 p.m. and was in bed by 8:30 p.m., as usual, so he could slip into the CDC headquarters on Clifton Road by 5 a.m. to get a few hours of work done before the meetings began and the phone started ringing. When he had a paper to write, Francis went to work at 2 a.m., sometimes running into Jim Curran, who would only then be on his way out of the office. Francis has learned such rigorous schedules when he was fighting smallpox in India. It was you against the disease, his ethos went, and the disease might win if you let up for one day.

This is not merely ridiculous; it is harmful and can't be justified on the grounds that it gains the attention of a mass audience or keeps even the thickest reader alert to a complicated narrative. What Shilts has done is to graft onto his story energies that belong to myth and ideology rather than to history or even political polemic.

An even more extreme case of Shilts's overdramatizing is his account (it gained *And the Band Played On* its most effective publicity) of "Patient Zero," Gaetan Dugas, the French-Canadian airline steward who had documented connections to a number of gay men who contracted the disease early in the epidemic. The implication of the story is that in Dugas, who persisted in a voracious career of bathhouse sex after contracting AIDS, researchers had tracked down—and Shilts had made public—the origin of the epidemic in America.

Shilts briefly concedes the improbability that the virus could ever be tracked to a single human carrier: "Whether Gaetan Dugas actually was the person who brought AIDS to North America remains a question of debate and is ultimately unanswerable." In fact, it is highly unlikely; the disease has been found in post-mortem tissue taken from a patient who died in St. Louis in 1969, well before Dugas's entry onto the scene. But this does not prevent Shilts from dramatizing him heavily, as an initially ignorant but ultimately willful angel of death. Dugas is first shown in 1980 in San Francisco on the day of a gay parade, just after the removal of his earliest KS lesion; eventually, diagnosed with AIDS and told he is spreading it, he becomes a gay Typhoid Mary: "It was around this time [mid-1982] that rumors began on Castro Street about a strange guy at the Eighth and Howard bathhouse, a blond with a French accent. He would have sex with you, turn up the lights in the cubicle, and point out his Kaposi's sarcoma lesions. 'I've got gay cancer,' he'd say. 'I'm going to die and so are you.'"

Shilts carefully avoids claiming these incidents really ever happened, or if they did that Dugas perpetrated them. But that reservation is likely to be lost on the reader who tracks the thread of Patient Zero's sinister course through the bathhouses and bars, as Shilts interweaves it among other narratives. Indeed, Dugas's story is particularly gripping (he appeared in a front-page *New York Post* headline as THE MAN WHO GAVE US AIDS). His story appeals to an immemorial superstition that insistently recurs in epidemics: the rumor of the anointer, the anonymous stranger who drifts into the city deliberately spreading the plague among the innocent.

Patient Zero, Gaetan Dugas, is a dream image, an allegory of our own terror. The image may (incidentally) be the truth, but it has the *frisson* of legend. The facts are a veneer, essentially beside the point; and despite its reportorial character, this is generally true of *And the Band Played On*. What the book really communicates is more the impact of the epidemic's spread on the emotions than its clinical and public health history. The documentary side of *And the Band Played On* is paradoxically what builds a façade of credibility over its underlying hysteria. It does tell some important truths, but its aim lies in the cheap sensationalism communicated by the potboiling prose in which these truths are clothed.

One of the book's recurrent themes is the gay community's early reluctance to shut down the baths, a cause for which Shilts was an emphatic advocate. In the effort to document this, however, *And the Band Played On* ultimately gives, as with Gaetan Dugas, the appearance of demonstrating objectively what it can't possibly know: that the disease spread mainly in the dark, seedy, disreputable shadows of on-premises sex clubs. Shilts never denies that AIDS can be (and perhaps mainly is) spread by people who meet socially or at work, fall in love, and have sex with each other by normal middle-class firesides. But that isn't mainly the role sex—at least the sex through which contagion is spread—plays in the book. It's dark, threatening, disgusting sex. No wonder, Shilts seems to be saying, such stuff leads to AIDS. An important early scene shows Kico Govantes, new to gay life in San Francisco, scandalized at his first trip to a bathhouse under the tutelage of a more experienced guide:

> Kico turned to his companion. Certainly, a psychologist would see that this was unhealthy, a corruption of the very gay love that this day was supposed to celebrate. The shrink eyed him curiously, as if he were a naive child. He seemed to enjoy guiding the twenty-two-year-old through the labyrinthine hallways.
> "That's fist-fucking," the psychologist said.
> "Oh," Kico said.
> Knowing the words for the acts didn't help him fathom the meaning of what he was seeing. Where was the affection? he wondered. Where was the interaction of mind and body that creates a meaningful sexual experience?

Shilts has been accused of internalized homophobia, and the charge gains credence from passages like this. Given the weight of such passages in Shilts's narrative, along with the Patient Zero story, AIDS, as he describes it, seems more a retribution for sin than a by-product of a virus blindly exploiting whatever opportunity it is offered to reproduce and perpetuate itself. It is as if, in the uncertainty and terror that a still unpredictable epidemic provokes, Shilts felt the need to plug the gaps in our knowledge with synthesized intensities: to testify to the experience of AIDS in ways more harrowing than mere facts would allow.

In the 1980s Shilts was far from alone in reacting this way to AIDS. Throughout the decade AIDS set loose the personal demons of virtually all who wrote about it. Try as they might to paint a portrait of the disease, what they ended up offering instead was covert psychoautobiography.

Nothing illustrates this tendency better than Larry Kramer's 1985 play *The Normal Heart*, the opening night of which figures as a landmark in *And the Band Played On*. Randy Shilts had campaigned for the closing of the bathhouses in San Francisco; Kramer did the same even more aggressively in New York, adding a course of political agitation against the Koch administration, which had essentially ignored the early phases of the epidemic. William Hoffman's earlier play, *As Is*, had dramatized the personal dimensions of AIDS, but *The Normal Heart* was frankly polemical, offering a history of the anti-AIDS movement in New York and, more than incidentally, a dramatic lecture on the disease. As Shilts had, Kramer rails against the early denial in both the scientific and the gay communities that allowed the virus to spread, and, in the preachy, improbable character of Emma, a wheelchair-bound physician, he offers advice on prevention: stop having sex. To that Kramer adds several vivid if melodramatic portraits of gay men coping with AIDS. Like *And the Band Played On, The Normal Heart* did mark a sociopolitical if not a creative breakthrough, and there is no question that it helped propel discussion of the disease into the world of public discourse.

But it too suffers from a division of soul: scene by scene it appears to unfold as a history of AIDS and a two-pronged diatribe against homophobia and the homosexual behavior that allowed AIDS to spread. But its dramaturgy reveals another and deeper-rooted preoccupation. The real crisis of the play has nothing to do with AIDS and everything to do with politics and the bottomless ego of the main character, Ned Weeks, widely reported to be a self-portrait of Larry Kramer. Much of the plot revolves around his founding of an anti-AIDS volunteer group at the beginning of the epidemic—as Kramer had founded Gay Men's Health Crisis. The play's climax comes when Weeks is humiliatingly drummed out of the organization (this also happened to Kramer with GMHC) because he is too loud, too confrontational, too willing to make a public issue of his (and his friends') gayness. The scene isn't as self-pitying as a description of it implies: Weeks admits he's an asshole, and begs not to be cut off from the group. But when he is left standing alone on stage at the end of the scene, the play has reached it apogee. Everything that follows this moment, including a deathbed marriage with his dying lover, Felix, is by way of denouement.

How is it that a diatribe against a disease and those who respond to it inadequately (at least as the play sees things) can devolve so thoroughly into a portrait of naked ego? *The Normal Heart* has one strong advantage over *And the Band Played On*: it is aware that it harbors and plays out violences of emotion not strictly related to AIDS. The stinging rebukes administered to Weeks by the other characters in the play, and his own self-criticism, demonstrate Kramer's recognition of this problem, but they don't solve it. We are left with the nagging sense that Kramer has exploited a general tragedy to ventilate a personal one.

Is such confusion peculiar to AIDS, or is it something to do with being gay? There have been, in the West, at least, arguably three contagious diseases in the twentieth century that match AIDS in psychological impact: tuberculosis (which was, at the end of the nineteenth century, still the leading cause of death in the U.S.), the 1918 influenza epidemic, and polio. But an implicit national faith in physicians and in the power of scientific medicine (which we have since lost) allayed some of the panic each provoked. In 1900 or 1918 or 1950, some of the angst unleashed by the fear of a fatal disease could be dispersed in the trust you felt in your doctor and his profession. In all the disease literature of the period, there is usually a potent physician, like Sir Luke Strett in James's *The Wings of the Dove*, who mediates between the character facing illness and the mysteries and horrors of the disease. But, for better and worse, we have since deconstructed organized medicine, leaving nothing between ourselves and the microbe, no social network to lessen the sense of isolation, powerlessness, and peril that a mortal disease brings. It's significant, and probably not an accident, that Emma Brookner, *The Normal Heart*'s doctor, is both female (hence off the map of gay male sexual territory) and confined to a wheelchair.

In his widely praised 1989 novel about AIDS (and the golden age of the zipless fuck preceding it), *Eighty-Sixed*, David R. Feinberg at first seems to apply satire as a distancing technique to avoid self-promoting emotion. His book is on the surface unsentimental, a tissue of stark and merciless comic contrasts. The first half, "Ancient History," follows the hero, B.J., through 1980. B.J.'s principal, though unmet, goal is a boyfriend, a search that takes him from trick to trick, and to all the loci of gay life after Stonewall in Manhattan—the St. Mark's Baths, the Ramble in Central Park, the gay stretch at Jones Beach, the New York University gym, the VD clinic (inevitably), and, as the stakes of disease rise inexorably, the still more surreal Greenwich Village lab which tested stool samples for intestinal parasites ("This is not the correct consistency," the Nordic technician icily informs B.J. after his first effort). The tone is sardonic, but B.J. is so obsessed with sex—albeit in the guise of romance—that his story, even as it cannonballs along through days of mindless libertinism, becomes claustrophobic and essentially joyless. B.J. comes up for air only for occasional rueful dinners with friends. But even they are most often ex-tricks, and, wherever the conversation ranges, it is eventually yanked back by B.J.'s lodestone: boyfriends, boyfriends, boyfriends.

Eighty-Sixed is most remarkable for the inevitability with which its unhinged first half predicts and ushers in the nihilism of its second half, "Learning How to Cry," which takes B.J.

through 1986, the year when the consciousness of AIDS became, at least among gay men in New York, a species of monomania. B.J., though an NYU graduate student, is essentially frivolous and brainless, remaining as driven as ever in the quest (still unsuccessful) for a lover; but to that preoccupation is added the gnawing fear of AIDS and the nagging strain of living with sick friends from debility to debility and finally to death. The book's comic edge sharpens here but nonetheless doesn't function as relief. It simply reflects the mockery by which an implacable fate reaffirms its power over the characters. The only real initiative B.J. manages is the firing of his insufferable cowlike assistant, Caroline—but even she returns, vampire-like, after intimidating his firm's personnel department and B.J.'s insouciant boss.

Eighty-Sixed is, in other words, despite its veneer of hard-boiled skepticism, as dedicated to the expression of its own mere extremity as either *The Normal Heart* or *And the Band Played On*. In Iris Murdoch's most recent novel, *The Message to the Planet*, a major character, dying of a disease which resembles AIDS (though we're told it's not), is brought back from the edge of death by a possible miracle. The book and its characters are as skeptical about the possibility of magic as the most hardened late-twentieth-century positivist could wish, and much of *The Message to the Planet* explores the possibility that the cure was a result of chance. But at least the hope for escape from necessity animates the story, lets in some air. Feinberg's despair, on the other hand, belies and ultimately vitiates the vitality of his imagination. His book is punctuated by short, usually comic, prose-poem riffs, but one, in "Learning How to Cry," is unforget-table for the black hole into which it sucks the reader, the writer, and, apparently, the novel. The poem is called "Sensitivity Exercises for Death," and it could serve as an epigraph for the whole book. In the poem we are exhorted to imagine ourselves floating through helium. Then fog. Then water. Then—finally—mud.

The mud is viscous. Gradually you make your way across the room. Watch out for rocks. The mud is warm and soothing. You

*hear muted music, the lower octaves from an organ. It gradually
fades away. The mud hardens. Now it is solid. You are encased
in concrete. Try to move. You can't....*
  Close your eyes.
  Now don't open them.
  Ever.

The book is so ferociously fettered to the experiences it
recounts, whether libertine or anhedonic (in Feinberg's world the
two blend inextricably) that catharsis becomes impossible. The
reader is afforded no distance, no perspective. The effect, as with
The Normal Heart and *And the Band Played On*, is ultimately
narcissistic. In each case the writer acts as if the only possible
way to respond to general suffering is to explore the tumult of his
own reaction to it and, either openly or covertly, clutch the
tumult to himself.

Nor is it only gay writers who have let the disease colonize
their imaginations (and in turn let their imaginations colonize the
disease). Michael Fumento's *The Myth of Heterosexual AIDS*
(1990) promises at first to be an exercise in debunking. Fumento
effectively deflates the panic-mongering sensationalism rampant
in press and broadcast treatments of AIDS; he describes the public
smarminess and private homophobia with which Hollywood has
faced the disease; he demonstrates how statistics have been
distorted to present future prospects for the disease in the worst
possible light. He is also refreshingly hardheaded about how
political interests on both the left and the right have manipulated
the crisis in pursuit of their own ends. Fumento's tone is so
commonsensical, so determined in its assault on the vapors that
afflict AIDS writing, that one might think he has finally escaped
the emotional distortion characteristic of the genre and that his
book is the herald of a more rational, less stress-laden way of
seeing AIDS.
  Unfortunately, *The Myth of Heterosexual AIDS* is simply panic
in reverse. Hard as he tries, Fumento can't make the statistics

back up his contention that the likely spread of AIDS among heterosexuals has been oversold. The problem is the one we began with—nobody knows exactly how AIDS spreads via sexual contact. It has clearly been demonstrated that it can be passed from man to woman and woman to man during normal heterosexual intercourse. These modes—the latter particularly—appear far less efficient than anal intercourse, a point Fumento emphasizes heavily. But how much less efficient remains unclear; the variable, and often very long, latency period of the disease means that epidemiological data about the nature and extent of its spread are slow to emerge. There are projections aplenty, but the disease is ahead of us, and the fact that so far it is a relatively minor risk for heterosexuals does not mean it will remain so.

To downplay the danger of AIDS to heterosexuals, Fumento makes heavy use of a flurry of 1986 press reports announcing that in one year the proportion of heterosexually transmitted AIDS cases has doubled from 2 to 4 percent of the total. As Fumento correctly notes, this rise was a statistical artifact. It occurred when the Centers for Disease Control decided to put Haitians and Africans who had recently moved to America first into a category in which the mode of AIDS transmission was "undetermined," and finally into the pool of heterosexually transmitted AIDS cases, thus doubling rates, as Fumento points out, without the emergence of a single new case. Reassuring. Or is it? It is true, as Fumento says, that rates did not really double, but it is also true, as long as you accept that AIDS cases among Haitian and African emigrés were heterosexual in origin, that such cases had been underestimated by half. The real source of Fumento's attack on these figures is his belief that many, if not most, of the Haitian and African AIDS cases were homosexual in origin or at least traceable to other factors than normal male-female contact. But when we turn back to Fumento's discussion of Haiti and Africa, his arguments weaken. He more or less simply asserts that most Haitian AIDS cases are really homosexual but not admitted as such (there is a brief but lurid picture of homosexual brothels frequented by Americans in Port-au-Prince). Fumento explains away the predominance of apparently heterosexual AIDS cases in Africa: unconfessed homosexuality, lack of circumcision, unsterilized hypodermic needles, a high general rate of sexually transmitted disease. Suggestive—and possible, but far less ironclad and not as reassuring as Fumento would have us believe.

Emotion remains the medium in *The Myth of Heterosexual AIDS*. We're still being yelled at. The screamer in this case is telling us to cool down rather than to gird for apocalypse, but he is shouting nonetheless, and it is ultimately his own passion that is being brought before us rather than the anatomy of an illness.

So what? one might reasonably ask. Isn't personal testimony a useful response to an epidemic? A natural and potentially cathartic part of the experience? Possibly. But all these books implicitly cross the line from testimony to prophecy. They are not merely saying, "This is my experience." They are saying, "My experience is the fountain of truth, and it is normative."

Of all the widely circulated books about AIDS, only one suggests a more useful, less punishing approach to AIDS: Susan Sontag's *AIDS and Its Metaphors* (1989). It is brief, virtually a pamphlet, and not entirely novel, because it extends to AIDS a discussion begun in Sontag's earlier *Illness as Metaphor*. But its point remains wholesome and tonic, and its warnings are amply documented by the abysmal quality of most mass-market AIDS writing. We are in peril, Sontag argues, of transforming AIDS from a viral infection into a devouring moral monster, laden with all our meanest and most destructive cultural prejudices. Sontag is the only widely read writer who observes a peculiarly danger-fraught feature of AIDS: the slipperiness with which it's been defined permits it to be invested with all kinds of pernicious metaphors. AIDS was first recognized not by its underlying etiological cause, the human immunodeficiency virus, but by the commonest (and worst) opportunistic infections that characterize the potentially fatal stages of infection: Kaposi's sarcoma and *pneumocystis carinni* pneumonia. Since the early 1980s, however, other infections and conditions have been added to the list as sufficient indicators for the diagnosis of "frank" AIDS, and other diagnostic devices (like T4 cell counts) have come into play as well. As a result, AIDS and its relation to HIV infection have repeatedly been redefined, confusing the statistical picture of the epidemic and turning the disease into a murky universal signifier, fuzzy enough in its outlines to become a touchstone for not one but a dozen kinds of terror. Sontag is astute on this point:

> That AIDS is not a single illness but a syndrome, consisting of a seemingly open-ended list of contributing or "presenting" illnesses which constitute (that is, qualify the patient as having) the disease, makes it more a product of definition or construction than even very complex, multiform illnesses like cancer. Indeed, the contention that AIDS is invariably fatal depends partly on what doctors decided to define as AIDS—and keep in reserve as distinct earlier stages of the disease. And this decision rests on a notion no less primitively metaphorical than that of a "full-blown" (or "full-fledged") disease. . . . "Full-blown" is the form in which the disease is inevitably fatal. As what is immature is destined to become mature, what buds to become full-blown, . . . the doctors' botanical or zoological metaphor makes development or evolution into AIDS the norm, the rule.

This isn't simply sharp; it is useful, in ways that none of the other books considered here can match. It gives us some perspective; it helps us to decide, amidst the dread and suffering surrounding the epidemic, which evils come from the virus and which from our own imaginations. It is perhaps surprising that literary criticism, Sontag's milieu, should prove so powerful a medium for discussion of AIDS. It shouldn't be. We still don't have the scientific, social, or political knowledge to assess AIDS satisfactorily. But we can evaluate the images we have been constructing of it, and these in turn can afford us the distance we need to render the challenge manageable, without minimizing it, but also without using it to empower our own most intractable mental demons. Sontag's book offers brief but highly useful discussions of the subversive and destructive ways in which AIDS has interacted with perceptions both of homo- and heterosexuality.

At times in her discussion Sontag succumbs to the reigning taste for apocalypse. She entertains more or less seriously, for example, Harvard biologist Stephen Jay Gould's speculation that AIDS may ultimately kill off a quarter of the human race. That speculation becomes the basis for a brief indulgence in some are-we-living-in-the-end-of-time rhetoric. But generally speaking, Sontag is the best kind of skeptic—neither overdramatizing the epidemic, like Shilts, Kramer, and Feinberg, nor, like Fumento, preoccupied with shooing it away. *AIDS and Its Metaphors* neither whistles nor screams in the dark; both its passions and its detachments are in the right places. It acknowledges the tentativeness of what we know about AIDS and doesn't, like so much other writing in this uniquely 1980s genre, renounce that tentativeness.

Josephine Hendin

FICTIONS OF ACQUISITION

The rich diversity of American fiction has always
made newness difficult to characterize. But the 1980s have seen
not only the arrival of fresh work by writers who have long
established that diversity, but also the fracturing of literary
culture along quasipolitical lines: the rise of a multi-ethnic
literature encompassing the work of Chinese Americans, Indians,
African Americans, and European ethnics, a growing gay literature, and new additions to feminist fiction. Powerful novels of
Vietnam and its aftermath, many by combat veterans, have added

Josephine Hendin is Professor of English at New York University. She is the author of *The World of Flannery O'Connor* and
Vulnerable People: A View of American Fiction Since 1945. Her
novel, *The Right Thing to Do*, received an American Book
Award from the Before Columbus Foundation in 1989.

to the cultural ferment. Yet all these often "radical" voices do not so much signal what has changed as serve the traditional end of extending our fiction's longstanding concern with the drama of marginal man beating at the doors of society. The literary revolution of the 1980s has erupted in a fiction of those who have already gained entry.

Perhaps nothing reveals what has changed more than the transformation of those heroes and antiheroes propelled toward mythic stature by an avid college market. The youthcult heroes of one period are made obsolete by those of another. Reflecting the aspirations and anxieties of coming-of-age, cult heroes dramatize the ethos of the day. The sweet brotherliness of Holden Caulfield in recoil from adulthood reflected the 1950s belief in authenticity, innocence, and family as bulwarks against the crassness of the social world. The sexual freedom of Robert A. Heinlein's *Stranger in a Strange Land*, whose Martian hero teaches the benefits of nonverbal communication, communal life, and abandoning possessive jealousy, reflected a 1960s rejection of competitive, acquisitive America. An attack on authority and authoritarianism figured in the feminist assault on the double standard, fueling mass-market bestsellers of the 1970s, from *Fear of Flying* by Erica Jong to the ambitiously belletristic novel of Francine Duplessix Gray, *Lovers and Tyrants*. But the comparable fiction of the 1980s seems to be giving up the counterculture attack on adulthood, authority, and repression. There is in progress a quiet but sharp recoil from the concepts of self and society, from the quest for authentic emotion, from the visions of individualism and possibility that have been animating forces in our literature. In the 1980s we encounter the new Self in its most extreme form: the Hero as Nostril.

In Jay McInerney's *Bright Lights, Big City*, he lives, or rather, inhales in a spiritual confusion in which day and night are confounded:

The night has already turned on that imperceptible pivot where two A.M. changes to six A.M. You know this moment has come and gone, but you are not yet willing to concede that you have crossed the line beyond which all is gratuitous damage and the palsy of unravelled nerve endings. Somewhere back there you could have cut your losses, but you rode past that moment on a comet trail of white powder and now you are trying to hang on to the rush. Your brain at this moment is composed of brigades of tiny Bolivian soldiers. They are tired and muddy from their long march through the night. There are holes in their boots and they are hungry. They need to be fed. They need the Bolivian Marching Powder.

The Hero as Nostril is nose without sense, an inhaling mechanism without the power of smell. His habitat is the toilet stall of an expensive restaurant or an *in* disco, for, together with cocaine, he inhales status sites and brand names. His distraught and destroyed senses, mirrored in McInerney's often impressive surreal style and speed-blurred descriptions, are incredibly precise at conveying name-brand identification. The Nostril is determined to inhale only the best.

McInerney has produced a distinctive literary effort: the compression of the novel of manners into an equivalent of upscale ads. In language there is a comparable constriction: the linguistic quest for T. S. Eliot's "objective correlative" is flattened into an exploitation of objects. There is no correlating link of attendant emotion or depth. His hero, who works as a fact-checker at a thinly disguised version of the *New Yorker*, considers himself vastly superior to the girl at the bar who believes the words "decadence and Dexedrine are the high points of the language of Kings James and Lear." He himself is a man who knows the titles of the best works: "*As I Lay Dying, Under the Volcano, Anna Karenina, Being and Time, The Brothers Karamazov*," even if he has kept himself innocent of their contents. The title is sign supreme, the label whose possession is meant to convey class.

*

In style and modes of characterization, the youthcult fiction of the 1980s is a fiction not of insurgency but of cultural collaboration. What stands out is an assimilation, to the point of wholesale adoption, of advertising culture. Labels, name brands, surface signs have become the sole social referents and methods of character definition. McInerney's characterization of a man of literary sensibility is effected not through a representation of consciousness but by the ownership of unread books, contempt for the underyuppie class, and the ability to give such imaginative names to cocaine as "Bolivian Marching Powder." What motivates the Nostril-hero is obscure; he has too little feeling for the gradual and now final withdrawal of his wife, a fashion model and perfect label-wearer. In a belated effort at explaining what drives his hero, when the book is nearly over, McInerney introduces his mother who, near death, wishes she could have lived the way he does. Not even a dying mother runs deep.

Bright Lights, Big City was not simply a successful novel. It was a publishing phenomenon. Produced as a paperback original in Random House's Vintage Contemporaries line, it was widely and enthusiastically reviewed, a first novel that rapidly sold out its first printing and justified the "NATIONAL BEST-SELLER" emblazoned on its cover along with that other label of distinction, "MAJOR MOTION PICTURE." Starring Michael J. Fox as the nose who knows, the film had the dazzling surfaces of the novel but not its ability to reflect a stream of consciousness that is itself filled with objects. Hailed by the *Playboy* reviewer as a "*Catcher in the Rye* for the MBA set," the novel's success underscored how aptly its talented twenty-nine-year-old author, in capturing a contemporary hero, had understood the culture's changing values and equation of materialism with the substance of being.

In this literature, character is entirely the product of acts of appropriation indistinguishable from buying. Serial purchases, episodic peaks and lows before scoring, make shopping the ultimate human act. Buying coke is the model for all experience: the purchase of self, the acquisition of other people.

The youthcult fiction of the 1980s differs from any we have

encountered before. Most of the fiction that has appealed to college students has involved a sense of social or generational conflict or advocacy of a hedonistic, experiential ethic at variance with the competitive work ethic of American culture. The youthcult novels of the 1980s reflect an enormous shift.

Rooted in the culture of acquisition, Bret Easton Ellis's *Less Than Zero* has an enraptured following among high school and college students. *Less Than Zero* hit national best-sellerdom and major motion picturehood in a film staring teen idol Andrew McCarthy. Ellis, barely into his twenties when the novel was published, was, like McInerney, hailed for producing "an updated *Catcher in the Rye*." And yet no one in his novel would know the meaning of Holden Caulfield's favorite pejorative, "phony."

For the eighteen-year-old hero of *Less Than Zero*, advertising posters mounted above his bed define his crisis of faith and emotional disconnections:

It's the promotional poster for an old Elvis Costello record. Elvis looks past me, with this wry, ironic smile on his lips, staring out the window. The word "Trust" hovering over his head, and his sunglasses, one lens red, the other blue, pushed down past the ridge of his nose so that you can see his eyes, which are slightly off center. The eyes don't look at me, though. They only look at whoever's standing by the window, but I'm too tired to get up and stand by the window.

Even old friends, the boys our hero went to high school with, have themselves become marketable objects inspiring one thought: Are they for sale? In this novel, the answer is usually yes. Virtually all are male models or prostitutes or both, who define themselves by their resemblance to David Bowie, their appearance on the cover or in the pages of *International Male* ("No nudes, just Speedos"), and by the singers they listen to. They go to college—UCLA or USC—and one even possesses Cliff's Notes to *As I Lay Dying*. They appear to have majored in the names of rock singers.

Ellis uses the names of rock groups to define self. Heavy metal? Soft rock? You are, in effect, who and what you hear. His characters have spent so much time listening to the Eagles, Joan Jett and the Blackhearts, and Killer Pussy that they have been rendered inarticulate. Ellis offers as a meaningful *cri de coeur* the ambiguous opening line of the novel: "People are afraid to merge on freeways in Los Angeles," spoken by a girl picking our hero up at the airport. In the light of the novel, it may refer more persuasively to traffic patterns at freeway entry points than to missed emotional rapport. The "force" of such emotional disconnection is withstood by the hero, by turning on MTV and wishing for a Valium. Passive consumption of rock, television, films, tranquilizers, and cocaine defines the world of the novel. Bleeding nostrils and tranquilized visions mark its emotional range. What distinguishes its vision of youth is primarily an enormous enervation on and off cocaine.

The youth culture fiction of the 1980s has virtually eliminated the conflict of generations. In *Bright Lights, Big City*, parents are dead or absent, and older women are of indeterminate age. Home for Christmas break in Ellis's *Less Than Zero*, the Nostril as affluent young Californian finds neither a constraining nor loving family, nor one in which there is a difference in values between parents and children. Parents are busy popping pills; fathers get face lifts and take their young homosexual lovers to family parties; mothers drink too much, little sisters easily displace mother's voice with Killer Pussy. Drinking white wine, the Nostril's mother

> tries to smile when she asks me what I want for Christmas. I'm surprised at how much effort it takes to raise my head up and look at her.
>
> "Nothing," I say.
>
> "You look unhappy," she says real suddenly.
>
> "I'm not," I tell her.
>
> "You look unhappy," she says, more quietly this time. She touches her hair, bleached, blondish, again.
>
> "You do too," I say, hoping that she won't say anything else.

She doesn't say anything else, until she's finished her third glass of wine and poured her fourth.

So much for Mom.

The young man of the 1980s is supposed to be infatuated with making money. But these youthcult novels reflect no such interest. The fathers of *Less Than Zero* differ from their sons in that they have been able to accumulate in the entertainment business enough to keep their children in cocaine and BMWs and to buy young men as lovers. Their sons have only contempt for their fathers' checkwriting abilities and no interest in finance. They know no modes of making money other than male prostitution, modeling, and drug dealing. Ellis's hero hires out as a voyeur while his friend turns tricks for a man who, Hollywood style, enjoys an audience most. In past youthcult fiction one found contempt for the treatment of sexuality as a commodity and for the phoniness of superficial looks, but in Ellis's the intertwined themes of sex, money, and voyeurism are celebrated as a descent to wallow in, disabusing the reader of literary expectations of youthful idealism, social criticism, or even physical pleasure. The body here is something to sell or see, not enjoy.

Sexuality has been the staple of mass youthcult fiction, reflected in fantasies of joy and freedom and in the pursuit of new sensations. Although our hero is bisexual, the likelihood of his waking up with either a man or woman does not multiply his fun. His most frequent contacts are with men and his descriptions of desired bodies are largely those of men. Yet with both men and women, the Nostril's experiences are rather like standing on line at the Motor Vehicle Bureau. It is only in the description of mutilated or exploited youngsters that some pathos emerges as our hero feels kinship with both male and female sexual victims. The definition of sexual worth alternates between excellence in the skin trade and, on the dark side, the capacity to eroticize exploitation and death.

Death is just another scene. No longer to be lamented, abhorred, or transcended, death is to be relished either as a spectacle or a justification for emptiness. In *Less Than Zero* all violence has been eroticized as pornography. At the close of the novel Ellis includes a scene of a group of beautifully built young men in a Malibu beach house watching a $15,000 snuff movie in which two adolescents are violated by a huge man who later castrates the boy and mutilates the girl. The film was of something real, the castration could not have been faked, someone says. They are excited; the high cost of the film seems additional proof that they have seen two actual murders. Later, Ellis throws in an anecdote about a Stanford student who gave a party in Rancho Mirage culminating in the repeated rape, mutilation, and murder of a girl whose throat "had been slit and her breasts had been cut off and someone had stuck candles where they used to be. Her body had been found at the Sun Air Drive-In hanging upside down from the swing set."

Less Than Zero has more dead and sexually mutilated young people than any novel I can remember that was not explicitly about war. Even Hubert Selby's *Last Exit to Brooklyn*, a milestone in the literature of disgust, developed its visions of sexual horror in terms that balanced physical pain with characterizations yielding a sense of psychological terror. But the superficial characterization employed here substitutes a rising body count for accumulated meaning. The expensive snuff movie reveals a culture of acquisition carried to an extreme in the notion that death and mutilation are highs for sale.

The moral sense is not entirely absent, but it might as well be in this fiction in which the enduring relationship is between the Nostril and his coke supplier. Ellis's Rip is not only a pusher but is also into violating innocence. Visiting Rip, our hero sees a naked twelve-year-old girl ("She goes to Corvallis"). "Her legs are spread and tied to the bedposts and her arms are tied above her head. Her cunt is all rashed and looks dry and I can see that it's been shaved. She keeps moaning and murmuring words and moving her head from side to side, her eyes half-closed. Someone's put a lot of makeup on her, clumsily, and she keeps licking her lips, her tongue drags slowly, repeatedly across them." She is drugged to the hilt (See, it doesn't hurt!) and about to be gangbanged in various ways by the three young men in the room who appear to have replaced film porn with a live act. To express his outrage, our hero asks Rip, "Why?" Rip replies the equivalent of why not: "If you want something, you have the right to take it. If you want to do something, you have the right to do it." Mulling this over, our Nostril walks out to powder his nose or, more precisely, to snort his newly purchased cocaine.

Is the Hero-as-Nostril only the aberrant creation of under-thirty writers who have come of age in the era of cocaine? The condition described in extreme ways in these novels cannot be dismissed so easily, partly because it differs in degree but not in kind from the worldview of many young writers who do not deal with cocaine but instead have tried to write about personal life. According to author David Leavitt, writing as the voice of the under-thirty literary generation in "New Voices and Old Values" in the *New York Times Book Review* of May 12, 1985, they have all "in general limited themselves to the short story, a form they seem to find appropriate to the age of shortened attention spans, fractured marriages and splintering families in which they grew up."

This youth fiction of personal life has been criticized for being insufficiently true to individual differences and for accepting commercially viable, collectivized notions of self. Bruce Bawer, in a pejoratively titled essay, "The Literary Brat Pack," accuses Leavitt, Elizabeth Tallent, Meg Wolitzer, Marian Thurm, Peter Cameron, and others of writing "exactly alike," of having forsaken an original voice to buy the modish sound purveyed to them by writing programs. Their collective, contrived voice is "especially big on the details surrounding 'relationships'. . . the set decorations— the bags of groceries, the copies of *GQ* and *People* . . . [that] tend, time and again, to overwhelm the frail narratives." At fault, Bawer believes, are "professors in university creative writing programs [who] tell their students that this is the way to write: load up on concrete details, relevant or not. The more particulars, the better." But what is at stake may be more than commercially oriented teaching or the vagaries of youth: these talented young writers are mirroring a striking change.

A new definition of the self, a new vision of subjectivity is being reflected in 1980s fictions. Cocaine-based novels are only the most extreme example of cultural change in which the traditional American faith in individualism, in insurgent selves transcending, withstanding, or at least withholding assent from unpalatable environments, is dying. This recoil from Emersonianism is not simply a crisis of youth. The world, constituted as a relationship and its artifacts, has slowly grown toward being treated as the only known territory; brand names have only now flowered into use as major social referents, whether what is being mentioned is the cookie bought in a supermarket or a luxurious fur. The self so circumscribed is not a youthcult invention but rather a postmodernist construction, a particular emptiness waiting to become a receptacle for the cultural artifacts that surround it. Like Paola, the young woman in Thomas Pynchon's *V.*, who can speak only in nouns, the characters find meaning only in objects. Just as McInerney's *Bright Lights, Big City* compresses the novel of manners to an upscale ad and Ellis's *Less Than Zero* reduces the novel of initiation to the equivalent of snuff-porn stills, so new fiction of "sensibility" operates to treat feelings through surfaces, breaking down the distinctions between people and things. In this phenomenological orgy, to borrow from Wittgenstein, the world is all that is the (Gucci) case.

The postmodern sense of fragmentation is now revealing itself in a vision of *emotions* as artifacts, of people as objects in a society whose common culture is increasingly standardized. What is being standardized is the self in fiction and perhaps in theory. This standardization is effected in several ways. Characters in search of a defining place or connection are seen against the linguistic and visual constructs mass culture provides. They seem almost to conform to a Lacanian theory of personality formation as the effort to discover oneself in "otherness," a differentiation of self as a "signifier" seeking to be assimilated into a purely symbolic order. Being is not intrinsic, not the existential *sine qua non*; individuals are only carriers looking for a sign, a billboard-self. Thus these characters seem doomed to equate personality with external objects, to discover self as and in objectified form.

Midlife Writing

These currents are evident not only in young writers, but also in the work of established artists who have achieved their widest audience in the 1980s and whose works reflect the various difficulties of intimacy in middle age. Even in this fiction it is clear that the primacy of individual experience is seriously in doubt. The author is unwittingly complicit in the externalization and standardization of feeling and seems to be writing from the center of a condition he or she cannot control.

The enervation apparent in youthcult fiction surfaces in new fiction of middle age as ongoing depression. Subjecting the ethic of experimentation to the scrutiny of characters abraded by a complex past of serial lovers, families, failures, this fiction explores the consequences of contemporary love. It does not aim for the power of *Anna Karenina*, with its apocalyptic passion and loss, or even of *Herzog*, with its histrionic magnifications of the betrayed husband. The fiction of personal life now emerges from a highly rationalized use of linguistic constructs as the vehicle for discovering humanity. It uses language to rationalize and institutionalize emotional trauma. It achieves this goal in several ways: through compressing and limiting explicit reference to trigger words such as "divorce," a label used as the justification for turmoil, through flattening affect by denying differences between minor and great misfortune, and by treating passionate situations as "relationships" to be worked on and over. It springs from the era of separation and divorce agreements, visitation rights, and custody arrangements. Family relationships float in that gray space where volition or emotion have been stripped of spontaneity. Such fiction ushers us into the world of negotiated lives.

In this fictional land, dramatic crisis has been subordinated to a texture of enervating hardships. Like the youthful protagonists

of Ellis and McInerney, middle-aged characters in these stories
do not see themselves as contributing to their difficulties. Trouble is something that happens to them. They emerge as affected
objects rather than initiators. Passivity, objectification, suppres-
sion and compression of pathos have transformed the tragedy they
experience to a serial flow of misfortune, not initiated or produced by flaws in character, but simply there to be lived through.

Raymond Carver, Ann Beattie, and Alice Munro are each
exceptional short story writers whose widest audiences have been
won in the 1980s. Raymond Carver received both critical acclaim
and commercial success in the 1980s. Ann Beattie has been a
star in the *New Yorker*'s constellation of writers. Alice Munro, a
Canadian, has won critical praise and an enthusiastic American
audience. Each of these serious writers, in short stories representative of their work as a whole, has revealed similar changes
in the conception of self and of tragedy; each has written
passages in which life is rendered as a list of objective events
projecting the rough texture of married life.

In Raymond Carver's "Boxes" a man says of his newfound
lover:

> Jill always says what's on her mind. She's thirty-five years old,
> wears her hair short, and grooms dogs for a living. Before she
> became a groomer, something she likes, she used to be a
> housewife and mother. Then all hell broke loose. Her two
> children were kidnapped by her first husband and taken to live
> in Australia. Her second husband, who drank, left her with a
> broken eardrum before he drove their car through a bridge
> into the Elwha River. He didn't have life insurance, not to
> mention property-damage insurance. Jill had to borrow money
> to bury him, and then—can you beat it?—she was presented
> with a bill for the bridge repair. Plus, she had her own medical
> bills. She can tell this story now. She's bounced back. But she
> has run out of patience with my mother. I've run out of
> patience too. But I don't see my options.

In this litany, the abduction of children is not distinguished from outrageous bills or physical abuse.

In Ann Beattie's "In the White Night," Carol and her husband have survived the death of their child, but that loss is subsumed in the mother's vision of life as precisely the succession of crises you cannot escape:

> What happened happened at random, and one horrible event hardly precluded the possibility of others happening next. There had been that fancy internist who hospitalized Vernon later in the same spring when Sharon died, and who looked up at him while drawing blood and observed almost offhandedly that it would be an unbearable irony if Vernon also had leukemia. When the test results came back, they showed that Vernon had mononucleosis. There was the time the Christmas tree caught fire, and she rushed toward the flames, clapping her hands like cymbals, and Vernon pulled her away just in time, before the whole tree became a torch and she with it. When Hobo, their dog, had to be put to sleep during their vacation in Maine, that awful woman veterinarian, with her cold green eyes, issued the casual death sentence with one manicured hand on the quivering dog's fur and called him "Bobo" as though their dog were like some circus clown.

This series of disasters serves to flatten affect by a process of trivialization. There is no distinction made between tragedy and annoyance: the death of a child, misplaced fear of serious illness, or someone forgetting the name of a dog. What seems to be important is not what happens to you, but how many items you can list to quantify and therefore establish your legitimate claims as a sufferer. Perhaps not surprisingly, this fiction has reached its widest audience in the 1980s, a period when quantification scales have also become modish in psychology. The Holmes-Rahe stress scale, for example, is widely used for measuring stress in life events. It gives points for the death of a parent or a change in eating habits. Are you stressed out on trivia or tragedy? No matter. What counts is the count. In this materialism of experience lies an analogue to the brand-name obsessions of McInerney and Ellis, a common urge to flee from interiority to surface.

Alice Munro's work discloses how the need to "work at relationships" may be analogous to the need to quantify misfortune. The end of spontaneity is written in the need to see intimacy as an achievement, the product of specific (and quantifiable!) steps taken to ensure and define success. Conversely, degrees of unhappiness and wrong moves can also be charted. The Beck Depression Inventory, also in vogue during the decade, often seems to be on the minds of characters who observe and count the pangs of love.

In Alice Munro's "Labor Day Dinner," Roberta is a book illustrator who has left her husband for George, a man who has given up his teaching job to live in the country, fix up his dilapidated farmhouse, and sculpt. Her daughter's diary lists Roberta's demise in the changing labor Roberta performs and in her loss of sexual confidence. Forsaking her art, Roberta has become enslaved to George's food needs and his moldering house. Her pleasure in her sexuality is destroyed by her fear of George's awareness of her declining looks. Yet her carefully noted misery brings a kind of enlightenment.

In her unhappiness, Roberta first understands the painful insecurity she caused her husband by having an affair with George and finally by leaving him for her lover. Now George, with his on-again-off-again interest, inflicts the pain of unstable commitment on her. "Isn't it funny . . . the idea of a pattern like that? I mean the idea is attractive, of there being that balance." The experience of ambivalent love is objectified and given a new bent by this sense of inevitability, a fated absence of what Carver calls "options." These lovers are caught in a cosmic pecking order of relationships, which, if miserable, seems part of the orderly progress of circumstance. More concerned than Beattie or Carver with the nuances of intimacy, Munro has nevertheless made it possible to understand how people can feel they do not "own" their own emotions.

There are, of course, other significant differences among these writers. Raymond Carver examines our cultural condition from the vantage point of paucity. An heir to the traditions of American naturalism, he sees the lives of his working-class characters as largely dictated by economic circumstance. In writing of the consequences to emotional life, he produces a meditation on the relationship between the power of circumstance and the meaning of personal responsibility. He makes us see a deeper aspect of the absence of generational differences than found in Ellis or McInerney.

In "Boxes," Carver focuses on the feelings produced by family relationships in a world in which generational differences between mother and middle-aged son have been eroded by shared experience. Mother has moved and leased an apartment to be near her son, which sounds conventional enough except for the fact that she is herself something of a rolling stone. Her son has little time for her, having met and become preoccupied with Jill, his new woman, and with trying to achieve economic stability. Mother has packed her possessions in boxes, but not left town. Yet her son's past and future are clearly her present life. Her son also regards possessions as always packed or packable; he too has had to be ready to move wearily on, looking for work and love without prospect of security. Each looking for love, each caught in relationships shaded by frustration, the mother, son, and Jill are equally insecure.

Uprootedness and drifting are virtually classical American motifs. But in an older literature they are attributes of counterculture characters, the young, the *isolato*, the beat, whose drifting reflected a rejection of bourgeois values. In "Boxes," they express the experience of working-class families propelled out of their niche by unemployment, out of family harmony by drinking or drugs, and able to find rest nowhere. The memory of home is of no home. On the phone with his mother, who has moved back to California, the son, pained by her chronic dissatisfaction, remembers the affectionate name my dad used sometimes when he was talking nice to my mother—those times, that is, when he wasn't drunk. It was a long time ago, and I was a kid, but always, hearing it, I felt better, less afraid more hopeful about the future. "Dear," he'd say. . . . "Dear, try not to be afraid," I say. I tell my mother I love her and I'll write to her, yes. Then I say good-bye and I hang up.

The future has arrived and seems without hope for the mother. But ironically, her future prefigures that of her son and Jill, who distracts herself by reading a curtain catalog.

Such spare recapitulation of sentiment and its packaging in the frail word "dear," that holds what the son knows of family love, reflect the essential containment of each of the story's characters. The "boxes" of the title symbolize the characters' compartmentalization of their own emotional life, the packaging of emotion as though it were second-class mail. Carver's story sensitively measures the impact on a family of the experience of futility. In the son's tearful recognition that he can do nothing for his mother, Carver discloses how a sense of filial responsibility can be reduced to an impotent yearning to be kind, even as all memory of love can be limited to the single word "dear."

Some fiction of middle age shares with youthcult fiction a denial of the tragic force of death. In Ann Beattie's "In the White Night," the death of a child from leukemia not only joins a list of trivial annoyances but also propels the child's middle-class parents toward being childlike themselves. Suffering does not enlarge character or understanding. This story uses language paradoxically to defy verbalization rather than to articulate feeling. Its controlling linguistic device is a word game in which the players are asked *not* to think about a suggested noun. Carol and Vernon, whose daughter, Sharon, died years before, visit their closest friends, Matt and Gaye. As Carol and Vernon leave after an evening with them, Matt calls out words from a Don't-Think-About-It game, terminating with, "Don't think about an apple." "Carol frowned. . . . Now she saw an apple where there was no apple, suspended in midair, transforming the scene in front of her to a silly surrealist painting." The snow swirls around the imagined apple. The chain of association, the color imagery of red apple/white snow, as professor Lucy Rosenthal has pointed out, leads toward the memory of Sharon's death from leukemia and of the imbalance of white blood cells and red. Yet the memory is displaced from the child onto the snow and to the friends whose advice was not to think. Vernon sees Matt and Gaye as buffers, "alter egos who absorbed and enacted crises, saving the two of them from having to experience such chaos." Yet it is their not-articulating word game that provides the buffer. The solution to both memory and snowstorm is a regression to not thinking and not speaking.

Reaching their house after the drive through the snow, the couple sleeps in the living room, Vernon in Carol's jacket on the sofa, Carol on the floor with Vernon's coat about her. The story's closing line sums up its peculiar effects: "In the white night world outside, their daughter might be drifting past like an angel and she would see this tableau, for the second that she hovered, as a necessary small adjustment."

The "small adjustment" is their recoil from adulthood toward the smallness of childhood, evidenced in such childlike symbolic actions as wrapping themselves in each other's coats and avoiding their bed. Real tragedy can only be dealt with indirectly by displacement onto surface images of the leukemia-snow and red apple. It does not torment so much as contract the soul into a "small adjustment." Death diminishes by a process that seems to be one of miniaturization in which surfaces both express and limit whatever pain there is.

Material Differences

Something new has been created from the union of materialism and emotion. In the past, object-laden fiction or a literature of objectified emotion was characteristic of such European experimentalist works as Robert Musil's *The Man Without*

Qualities or the fictions of Alain Robbe-Grillet and Nathalie Sarraute. In this country, it has been most associated with the experimentalism of such intellectual artists as Thomas Pynchon. Its appearance in 1980s fiction with a broad, even mass-market appeal suggests both its new importance and its changed emphasis.

This 1980s fiction discloses a fascination for advertising culture most simply in the use of brand names in character definition, but more profoundly in utilizing and adapting its processes: compression, packaging, and quantifying. In embracing commercial culture, 1980s fiction focuses on both the illusions it sustains and the manipulative power of its techniques. On the dark side, it seems to embrace the illusion that the unknown can be ruled out and the self defined by packaging glitzy or strong enough to contain and label it. On the brighter side, 1980s fiction finds, in the operative processes for sustaining such illusions, coping devices.

In the movement toward surfaces there may be a search for ways of relieving what is perceived as unalterable in the inner life. Characters seem actively to seek freedom from uncertainty, self-hatred, and pain. The vision of people as victims rather than masters of their own lives may involve a rejection of the power of individual will but also relieves the burden of rage or guilt. Hoping for release into the pictorial surface, the impersonal course of troubled love (quantifiable too as midlife crisis), or the powdered high, cocaine, are ways of pain-killing through different forms of depersonalization. The spectacle, the object, the impersonal texture, and, as Munro puts it, "the pattern," have become synonymous with experience itself. Each of these writers seems to disclose, in visions of standardization, qualified relief from solitariness.

Knowingly or unwittingly, 1980s writers are our pollsters of the contemporary soul. Delving into its ambivalences, they report that collisions between emotion and materialism, individualism and commercial culture, youth and middle age, have forged a new consensus about our shared limitations and vulnerability, a consensus in the shape of a birth: a shelter-seeking self.

Irving Howe

THE END OF THE COMMON READER

Few aspects of 1980s literary life seem more important than the loss of faith, perhaps even interest, in the idea of the common reader. Most literary people now live and work in universities, and not many of these still write for the common reader. It sometimes seems almost as if that figure has been banished, at least in the academic literary world, as an irritant or intruder, the kind of obsolete person who still enjoys stories as stories and still supposes that characters bear some resemblance to human beings.

"I rejoice," wrote Dr. Johnson in his life of Gray, "to concur

Irving Howe is a founding editor of *Dissent*. His books include *The American Newness*, *World of Our Fathers*, *A Margin of Hope*, and *Politics and the Novel*.

with the common reader: for by the common sense of readers, uncorrupted by literary prejudices, after all the refinements of subtlety and the dogmatism of learning, must finally be decided all claims to literary honors." As tantalizing as it is famous, this remark has occasioned an abundance of scholarly investigation, much of it illuminating, almost all of it scrupulously inconclusive. Did Dr. Johnson really know who this common reader was? Did he have in mind a distinct social group, or did the common reader serve as an emblem, a shorthand convenience, for the Augustan belief that the culture of England was still bound by shared understandings? Or was the common reader simply a mask behind which Dr. Johnson could deliver his authoritative judgments?

Eighteenth-century scholars can locate with fair accuracy, if not through quantitative weightings, the publics for which Dr. Johnson wrote in his own and other periodicals. There was evidently a small remnant of the aristocracy and the gentry with cultivated tastes; there were prosperous members of the commercial classes, part of a new reading public reaching out for breadth of cultivation; and there were literary people of indeterminate social standing. Especially noteworthy, remarked Dr. Johnson, was the growing number of women readers. But it seems clear that he did not see, indeed could not see, the common reader as we might.

James Basker, a scholar of eighteenth-century English literature, has written that Dr. Johnson's common reader should not be seen as "a single entity. . . . [Dr. Johnson] imagined many different kinds of readers. . . . Within a given work he would vary his rhetorical register to address now one group, now another, at moments perhaps all together." This varying of the "rhetorical register" is, of course, a common practice among journalists; and Dr. Johnson was, among other things, a journalist. Another scholar, Clarence Tracy, believes that what Dr. Johnson saw in the common reader was "the basic man," that generic figure "who was so much the preoccupation of 17th- and 18th-century thinkers," though in practice Dr. Johnson "seems often to have thought of [the common reader] as belonging to the lower middle class, to the vulgar, a word that he defined in the *Dictionary* as 'the common people.'" And in the eyes of still other scholars, Dr. Johnson's common reader simply referred to someone who read for pleasure, without a friend to boost or a cause to promote.

What can we conclude from this pleasant haze? That what mattered most to Dr. Johnson was a negative trait: the common reader was not a professional, not a university man, and usually had no Latin. Perhaps also the common reader was partly a creature of desire, a postulated figure made to represent some widely shared sentiments of a culture.

By the time Virginia Woolf picked up the term, the common reader had acquired a more precise social physiognomy. Woolf had in mind a community of literate persons who were not, in the narrow or professional sense, literary. They were drawn to, and held by, literature, but they did not stand within literary life. The common reader had also begun to suggest ambitious young plebeians eager to claim their portion of the cultural heritage; real-life versions, say, of Jude Fawley or Leonard Bast, the sort of people Woolf would have met at the evening educational institutes for working people at which she occasionally (and uneasily) lectured.

Woolf was not without a touch of condescension toward the very reader whom she placed in the forefront of her audience. He "differs from the critic and the scholar. He reads for his own pleasure rather than to impart knowledge or correct the opinions of others." By the time Woolf was saying these things, she and her Bloomsbury friends may have begun to suspect that the common reader was slipping out of sight, just as the parallel figure of the man of letters was. Neither of these could withstand the increasing professionalism of literary life that began around the First World War.

From the more advanced literary circles of the time, there emerged the verdict that the common reader and the man of letters had sealed a pact in behalf of a genteel amateurism, the decline of literary criticism into impressionist chatter. Pound and Eliot were among the outstanding figures who wrote as if the premise of the common reader had been pretty securely overturned. Was not this figure, or the notion behind this figure, a barrier in the way of the new, the revolutionary innovations of literary modernism? Modernist literature, by its very nature, could attract only a specialized readership, and a readership narrowing into those who steadily "worked" on it—this last, of course, an exaggeration, but not a pointless one. (The common reader could hardly be expected to devote a lifetime to the study of Joyce's fiction in order to satisfy the demand that Joyce made for such attention.)

Still, in the United States as late as the 1950s, many of the leading critics, both New and New York, continued to take seriously the idea of the common reader. Meanwhile this protean, elusive figure had undergone a change. For the *Partisan Review* and *Kenyon Review* critics, the common reader now signified a small audience of nonspecialist people: say, university teachers in the social sciences and humanities, scientists interested in culture, left-wing politicals of some cultivation, students hoping to become writers, and so on. These critics wrote as if they still had readers other than other critics, as if there still were people who turned to critics for illumination while keeping an optimal distance from those noisy disputes in which critics seem fated to indulge.

Such readers of the 1940s and 1950s were likely to follow Clement Greenberg on the new painting, Eric Bentley on theater, James Agee on film, Randall Jarrell on poetry, Edmund Wilson, Philip Rahv, and Lionel Trilling on the novel, as well as reviewers like Robert Fitzgerald, Marius Bewley, and Dwight Macdonald. These readers had, by now, probably read Eliot's poems and essays, which had gained academic respectability and were being taught in the colleges, and they were also reading Hemingway and Faulkner, among American writers, and Joyce, Proust, and Mann, among European. But they were decidedly not interested in the writings of the Chicago neo-Aristotelians, or in the "heresies" and "fallacies" unearthed by some New Critics.

Just as Dr. Johnson had shifted his "rhetorical register" because he knew (or sensed) that he wrote for a variegated public, so the contributors to the major quarterlies of the time were prepared, no matter which "school" they adhered to or kept apart from, to accept a division between topics that mattered to their small but crucial public (really *un*common common readers) and topics best left to graduate seminars. As I recall, there was certainly a touch of anti-academic prejudice in these literary circles, but it was neither pervasive nor inescapable.

The more clever among the critics, aware that there was no single kind of common reader, that the category actually covered a span of figures and interests, tried to direct their work to both outsiders and insiders, amateurs and professionals, sometimes in alternation and, when really ambitious, simultaneously. I doubt that many common readers kept turning eagerly to John Crowe Ransom's *Kenyon Review*, with its few thousand readers forming a public no larger, proportionately, than the five hundred of Dr. Johnson's *Rambler*. But at least some of Ransom's contributors, though writing for and quarreling with one another, also shared a desire to reach some portion of the publics we designate as common readers. I recall conversations among admirers of R. P. Blackmur's criticism who were distressed at the increasing opacity of his later work: Who but themselves (and even then . . .) would try to make it out? Difficulty was accepted as necessary at times, but obscurity not. Almost every critic would have agreed with Allen Tate's remark that "critical style ought to be as plain as the nose on one's face."

If the quarterlies could at times also put off many common readers with their internal debates and mandarin styles, there were still the book pages of the political weeklies in which the New York critics appeared. A few of the New Critics did also, very occasionally; but some of those I knew wanted to, and regretted their seeming inability to write in a way that would be at once serious and accessible. It was then generally assumed that the line of great English critics, from Dr. Johnson and Hazlitt to Arnold and Eliot, had cultivated, as a matter of course, a certain journalistic bent (critics often *had* to be journalists) and that the migration of critics to the universities that began in the early 1950s, while a practical advantage, was still a somewhat uncomfortable development. Surely in the history of American literary life, this was a major turning point. The new circumstances of our economy made it close to impossible for a free-lance man (or woman) of letters to survive. And this change must be one of the major reasons for the shift in attitudes toward the idea of the common reader.

Let me propose the hypothesis—it could be tested adequately only in a comprehensive cultural history—that in the years between the two world wars there occurred a fracturing or proliferation of literary publics. There were now perhaps more kinds of common readers than ever before, ranging from the few who saw themselves as devotees of the literary quarterlies to those who read magazines like *Harper's* and the dreary *Saturday Review*. And somewhere in between was the *New Yorker*, with at least a portion of its readers interested in cultural criticism.

After the Second World War, as gifted writers like Edmund Wilson, W. H. Auden, Dwight Macdonald, and Mary McCarthy began to appear in the *New Yorker*, it became harder still to make clear or sharp distinctions among common readers. Perhaps one distinction that still holds is that the literary quarterlies and political weeklies involved their readers in intellectual exchange and debate, or at least opened their pages to such exchange and debate, while the *New Yorker* presented the work of its contributors as finished products, not as something open to scrutiny through question or polemic within a community of letters. The kind of common reader who took the *New Yorker* was, in that capacity, a consumer. The kind who read *Partisan Review*, the *Nation*, the *New Republic*, and later the *New York Review of Books* was now and again a participant in an ongoing life of cultural exchange. This distinction is not an absolute one, since it seems probable that at least some readers of the quarterlies and weeklies took on the role of passive consumer quite as the readers of the *New Yorker* did. But the point to be stressed here is that radically different views of the life of culture were reflected in the divergent attitudes toward controversy between the quarterlies and weeklies, on the one hand, and the *New Yorker*, on the other. Even when the *New Yorker* printed something as deeply controversial as Hannah Arendt's work on Eichmann, it would not print any refutations or commentaries.

It's possible, of course, that the idea of the common reader, from the time of Dr. Johnson to our present moment, was mostly an enabling hypothesis that enticed critics into exegesis and lucidity. But it must have been more, too: there were people I knew in the American socialist milieu who, often somewhat shyly, immersed themselves in Proust, Kafka, and Eliot. Especially in recent decades, when the great works of literary modernism were still fresh, and it had not yet become the dubious custom to minimize their difficulty, even learned and sophisticated people, some of whom rather foolishly looked down on critics like Edmund Wilson, could profit from the kind of exegesis and lucidity he exemplified.

Thus, even if the common reader was a contrivance of critics to satisfy their desire for an audience other than fellow critics (and I don't think it really was such a contrivance), the *idea* of the common reader served a useful purpose. At least during the first decade or two after the Second World War, there were critics who kept one eye on the reader outside the classroom. All of them, while naturally concerned with the responses of their colleagues, still wanted to reach someone "out there," one kind of common reader or another.

But things have changed radically in the last decades. There now flourishes an academic community of younger, accomplished, and, as it appears, self-assured professors of literature for whom the idea of the common reader seems to be of small interest. Such professors are likely to regard the common reader as an indulgence of an earlier generation of litterateurs that resulted mostly in ephemeral journalism. Today most of the ambitious and talented young people within the literary academy publish only in journals read by their colleagues, and they seem to find this an acceptable, indeed a normal, condition.

I was just about to use an unfriendly phrase, "within the narrow confines of the literary academy"; but that would no longer be quite accurate. Those "confines" are no longer narrow. The American university system has expanded so rapidly that it's possible for aspiring professors to feel that their colleagues *do* form a sufficient audience. And in a way, they do: an audience that is attentive, self-absorbed, and with a vocabulary of its own. Give a paper at the Modern Language Association on Heidegger or de Man and you will probably enjoy a larger and more responsive audience than if you write about Ashbery's poems or Naipaul's novels in a literary magazine.

Why are literary academics so keenly drawn to purely "theoretical" theory? It is a question that could take us far afield, but since it has a bearing on my topic, I offer a few quick speculations. There has been a growing tendency toward internal specialization in all academic fields, and this holds true for the literary academy as well. Each guild, or guild of guilds, lives absorbed in its own rituals, norms, disputes. There has been a general decay of strong beliefs, if not ideologies, among the intellectual classes; and the sophisticated skepticism, sometimes slipping into nihilism, that now dominates literary theory seems made to order for the mood of the moment. And then, to be fair, there are some powerful minds at work in literary theory who naturally win over younger people (who, decades before, might have been converts to earlier theories, earlier schools).

What results is a conviction that the literary theorist, rid of the grubby tasks of practical criticism and not obliged to pay very much attention to literature itself, can find satisfying expression by remaining within the academy, speaking to fellow theorists, and not having to worry about that nuisance, real or imagined, known as the common reader. The freewheeling literary intellectual of an earlier day, reaching several audiences and coping with a number of subjects, is all but gone. Our literary academics stay academic to the last, or to the last theory. And they find it good.

To avoid misunderstanding, I should say that it seems entirely appropriate for scholars to publish mainly in scholarly journals. So it has been, so it should remain. But when it comes to literary people who teach in universities and are not exactly or primarily scholars, the tendency to turn inward is disheartening. It means that the teaching of literature falls increasingly into the hands of people who lack a vital relation to, or strong feeling for, the writing of the moment, into the hands of professors for whom Hélène Cixous is more interesting than Nadine Gordimer and Jean Braudrillard more important than Milan Kundera. It means that literary academics, or at least some of them, are inclined to a mild—and not always mild—condescension toward critics who still find it desirable to review novels and books of poetry. And what is quite as disturbing: a snobbish disdain for students who prefer to read novels and poems.

One reason for the inward turn of literary academics may be that recent American writing has not been especially "great." But "great" is a loaded word, and writers to whom it can be applied don't appear every day. There *are* interesting American writers, some talented and many serious, perhaps no fewer than at other times; and it's hard to envision a vigorous culture in which some of the most influential and the most talented literary people pay little attention to living writers. True, the academics of the 1920s and 1930s, when the United States could boast of a major literature, weren't greatly concerned with living writers, either; but in those days it hardly mattered, since good critics flourished outside the academy, grouping themselves around such magazines as *The Dial* and *Hound and Horn*.

The very idea of a literary community, one that would encompass the literary academy but not be confined to it, has now come into question. Which brings me to another, perhaps central, question: What happens to the idea of a democratic culture, advanced by almost every major American critic since Emerson and Whitman, if the increasingly powerful and self-assured literary academy, barely challenged by critics outside its walls, remains aloof from the larger culture, remains content to live and work within its own space?

To hope for a democratic culture, we need not cherish earlier populist or Marxist notions about the masses. The vision of a public spiritedly and independently engaged with literature has always been a precarious, if also a precious, one. Whoever thinks back to the vulgarities and the buffooneries of the 1988 presidential campaign knows it would be foolish to indulge in high rhetoric about the prospects for a democratic culture (perhaps even for a democratic politics). Clearly the decline in the public of informed, discriminating, yet nonspecialized readers— or, more likely, the decline of concern with that public among academic literary people—has not been caused by recent trends within the academy, though it may have been hastened by them. The spreading blight of television, the slippage of the magazines, the disasters of our school system, the native tradition of anti-intellectualism, the cultivation of ignorance by portions of the counterculture, the breakdown of coherent political and cultural publics, the loss of firm convictions within the educated classes— these, in merest summary, are among the reasons for the decline in both the presence and the idea of the common reader.

And yet the idea of a democratic culture, which must mean a culture that extends beyond the academy, is one that we cannot afford to surrender, not if we remain attached to the idea of a democratic politics. Indeed, it's hardly within our power to abandon such ideas, so deeply rooted are they in the traditions of this country. Emerson asked for "confidence in the unsearched might of man. The literature of the poor, the feelings of the child, the philosophy of the street, the meaning of a household life, are the topics of the time." Whitman spoke for those "within whose thought rages the battle between democracy's convictions and aspirations, and the people's crudeness, vices, caprices." Toward the end of this wretched century it's hard to summon the buoyant tones of Emerson and Whitman; but we remain, with whatever

244 · Irving Howe

modulations, their cultural offspring, whether we acknowledge it or not.

The inward turn among literary academics has not been accompanied by a large-scale or explicitly reactionary politics, such as several decades ago was being advanced by Eliot and Pound. What flourishes in the academy now is a craft elitism, expressed at times as a readiness to look on the large society as incorrigibly debased, or to dismiss it as inconsequential. The academy, it seems, is enough.

Sometimes this self-satisfied acquiescence even comes with assertions of radicalism. A number of those drawn to deconstructionist theory, for example, feel that their writings have political implications, though that does not lead them, so far as I can tell, to any visible politics available in the United States. A small academic group describes itself as Marxist, but that strikes me as a bit comic: whatever Marxism may have been, it always saw itself attached to, or in search of, a mass movement of the working class. It was not merely a "method" for literary criticism. But Marxism has gone to the universities to die in comfort.

It is true that the idea of a democratic culture remains, historically, a novelty not fully tested, and may even turn out to be no more than an attractive yearning. It may refer to several aspects of literature or the literary life. We may have in mind the dominant voices or ideas of a literature, so that we can speak of a democratic culture even with regard to writing (some of Melville, some of Henry James) that has little popular appeal, is alienated in spirit, and sets itself up as an adversary to the society's dominant values. In that somewhat restricted sense, we have had a democratic literature since the days of Emerson, and probably into, or close to, our own time.

But the idea of a democratic culture may also refer to something more ambitious and difficult: to the relations between writers and an active, autonomous public, neither academic nor professionally literary, perhaps small, but providing writers with a flow of sentiment and response. The odds against maintaining a vital link between a literary community and a literary public are pretty high these days. If we cannot locate the common reader, however, we must try to help him/her/them reappear. Critics might learn once more to speak to the common reader, as if he still matters, as if she will soon respond; and to speak in English, a language that for some time served criticism well.

Alessandra Stanley

PRESIDENCY BY RALPH LAUREN: CLOSING THE DECADE IN STYLE

The exterior shot: A tiny blond girl in a pastel-blue dress totters in slow motion across a gleaming freshly mown lawn. As Vangelis-like (*Chariots of Fire*) music swells, a tall, fine-boned man wearing a blue striped shirt turns, opens his arms, and sweeps the child high in the air.

The interior: In a large, old-fashioned country kitchen, the same man tosses ingredients into a simmering lobster pot, surrounded by helpful, happy grandchildren, attractively arrayed in faded all-natural fibers.

Alessandra Stanley is a senior correspondent for *Time*. Her writing has appeared in the *New Republic, Gentlemen's Quarterly*, and *Vogue*.

Picnic exterior: Sun-dappled adults and children loll on the grass, circling the gentleman, who sits cross-legged on the ground. A small granddaughter hugs his back, and her tiny arms reach around his neck like the sleeves of a carelessly tossed tennis sweater. The smiling patriarch talks animatedly and eats, but he chews with his mouth closed.

Tradition. Family. Manners. Freeze any frame, and you have an instant Ralph Lauren advertisement, one of those lush tableaus of well-bred families at play that spread across many pages of glossy magazines, moodily evoking class and quality and grace, without ad copy or price tags. Actually, the picnic commercial was filmed at Kennebunkport, Maine, the male model is George Bush, and the improbably well-behaved children and grandchildren are all unpaid members of the Bush extended family.

The credit line in the commercial goes to Roger Ailes, Bush's media adviser, but an acknowledgment is due to fashion designer Ralph Lauren. Without Ralph Lauren and his expert molding of American taste, George Bush, Andover '42, Yale '48, a.k.a. "Poppy," might never have been elected. For more than a decade, Lauren has been hooking middle-class and lower-middle-class Americans on WASP aesthetics and pseudo-English gentility; the country has gone from Ralph Lauren clothes, to Ralph Lauren home furnishings, to Ralph Laurenesque architecture, design, and art. Get ready for the Ralph Lauren presidency.

Ronald Reagan also deserves some credit since he blurred for good the line between commercial advertising and political philosophy. Reagan's Norman Rockwellesque 1984 "Morning Again in America" commercials were virtually indistinguishable from television ads hawking Pepsi, cars, or insurance; the message in both was bring back the good old days of Main Street, white picket fences, and newspaper boys on bikes. No matter that nobody did bring them back; in 1988 Bush's early ads borrowed heavily from Reagan and played on the same themes. That's because Bush aides thought they had to sell a product nobody but his mother would buy, George Bush, Uber-prep. They were wrong. Fortunately for them, they discovered their error in time.

The ads started to change. The brief, blurry glimpses of Bush family life at the summer retreat along the rocky coast of Maine are tantalizing—and dreamily familiar. White wicker chairs on the porch, a pedigree springer spaniel, little girls in Liberty print dresses, vast lawns, patchwork quilts, leather-bound books. Casual, yet understatedly elegant: the "whole atmosphere of the good life" that Ralph Lauren says he conjures in his ads, and that millions of Americans have learned to covet. George Bush has it, and now the country has George Bush.

Bush lucked into more than a trend. He is the direct beneficiary of a national obsession. The United States has been on a ten-year binge of crested blazers, polo matches, and English hunting prints, an insatiable mass-market hunger for upper-class totems. Shopping malls that used to be filled with Sears, Syms, and J. C. Penneys are now vulgarity-free zones: from New Jersey to Alaska, five-and-dimes have been replaced by neo-Edwardian outlets of Alcott & Andrews, Ann Taylor, Victoria's Secret, Brooks Brothers, shops that look less like a retail store than a Hollywood set designer's notion of Harvard's Porcellian club. These are interiors that mimic the grandiose Polo store on Madison Avenue, the old Rhinelander mansion that Lauren turned into his flagship shop, which in turn mimics the grand old houses that George and Barbara Bush grew up in.

Snobbery had always sold well. But no one had ever mass-marketed the mystique or so widely popularized the yearning as Bronx-born Ralph Lauren, né Ralph Lipschitz. At $70 a shirt, Ralph Lauren is a household name, but hardly a household product. Like a great politician, he set out his vision. Eager imitators scurried to supply consumers with affordable cachet: The GAP, which has 714 outlets across the country, sells hundreds of thousands of monogrammed shirts a year and has its own brand of sports shirts, white cotton T-shirts emblazoned with a phony rowing crew insignia—tiny oars crossed across a circle.

The English may snobbishly call it "aping the gentry." In America it's called "instant classic."

The Laurenification of America reaches far beyond clothing. Surveying the neoclassical opulence of Philip Johnson's AT&T building in New York and Robert Stern's neo-Georgian mansions, *New York Times* architecture critic Paul Goldberger recently concluded that Ralph Lauren is the "real design symbol" of our age. He calls the clothes designer a "one-man Bauhaus." Forget high tech. Upscale health spas, like the "Regency" in McLean, Virginia, look like corporate board rooms, with jade-green marble, carved balustrades, upholstered armchairs, and Oriental rugs. Even law firms want to look like law firms. They are exchanging abstract art and the "go-go" spirit for luxuriant nineteenth-century English and American landscape paintings. Magazine entrepreneur Chris Whittle recently commissioned New York designer Peter Marino to design a new Whittle Communications headquarters in Knoxville, Tennessee. It will be a replica of Christ Church College at Oxford.

Bush would never fall for such falderal. As Nancy Mitford painstakingly explained in a collection of essays, *Noblesse Oblige*, it is strictly non-U, that is, not upper-class, to strive or show off wealth. The Bushes come by their subdued fashion sense the old-fashioned way. They inherited it. To the happy few, Ralph Lauren is of course hopelessly non-U. As president, Bush will be too polite to point out the difference.

WASPS are fashionable again. Playwright A. R. Gurney started writing sly contemporary drawing-room comedies about them and became the toast of Broadway. Glitz-and-glitter TV shows like "Dynasty" went out with Nancy Reagan. The creators of "Hill Street Blues" have turned from blue-collar cops and robbers to prep school heroes in a new TV show, "Tattingers," in which Old Money triumphs over vulgarity week after week. In the first episode, Blythe Danner briskly instructs her marriage-minded debutante daughter, "Go to Yale and get on with your life." Prescott Bush couldn't have said it better when son George returned from the war.

You can't even buy a jug of cheap wine anymore without bumping into the Ralph Lauren sensibility. The "All the Best" Gallo wine TV commercials, in which a gauze-covered camera pans slowly across sunlit vineyards, grandmothers, brides, oak tables, and eternally glistening lawns, are confusing. Is it Gallo, Polo, or Bush for President? Only the narrator knows for sure, and even then, one has to listen carefully: the golden baritone that sonorously recounts the life history of George Bush in political advertisements sounds exactly like the hushed grave tones used to ennoble Gallo wine.

George Bush never explained what he meant by "Family Values," nor did he really need to. Advertising firms have been making it up for years. Ira Zucherman, senior vice president at Hal Riney and Associates, the firm that peddled Gallo, Perrier, and helped create "Morning Again in America" (Hal Riney himself is that wonderful gravelly voice in the Gallo ads), sums up the message that now dominates commercial advertising: "Traditional Values, Quality, Taste, and a Certain Sense of Heritage." George Bush couldn't have defined his "vision thing" any better. When he informed an Ask George Bush audience that he was running for president "because I believe in the honor of it all," his lips read: "noblesse oblige." His loose-fitting suit, striped tie, and attractive family screamed BCBG, or "Bon Chic, Bon Genre," yet another French expression connoting elegant good breeding.

Digby Baltzell, professor emeritus at the University of Pennsylvania, coined the term WASP in his 1964 book *The Protestant Establishment*, and has been studying the caste ever since. He despises the voter's preference for log cabin myths and self-made politicians, arguing that the best presidents came from "high backgrounds." Baltzell, who currently detects "a manifest disdain and latent yearning for patricians," is pleased with Bush's election—up to a point. "All the great patricians led the masses against the middle class," he huffs. "Bush seems to be leading the middle classes against minorities."

Politicians are slower on the uptake than merchants. Two summers ago, when Bush aides were fretting over how to overcome the vice president's upper-class twit demeanor, Hugh Barnard, publisher of the "Retail Marketing Report," was advising his subscribers that "fantasy marketing spells big bucks." His newsletter helpfully defined the requisite props: "steamer trunks, antique armoires, life-size paintings of military officers of long-ago wars, upholstered chairs by tables laden with books." Barnard knew instantly that Ralph Lauren had his fingers on the purse, er pulse of the nation. "The American public has become more conservative and tradition-conscious," Barnard says. "People are less impressed with outward glitter, they want stability and classiness." Fifteen years ago, even George Bush didn't want to be George Bush—he chaired the Republican National Committee in sideburns and wide psychedelic ties.

The lesson from Madison Avenue got lost in the downward mobility contest of the Republican primary. Bob Dole was lording his father's overalls all over everyone else. Pete du Pont tried to claim that his aristocratic ancestors had been mere "scraggly French immigrants" who came to the United States barely better off than the Vietnamese boat people. (Du Pont conveniently forgot that his people arrived with a letter of introduction to Thomas Jefferson from Talleyrand.) Bush aides mistakenly assumed Americans would be turned off by Skull and Bones, vacation homes in Maine, and preppy idioms.

Bush took to bragging about eating pork rinds and listening to country-Western music. He became aggressively low-culture. He even insisted at one point that he didn't know the meaning of the word "patrician." He campaigned in Illinois alongside Loretta Lynn and Crystal Gayle and hotly defended his love of Country, at one point challenging *New York Times* reporter Maureen Dowd to enter his bedroom and see for herself that his clock radio was tuned to the country music station—rather like Gary Hart recklessly challenging the newspaper of record to "put a tail on me" and check out his womanizing.

The Bubba vote may have been mollified by Bush's pork rinds

and Western props, but nobody else was fooled. Ralph Lauren likes country too, witness his highly successful line of stone-washed denims, earth-tone Western shirts, and pastel bandanas, always artfully laid out against a background of iron cattle gear and Santa Fe–style ceramics. Even Bush's pork rind habit had an *épater le bourgeois* ring to it—it suggested the kind of reverse snobbery that drives Beacon Hill matrons to turn up their noses at Mercedes and buy Chevettes. Besides, WASPs have notoriously gross eating habits. Nouvelle cuisine is aptly named: only the nouveau riche really eat it.

Bush's populist message was always there, voiced in shrill attacks on Dukakis. He painted the governor of Massachusetts as the liberal "elitist" from Harvard Yard, and he wasn't just talking about the Pledge of Allegiance and the American Civil Liberties Union. Bush derided Dukakis as an intellectual snob, a dour Cambridge don who sneers at bourgeois pretenses. Dan Quayle, for once, summed up the aspiring classes' fears the best, saying that Dukakis was "conceited." Dukakis, Quayle argued, "looks down on America." Reagan had turned America into a nation of shoppers, and Dukakis seemed poised with scissors, ready to snip overextended Bloomingdale's credit cards in two. If Mike Dukakis came off as an unreconstructed Ralph Lipschitz, a self-made man who buys his clothes at Filene's basement and despises those who pay more, Bush was The Real Thing, the personification of everything that Ralph Lauren yearns for. Bush, for one, shops at the proper but hardly extravagant Arthur Adler men's store. But then, the rich are different from you and me; they spend less money.

By the time Roger Ailes got around to filming the Bushes *en famille*, the campaign had wised up. Aides who once used to ban still-photographers from filming the outside of the Kennebunkport house—or, as press secretary Sheila Tate instructed reporters, "minimize the edifice, maximize the people"—relaxed.

Certainly, the half-hour George Bush documentary that Ailes aired nationwide the evening before the election was a paean to Bush's patrician background. In one arresting bit of footage, a tanned, chiseled George Bush, Jr., sat on a flowered chintz sofa in Kennebunkport, his wife smiling serenely at his side, and ruminated about "Dad." He recalled being accosted by a night bellman in a Cooperstown, New York, hotel who wanted to show him his "most treasured memento": a letter from George Bush, thanking the bellman for getting his pants pressed at an unusual hour. Was it the thousand points of light or the sixty thousand thank-you notes that put Bush over the top?

After the Republican convention, Bush's aides claimed that the candidate felt "liberated." He soon reverted with relief to Poppy-speak. He referred to negative ads as "the naughty stuff," and in a speech decrying chemical warfare described the effects of nerve gas as "ghastly." Bush dropped pork rinds altogether after election night and returned to his roots, hightailing over to the Florida summer home of William Stamps Farish III, a Kentucky horse breeder and polo player who also manages Bush's blind trust, for a little fishing, tennis, and golf. His choice of locale, Gulf Stream, near Hobe Sound, is a private enclave so exclusive its 550 residents look down at Palm Beach as trashy. On Sunday, Bush attended services with his eighty-seven-year-old mother at Christ Memorial Church, which sits conveniently enough on the seventh hole of the Jupiter Island golfing green. Mother Bush, natty in white shoes and a sea-green dress, greeted him while perched regally on a golf cart, a real-life Katharine Hepburn, frail but yar.

The cult of the Haute Bushoisie was helped along, of course, by Ronald Reagan, who made America safe for the rich again. By Inauguration Day, it was "Morning Coat Again in America," a hostile takeover of dowdy Democratic Washington by top hats, tails, furs, jewels, limousines, and the Hollywood Mafia. But Reagan's era glorified style, not taste. Now the pendulum has swung away from Frank Sinatra, Galanos, Chuck Heston, and the Hollywood make-believe glamour that Sidney Blumenthal, co-author of *The Reagan Legacy*, calls a "neo-kitsch aesthetic." After eight years America yearned for better breeding.

Barbara Bush proudly tells friends that the three strands of clam-sized pearls she always wears are fakes, worn mainly to conceal the wrinkles around her neck. Like her husband, Mrs. Bush has no snooty airs. She is too self-assured to stoop to Nancy Reagan's habit of "borrowing" diamond necklaces from Van Cleef and Arpels and passing them off as her own. The appeal of the Reagans partying until dawn with nouveau riche septuagenarians is spent. Bush represents what a glitz-sated but still socially aspiring nation has been taught to yearn for in the 1980s: a kinder, gentler snobbery.